Guide to North American
Brewpubs and Craft Breweries

by
Steve Johnson

with a foreword by Michael Jackson

Vol. 1
U.S. East of the Mississippi and Canada

2nd edition

WBR Publications
Clemson, South Carolina

On Tap: Guide to North American Brewpubs and Craft Breweries

ISBN   0-9629368-2-0 -- set   (pbk.)

0-9629368-3-9 -- Vol. 1   (pbk.)

WBR Publications
P.O. Box 71
Clemson, South Carolina 29633

tel.   (803) 654-3360

fax.   (803) 654-5067

Cover photo by W. J. Penberthy: customers are served craft-brewed beer at the Allegheny Brewery & Pub, Pennsylvania Brewing Co., Pittsburgh, Pennsylvania.

TABLE OF CONTENTS

Acknowledgements

The creation of this book would not have been possible without the coopera-
tion of many people, especially the many brewery and brewpub owners, presi-
dents, brewers, managers, chefs, and wait staff, who provided me with the information I needed. Also, I am thankful to the many subscribers to my newsletter,
World Beer Review, who alerted me to brewery openings and closings.

It would be impossible to mention them all by name, but I will list some that
come to mind.

Phil Alley; Lynn Anderson; Phil Atkinson, CAMRA Victoria; Steve
Beaumont; Wayne Blanchard; Louis Bregger; Rosemarie Certo, Dock Street
Brewing; Sandra Clipp; Pat Conway, Great Lakes Brewing; Alan Ditky,
BRD; Jim Dorsch; Michael Dowding, Teri and Shawn Dunn; David Edgar
and Jeff Mendel, The Institute for Brewing Studies; John Fryer; Ed Hacala;
John Hall, Goose Island Brewing; Herb Haydock, Oldenberg Brewing; David
Hull; Michael Jackson; Maria Johnson. Roger Kirkpatrick; Alan Knight,
Hanwells Brewing; Jim Koch, Boston Beer Co.; Roger Levesque; Marty
Nachel; Tom Pastorius, Allegheny Brewery & Pub; Greg Noonan, Vermont
Pub & Brewery; Brett Peruzzi, the *Yankee Brewer;* Jim Robertson; and Ed
Stebbins, Gritty McDuff's.

Dedication

I dedicate *On Tap* to my old college classmate, Bill Clinton,
Georgetown University, class of '68. While I was drinking
beer at The Toombs, Bill was hitting the books . . . and look
where it has led us: Bill, to the White House, and I, all to
often, to the Out House. Now Bill has moved from Arkansas
(which has a brewpub) to Washington (which also has a
brewpub) . . . aah, it sounds so regal. And I, ironically,
reside in South Carolina, where brewpubs are still illegal.

Steve Johnson
May 7, 1993

Foreward
by Michael Jackson

While each of Europe's great brewing regions sticks mainly to its own types of beer (flowery Pilsners in the Czech Republic and Germany; tart wheat beers in Germany and Belgium; fruity ales in Belgium and Britain; dry stouts in Ireland, and so on), all of these styles are now being produced in America. Neither Europeans nor North Americans believe it when I tell them, but the truth is that the greatest stylistic variety of beer available in any country is today to be found in the United States and Canada. In some instances, too, the European classics are challenged or exceeded by the new American beers.

This is a result of the brewpub and microbrewery renaissance, which began in Britain in the 1970s but has spread most vigorously to North America.

European immigrants made this variety of beers on this small scale before Prohibition; now their grandchildren are doing it again.

This means that beer is no longer simply a cold, pale, rather gassy, refresher. It is now possible to choose one brew to quench your thirst, another as a reward after a tough day; one as an aperitif, another with your meal. Some beers better accompany fish, others suit meat, or even a dessert. Another might be best suited to take home for a nightcap with a book at bedtime. In some cases, examples of each style can be found under the same roof.

People disbelieve this, too, because they have never found such an establishment. The landscape is dominated with ads reminding us about beers of which we are all already well aware, but how do you track down the more individualistic alternative? You have to know where to look.

It may exist even in your own home town, without having come to your attention (small brewers do not have big advertising budgets). I have visited cities and discovered that my cab-driver was unaware that there was a local brewery. Could you imagine a cabbie in France not knowing that his town made wine? If you travel, part of the experience should be the enjoyment of local food and drink, but how do you find it? Even the most worldly of us needs a guide.

I myself wrote an international *Pocket Guide to Beer* at the beginning of the 1980s, and the U.S. coverage, which was comprehensive, listed only 40-odd breweries. At that time, there were only four or five of the new generation for me

V

to cover. As I have seen new breweries rise, in dozens and twenties, and now hundreds, my *Pocket Guide* now features almost 300 breweries in the U.S. and Canada, but I have had to become more selective.

I have longed to produce my own guide dealing only with North American breweries, with the space to give more detailed information on each, but supposedly aware New York publishers still have difficulty in persuading themselves that anyone who drinks beer could be literate. Worse still, the publishing industry, being centered in the East, has difficulty in acknowledging or understanding a renaissance that has been most vigorous in the West.

The author of this work solved that problem in the most American way: he is his own publisher. He was kind enough to dedicate his first edition to me, as an inspiration, though I was not aware of that intention until I saw the book. I am now delighted to return the compliment by introducing this edition.

Having been a first-hand witness of the beer renaissance on both sides of the Atlantic, from Day One, I am in a perfect position from which to confirm the remarkable usefulness and thoroughness of *On Tap: Guide to North American Brewpubs.*

It will be a great success, and it deserves to be.

Michael Jackson's Pocket Guide to Beer *is published by Simon & Schuster, of New York. His latest book, Michael Jackson's* Beer Companion *is published by Running Press, of Philadelphia. Jackson presents on-screen* The Beer Hunter *(Discovery Channel), and is the world's leading writer on the subject.*

Introduction

North America is experiencing a beer renaissance. After a century of brewery con-solidations, a "noble experiment" with national Prohibition, the disappearance of many beer styles, and a gradual trend toward blander and blander beer, Americans and Canadians are rediscovering the pleasures of good beer along with their brew-ing heritage.

Small breweries are leading the way. These new breweries, alternately called microbreweries, craft breweries, or brewpubs, are providing an amazing variety of fresh beers with assertive flavor and made with natural ingredients. While the major breweries are still producing more than 99% of the beer, the craft breweries are producing more than 99% of the interesting beer.

The beer renaissance is a grassroots movement and a reactionary one at that. The participants want to return to beer the way it used to be made. At the same time, it is dynamic, with many of the brewers experimenting with new ingre-dients and brewing methods. They are using more and fresher ingredients and few, if any, adjuncts and additives. They employ only minimal filtration and almost none pasteurize their beer. The craft breweries are providing what a small but growing number of Americans and Canadians have been searching for. Their beers are handcrafted in small batches by people who care about good beer.

If you have not already taken part in the beer renaissance, it's time you got started. But, where DO you get started? Exactly how do you find these brewpubs and craft breweries? This guide book is your answer.

As the publisher of a beer connoisseur's newsletter (the *World Beer Review*) focusing on brewpubs and craft breweries, I became acutely aware of the difficul-ties and frustrations of trying to locate the more than 370 brewpubs and craft breweries which now exist in North America. With that in mind I put together this guide, which tells you where the brewpubs are located, how to find them, when they are open, what beers they serve, what type of food is served, and other useful and interesting facts about the pubs. I have also included craft breweries which serve free samples or give tours.

One thing I purposely avoided was rating the beers. This is because of the dif-ficulty of rating so many beers (more than 2,000 brands now and dozens of new ones coming out every month) and because they vary in quality from batch to batch. So be warned, although some of the best beers are being produced by these new breweries, sometimes the suds are duds.

One thing I have learned about brewpubs, you have to take the good with the bad. But there will never be a dull moment. So, it's time you started on your brewpub adventure.

Cheers!!!
Steve Johnson

A MAN FOR ALL SEASONS.

From the brewers of
SAMUEL ADAMS BOSTON LAGER,
the Best Beer in America,™ several reasons to be optimistic
about what the future holds.

Spring
Samuel Adams Double Bock
•
Summer
Samuel Adams Dark Wheat, Samuel Adams Wheat
•
Fall
Samuel Adams Octoberfest
•
Winter
Samuel Adams Winter Lager
Samuel Adams Cranberry Lambic

Along with our six seasonals, we offer the discerning beer
drinker four year-round brews: Samuel Adams Boston Lager,
Samuel Adams Boston Ale, Boston Lightship, and our newest
introduction, Samuel Adams Cream Stout.

What is a Brewpub?

A brewpub is an establishment which brews and sells beer for consumption on premise. Different people, looking at brewpubs from different perspectives, define them differently. A pub-bar-tavern keeper looks at it as a pub with a brewery. A brewer looks at it as a brewery with a pub. A restaurateur looks at it as a restaurant with a brewery. However, when these activities take place at the same location, as far as the consumer is concerned they are brewpubs, regardless of what the owners may call them.

A brewpub is basically a bar with a brewery in it. Beyond that there is an almost infinite variation in styles. Some are old and quaint, others, modern; some are open and airy, others, small and cozy; some are primarily restaurants, featuring fine dining; some serve only their own beers, others have fantastic selections of draft and bottled beers from other breweries; some have substantial selections of wines, and still others offer the entire range of alcoholic beverages. However, they all provide a place where you can relax, socialize, and drink fresh beer.

For the purposes of this book, I have stretched the meaning of a "brewpub" slightly. Namely, I have included breweries with outlets for their products in adjacent buildings. There are many small breweries across the country which for various reasons, usually legal, have a brewery and a pub next door to each other. Sometimes they are owned by the same person, sometimes they are owned separately by a husband and wife, usually in order to get around a state or local legal restriction, and other times they are owned by different people who are informally working together. Regardless of legal and business differences, for the consumer they are still brewpubs. And many of these brewery-pubs also have windows between them, creating an authentic brewpub atmosphere.

Unlike earlier editions of *On Tap*, all breweries included in this edition were open at press time and serving beer brewed on premise, with three slight exceptions. These were Lone Star Cantina and Brewery in Roanoke, Virginia, Chapter House Brewing in Ithaca, New York, and Bardo Rodeo in Arlington, Virginia. The first opened as the Blue Muse, closed, reopened as the Lone Star, and the new owners have reapplied for licensing. The second brewed, then discontinued the brewing operation, and have since reapplied for licensing. The third is brewing test batches and will probably be serving house beers by the time this book is distributed.

Is it a Brewpub or Is it a Craft Brewery?

In order to keep things simple, I use the term "brewpub" for any craft brewery which sells its beer for consumption on premise. But, you might ask, what about a craft brewery which sells beer both on and off premise? My answer is that these establishments are both craft breweries AND brewpubs.

4

Several people suggested that a microbrewery should only be called a brewpub if <u>most</u> of it's sales were for on-premise consumption. The problem with this definition is some microbreweries would be changing from one category to the other, depending on their sales ratio, and would only serve to confuse the reader. Yakima Brewing & Malting (Grant's Brewpub) is a good example. For the first few months after opening, most of it's sales were on site, so it would have been called a brewpub. After that, most of its sales were off site; so, it would have been called a microbrewery. Now, it has added a second brewing operation across the street from the original brewery, which is a brewpub; so, it should be called a brewpub again. Confusing?

Many craft breweries are located in or next to restaurants or bars, where their beer is served. Such establishments offer the same services as a brewpub, but are not legally considered to be brewpubs, and, to the confusion of the consumer, have different names than the restaurant or bar. When asked if they are brewpubs, they frequently reply they are not, furthering the consumers' the confusion. Following is a partial list of such establishments.

Appleton Brewing - Dos Bandidos Restaurant - Johnny O's Pizzeria
Bayern Brewing - Missoula Northern Pacific

photo by Tom Bernard

Dock Street Brewing
Philadelphia, Pennsylvania

Beach Brewing - The Mill
Columbus Brewing - Hagen's - Gibby's
Hale's Ales - Kirkland Roaster
Kennebunkport Brewing - Lobster Deck - Federal Jack's
Miles Town Brewing - Golden Spur
Widmer - B. Moloch - The Heathman

Is It a Small Brewery
or Is It a Craft Brewery?

When the new breweries began to spring up in the late seventies they were called either craft breweries or boutique breweries. Then someone coined the term "microbrewery" and defined it as any brewery producing not more than 10,000 barrels of beer annually. This definition was limited, but, of course, the breweries' production was not limited. Now many of these "microbreweries" have far surpassed this limit (Sierra Nevada and Redhook were the first to do so).

Recently, people have been speaking of a 15,000 or 20,000 barrel limit. The term microbrewery seems to be racing to keep up with the breweries' production. It is becoming apparent that "craft brewery" would have been a more useful term.

For this reason, I have discarded the term microbrewery altogether and use the term "craft brewery," instead. Anchor Brewing of San Francisco, California, is a good example of a craft brewery which is not a microbrewery. Anchor is most definitely a craft brewery, producing highly distinctive interpretations of classic styles. In the early days of the microbrewery movement, Anchor was a source of inspiration and a model for the new brewing entrepreneurs. August Schell Brewing of New Ulm, Minnesota, was not included because, although a craft brewery producing beers every bit as good as Anchor's, it did not play the crucial role in the microbrewery movement that Anchor did.

Because of the fuzziness in definition, we are in the process of determining what qualifies a brewery to be called a craft brewery. In future editions of *On Tap* we may include breweries which have not heretofore been considered craft breweries (and we might eliminate some breweries as well).

Are There Craft Breweries and Brewpubs
Which Are Not Included in the Guide?

The answer is yes. To be included in the guide the consumer must at least be able to visit the brewery and taste the beer. Some of the breweries contacted didn't allow tasting on premise or offer tours, others were private clubs. An example of the former is Beier Brewing in Boise, Idaho, and of the latter, New Albany Brewing, located near Columbus, Ohio.

Then, there are the contract breweries. Although there are several variations of how this works (some have their own brewer, some have their own recipes, and

some merely put their labels on someone else's brand), basically, these are breweries in name only. They brew their beer (or have it brewed for them) at someone else's brewery.

To complicate things even further, some breweries are contract breweries, microbreweries, AND brewpubs. Boston Beer is a good example of this--it has a microbrewery in Boston, a brewpub in Philadelphia, and also brews beer at Pittsburgh Brewing in Pittsburgh, Pennsylvania, and at Blitz-Weinhard Brewing in Portland, Oregon. Pike Place Brewing of Seattle, Washington, is a craft brewery, but also has one of its beers brewed elsewhere as well.

Finally, there are pseudo-brewpubs. They call themselves breweries; they may even have brewing equipment on display; but, they don't brew beer. Some of these are innocent--they are trying to create a "beery" atmosphere, without claiming to be a brewery. But others are trying to deceive the public, and will only admit that they do not brew their own beer when challenged. I have tried, and I hope successfully, to keep such establishments out of the guide.

Gritty McDuff's, Portland, Maine   photo by Kevin Leduc

How Did Brewpubs
Get Started?

Background

About a century ago there were many small breweries in the United States producing fresh, hand-crafted beer for local distribution. The more than 2,200 breweries were making a great variety of styles, from English porters to German bock biers.

A hundred years later, even though much more beer was being produced, almost all the styles had died out but one: American Pilsner, a watered-down and very bland beer. And almost all of the small breweries had disappeared as well. In 1980 there were only 40 brewing companies left.

What happened during those 100 years? Most of the old breweries were very small, using traditional methods of brewing, and marketing to a local geographic area. Ironically, even though brewing output was increasing, the number of breweries began to decline and continued to do so for the next 100 years. As improved methods of storing beer (refrigeration), preserving beer (pasteurization), and transporting beer (railroads) took effect, breweries began competing in each other's territories. The weaker breweries closed or were gobbled up by their competitors.

By 1920 only 583 active breweries remained. Then on January 17, 1920, Prohibition became the law of the land, with the passing of the Volstead Act. Of course, brewing didn't stop, it just became illegal-- home brewing became a popular past-time and more than 50,000 speakeasies selling beer, wine, and spirits sprang up. One little ditty from the times goes like this:

> *Mother's in the kitchen*
> *Washing out the jugs;*
> *Sister's in the pantry*
> *Bottling all the suds;*
> *Father's in the cellar*
> *Mixing up the hops;*
> *Johnny's on the front porch*
> *Watching for the cops.*

When Prohibition was repealed in 1933 many small breweries reopened, but the new business environment favored even larger breweries. In this new age, advertising was becoming increasingly important to a brewery's success. Americans were more mobile than before and when they moved to a new community, they frequently preferred to stick with a familiar brand, such as a national brand, rather than switch to a local, unknown one. It also became easier for the new national supermarket chains to sell a national brand than it was to carry many different regional and local beers.

Another important change which took place after the repeal of Prohibition was the setting up of the "three-tier" system of beer distribution in all of the states. Before Prohibition, there had been much criticism of the "tied house" system, whereby breweries bought taverns and allowed only their beers to be sold in the taverns. This is similar to the situation that exists in England today. When Prohibition was repealed, state lawmakers took the opportunity to break up the tied houses and required that those involved in the beer business (breweries, beer wholesalers or distributors, and beer retailers) be owned independently. In many cases it was illegal to have family members own different segments of the industry. This proved very effective, but it also prevented the creation of brewpubs (where beer is brewed, sold, and consumed under the same roof). When the brewpub movement came to the United States, one of the first things that had to be done was to modify the three-tier system.

The small breweries struggled through the thirties and forties, but by the fifties they began to disappear precipitously. In 1950 the total number of active breweries had dropped to 407; by 1960 only 229 had survived; by 1970, only 142.

In 1980, a century after the high-water mark for breweries, only 82 breweries remained in the United States, and these were in the hands of only 40 companies. They were producing more beer than ever, but it was uninteresting and homogeneous.

BEERTOONS
by phil alley

Time for sports, brought to you by **Stale Ale** . . . It's for folks who'll <u>drink anything</u>. And at 39 cents a pack, it's a real bargain!

At the same time consolidation was taking place, beer was becoming lighter and less flavorful. The 3.2 beer served to American GIs during World War II created a ready market for the more insipid beers when the War was over. In the 1970s lighter, lower calorie food was the rage, and beer followed suit with light beer. The breweries substituted adjuncts, such as corn and rice, for malted barley and used less hops as well. In addtition to lowering the calorie content of the beer, it reduced the cost of the raw materials for brewing. Arguments have been made that (1) breweries were trying to cut costs by brewing light beer, and on the other hand, that (2) breweries were simply responding to consumer demand. I do not know the answer to this debate, but it could conceivably be a combination of both factors.

The Beer Renaissance

From these "dark ages" in brewing, interest in fresh and flavorful beer sprung anew. This, in turn, led to the birth of craft breweries and brewpubs. Several factors contributed to this renaissance. They are as follows:

1. Consumer backlash: Chief among the factors was the low level to which American beer had sunk. It had become so insipid that a small but noticeable consumer backlash was created. A few Americans switched to other types of beverages, some started to drink imported beer, and yet others began to brew their own beer. Some people sought out regional and local brewery products, but were usually disappointed because these small breweries, like the larger ones, had followed the same trend toward American Pilsner. Two breweries which were bucking the trend were August Schell Brewing of New Ulm, Minnesota, and Anchor Brewing of San Francisco, California.

2. Imported beer: Some people began to notice the difference when they travelled abroad and tasted beers brewed in foreign countries. This created an interest in imported beer during the 1970s. The interest was both in the flavor and in the variety, even though the imports generally lacked freshness. This lack of freshness was a contributing factor to the creation of American craft breweries.

3. Homebrewing: At the same time there was an increased interest in homebrewing. This, in turn, led to the passing of a federal law in 1979 legalizing homebrewing. Some of these early homebrewers later became pioneers in the microbrewery revolution.

4. Concern about health and safety: In the 1980s there developed a growing concern for health and safety. Beer, being a drink of moderation, became an increasingly attractive option for Americans.

5. CAMRA: In 1971 a group of Englishmen formed The Campaign for Real Ale, a consumer group aimed at protecting small English breweries and beer quality. They were combating the major breweries which were gobbling up the local breweries and their pubs (tied houses) and then eliminating many of the local beer brands and styles. Once the major breweries had achieved a monopoly in a particular locale, they tended to raise prices. Another unpopular practice of the major breweries was to inject carbon dioxide into the beer and to store and serve it at colder than cellar temperature, in order to preserve the beer from spoilage for a longer time. Ale treated in this manner is known in England as "keg ale," as opposed to "cask ale" or "real ale." The purists argued that this ruined the drinking quality of the beer. CAMRA has been very successful in attracting support among the citizens and in publicizing its concerns. CAMRA forced at least a temporary reversal in brewing practices in England and slowed the trend toward keg ale (draft beer pumped under carbon dioxide pressure and served at colder than traditional serving temperatures). CAMRA attracted the attention of several homebrewers and beer enthusiasts in America who saw the need to foster an interest in good beer in this country.

6. Rebirth of brewpubs in England: David Bruce opened the first modern home-brew pub in England. Bruce had worked in a series of jobs in the brewing/ pub/entertainment business, but nothing seemed to work out. In 1979, while on the dole, he devised a plan to refurbish and install a small brewery in a boarded-up pub on Bourough Road in Southwark. Most people regarded Bruce's scheme as hair-brained, but he was able to fast-talk a bank manager and two breweries into lending him enough money to open. He changed the name of the pub from the Duke of York to the Goose and Firkin and lacking funds, he kept the furnishings inside the pub to the bare essentials. The pub was an instant success and within four years Bruce had a chain of six brewpubs in southern England. Bruce's success provided an inspirational model for many would-be brewers in England and North America. Incidentally, the name used in England "home-brew pub" was also the origin of the term "brewpub" in America.

7. Rising interest in gourmet food and drink: The spread of good beer has definitely benefited from the interest in gourmet foods and beverages. Drinking a quality beer is now the "in" thing to do. If you want to be conspicuous about it, taverns and restaurants are among the best places to do so.

Fritz Maytag, President, Anchor Brewing Co., San Francisco, began the beer revival in the early seventies by producing hand-crafted, traditional styles of beer, such as steam beer, porter, pale ale, wheat beer, barley wine, and spiced holiday ale.

The Birth of Craft Breweries and Brewpubs

The craft brewing revolution began in the United States in the summer of 1977 when the first bottles of New Albion Ale went on sale in Sonoma, California. The brewer of this beer was Jack McAuliffe, a local homebrewer.

While stationed in Scotland with the U.S. Navy, McAuliffe had developed a strong liking for the distinctive English and Scotch ales he found there. After returning to the United States McAuliffe began brewing his own beer at home, trying to duplicate the styles he had found in Scotland. McAuliffe's friends spoke so highly of his homebrewed beer that he decided to brew it commercially. On October 8, 1976, Jack McAuliffe, Suzy Stern, and Jane Zimmerman incorporated under the name of the **New Albion Brewing Co.** The word "Albion" is Gaelic for "England," which reflects McAuliffe's interest in English ales.

Like many craft breweries to follow, the tiny brewery, with a 450-barrel annual brewing capacity, was started on a shoestring and constructed entirely by McAuliffe, Stern, and Zimmerman. New Albion went up in a rural area about three miles south of Sonoma. Test brewing began in July 1977 and New Albion Ale was ready for bottling shortly thereafter (a Porter and a Stout were introduced in short order). The bottle-conditioned beer was hand-capped and at first distributed by New Albion in wooden cases, which had to be returned to the brewery afterward. From the meager earnings the three partners were able to pay themselves a monthly salary of $150. McAuliffe was able to save on rent by making a makeshift apartment above the brewhouse, reached by a ladder, where he "lived like a spider."

New Albion operated profitably for a period, but its resources were too meager to fund a planned relocation and expansion in 1981. The financial strain was too much and brewing ceased late in 1982. The Mendocino Brewing Co. purchased the brewing equipment and early in 1983 Jack McAuliffe, along with New Albion employees Don Barkley and Michael Lovett went to work for Mendocino.

Although New Albion experienced rough going from the start and ultimately failed, craft brewing was an idea whose time had come, and New Albion was the spark to ignite the brewing explosion.

By the time New Albion officially closed in early 1983, eight craft breweries had sprung up across the country. The first of these was **DeBakker Brewing** of Marin County, California, started in 1979. Brewer/owner Tom DeBakker had been a homebrewer for ten years before he opened a commercial brewery. From 1979 until 1981 DeBakker produced a pale ale and a porter. DeBakker worked as a fire fighter during the week and brewed beer on the weekends. Unfortunately, the DeBakker Brewery closed within two years.

The Boulder Brewery in Boulder, Colorado

(now Rockies Brewing)

During 1980 two breweries opened outside of California: **Boulder Brewing** (now Rockies Brewing), in Boulder, Colorado, and Cartwright Brewing, in Portland, Oregon. Boulder's original brewing operation was located on a goat farm near Hygiene, Colorado. Founders David Hummer and Randolph Ware actually began in 1979 by selling their homebrew at a liquor store in Boulder. One thing led to another and by 1984 they had built a beautiful cathedral-looking brewery in Boulder. Boulder brews Extra Pale Ale, Porter, and Stout. Of the first four craft breweries to open, Boulder, renamed Rockies Brewing in 1993, is the only survivor.

Cartwright Brewing was founded by Charles Coury, who had had experience running a winery. It took him 18 months of hard work before he was able to open his own brewery in 1980. The brewery was named after his wife, Shirley Cartwright. The brewery's Cartwright Portland Beer was inconsistent at best and sales were not sufficient to keep the brewery profitable. The brewery was closed by the City of Portland in 1982 for failure to pay back taxes.

1981 brought a crop of four new craft breweries, including three in California and one in New York. **Sierra Nevada Brewing** was opened in Chico, California, by two young homebrewers, Ken Grossman and Paul Camusi. The company was founded in 1978, but it took Grossman and Camusi almost three years to raise the money and construct the brewery themselves. Soon after

BREWED AND BOTTLED BY SIERRA NEVADA BREWING CO., CHICO, CALIF.

opening in early 1981 they were brewing Pale Ale, Porter, Stout, and seasonal Celebration Ale and Bigfoot Barleywine-Style Ale. They have won numerous awards for their beers. The brewery has since expanded and opened a brewpub.

River City Brewing was opened in Sacramento, California, by Jim Schlueter and his wife Chris Hoover. Schlueter was an ex-Schlitz brewer who felt there was room for craft brewed lagers. Up to this time, all craft brewed beers had been top-fermented ales. He produced a very good, all-malt lager called River City Gold. River City closed in the eighties and Schlueter went on to found Hogshead Brewpub in 1986.

Charles and Diana Rixford began brewing beer in their basement in Berkeley, California, in October of 1981. They called their company **Thousand Oaks Brewing**. The beer was made with malt-extract and fermented in 52-gallon industrial barrels. Their four beers (Thousand Oaks Lager, Golden Gate Malt, Golden Bear Malt Liquor, and Cable Car Lager) were distributed in the San Francisco Bay area. The Rixfords have since ceased their brewing operation but are having some of the brands brewed under contract.

When Bill Newman became interested in real ale, he went to work at the Ringwood Brewery in England so that he could learn how to make it well. When he opened **Newman's Brewing** in Albany, New York, in late 1981, he became the first craft brewer in the United States to produce cask-conditioned bitter, or "real ale" as it is called. This was called simply Pale Ale. Later Newman added a Winter Ale and then began marketing a contract-brewed beer called Newman's Albany Amber Beer. The brewery has since closed, but the contract brewed beer is still available.

The year 1982 saw the opening of the first two brewpubs in North America as well as one more craft brewery. Also, in that year a law was passed in California allowing brewpubs.

Bert Grant
founder of the Yakima Brewing & Malting Co.

The first brewpub was **Horseshoe Bay Brewery/Troller Pub** in Victoria, British Columbia, which opened in June (for more information, see the chapter on Canadian breweries). In July, Bert Grant opened **Yakima Brewing & Malting**, located in the old Switzer Opera House in downtown Yakima, Washington. Grant had worked in the brewing business since 1945, first for breweries and later as Technical Director for S.S. Steiner, a hop merchant. Given his outstanding technical knowledge of, and experience with, brewing, Grant decided to be his own brewmaster. When Yakima Brewing opened in July of 1982 it was the first brewpub to open in America. Brewers, homebrewers, and reporters flocked to see Grant and his new brewpub. His beers were assertive and Grant said, with a smile on his face, "I make my beers the way I like them and it happens that a lot of other people like them that way, too." Grant's beers have won several awards and he opened another brewpub across the street in 1990.

Washington got its second brewery shortly afterward, with the opening of the **Independent Ale Brewery** (now **Redhook Brewery**) in Seattle. President Paul Shipman had been a marketing representative for the Chateau Ste. Michelle winery when he developed an interest in opening a brewery. The brewery expanded and moved in 1988. It now has a taproom called the Trolleyman.

Michael Laybourn
founder of Mendocino Brewing

The year 1983 saw the opening of the first three brewpubs in California. **Mendocino Brewing** was the first to open in Hopland, on August 14, followed within a few weeks by Buffalo Bill's in Hayward. Mendocino's general partner, Michael Laybourn, was able to pick up brewers Don Barkley and Michael Lovett from the failing New Albion Brewery. Laybourn had been a homebrewer for many years and had become inspired by the New Albion Brewery. The brewhouse also came from New Albion. The brewery opened in the old Hop Vine Saloon and produced ales named after the various birds which inhabit the area. A bottling line was added in 1985.

Bill Owens, founder of Buffalo Bill's Brewpub.

Buffalo Bill's opened in September. Owner/brewer Bill Owens had been a commercial photographer who developed an interest in brewing. In 1982 he published a book, *How to Build a Small Brewery*. Owens has since opened two more brewpubs in the San Francisco Bay area and is the publisher of *American Brewer* magazine.

Palo Alto Brewing opened in November, but closed within months.

The other brewery to open in 1983 was **Hale's Ales**, in Colville, Washington. President/brewer Mike Hale travelled to England in the early 1980s and fell in love with English ales. He stayed in order to learn the art of brewing. When Hale returned to the United States he built his small brewery single-handedly and he still does almost all of the work around the brewery by himself. Hale's Ales produces only draft beer.

By the end of 1983 there were eleven craft breweries and brewpubs. At this point the pace picked up speed. During 1984, 17 more opened and by the end of 1986, 55 were operating in the United States. Four years later, at the end of 1990 there were more than 200 craft breweries and brewpubs, and several brewpub chains had sprung up.

What is Beer?

Beer is a fermented beverage made from cereal grains. In the modern world it has been traditionally made from malted barley. Other grains used in brewing include corn (from which the South and Central American chicha is made) wheat, oats, and rice (from which saké is made). These grains are frequently used in addition to barley to change the character of the beer. In the United States beer is still made from malted barley, however, the use of unmalted corn and rice as adjuncts has become almost universal by the larger breweries. Corn and rice serve to lighten the body, diminish the malted barley flavor, and decrease the production costs because both are less expensive then malted barley.

Fermented beverages can be made from things other than cereal. Wine, for example, is made from fermented fruit. Although some beers have fruit in them, such as the Belgian fruit lambics, they are still brewed with malted grain. Hard cider, although popular in many pubs, falls in the wine category, because it is made from apples. Mead, made from fermented honey, is neither beer nor wine.

Two other necessary ingredients in beer are water, which constitutes up to 92% percent of the finished beer, and yeast, which creates alcohol. The alcoholic strength of beer can range anywhere from less than .5% (in the so-called "non-alcoholic" beers) to a high of almost 15%. Yeast can also give an estery character to the aroma.

Samichlaus Bier, brewed by Brauerei Hurlimann of Zurich, Switzerland, holds the world beer alcohol record at 14.93% by volume. Two other contenders for the alcohol record are Kulminator Urtyp Hell (also called EKU 28) brewed by the EKU Brewery in Kulmbach, Germany, (13.5% by volume) and Thomas Hardy's Ale, brewed by the Eldridge Pope Brewery in Dorchester, England (12.48% by volume).

A fourth ingredient in almost all modern beer is hops. Hops give bitterness to beer (although over-roasted barley can make beer bitter also) and serves to counterbalance the natural sweetness of the malted barley. Hops can also contribute greatly to the beer aroma, giving it a floral character. Before pasteurization and industrial refrigeration were invented hops served somewhat as a natural preservative for beer.

Craft brewers tend to be purists. They want their beer to be made with the the best ingredients, without

BEERTOONS by phil alley

This is a new beer...brewed with Barley, Malt, and Lettuce! Should be a big seller in any Salad Bar!

adjuncts, additives, pasteurization, or microfiltration. For this reason many of them adhere to the *Reinheitsgebot*, or German purity law. In 1516 William VI, Elector of Bavaria, declared that only water, malted barley, and hops could be used to make beer. Yeast was not included in the ingredients, but taken for granted. The purity law was amended later to allow malted wheat. It was so important to the Bavarians that they made the continuance of the purity law a condition to their joining the German Republic in 1919. The purity law was struck down in 1987 by the European Court for being protectionist in nature (i.e., not allowing the importation of many foreign beers, which used all kinds of dreadful things in their beer). Despite the reversal in the European Court, German brewers have pledged to continue to adhere to the *Reinheitsgebot*.

How Is Beer Made?

There is a lot more to making beer than just throwing some barley and yeast into water and letting it ferment. If you take this more laissez faire approach, and don't mind off-flavors and inconsistent beer, you can make it this way. But if you want to consistently brew a particular style of beer with an unadulterated flavor and aroma, which your customers will learn to like and return for again and again, you will have to be methodical and exact in the way you brew it.

The barley must first be malted, dried, and then roasted. The way in which it is roasted affects its flavor. The hops have a very important effect on the beer's nose and palate, and, of course, they must be kept fresh if they are to be any good. The type of water can also influence the quality of the beer, although, some marketing departments have overemphasized its importance to the beer's quality. The type of yeast used (and there are dozens of varieties) can profoundly influence the flavor of the beer. Finally, beer is very prone to spoilage, caused either by bacteria or wild yeast. All of these things and more, can affect the flavor and character of the finished beer. For this reason, brewing has become a very precise science, but still allows for the "artist" to express him or herself in the formulation of recipes.

Once the beer has been brewed it must be stored and dispensed properly in order to guard against spoilage. Being a very perishable product, if you don't pasteurize it, cover it with a pressurized blanket of carbon dioxide, and microfilter it, like the big breweries do, you have a product which is almost spoiling before your very eyes. Like a freshly-baked loaf of bread, good beer is delicate and short-lived. The best beer is fresh, unfiltered, unpasteurized, and unpressurized. This is what makes brewpubs so attractive. A fresh, well-designed, well-brewed, and well-stored beer is a thing of indescribable, but simple beauty. It almost brings tears to my eyes to think that real beer had been fast disappearing from American breweries.

The Ingredients

Beer is made from the following four primary ingredients:
> barley
> water
> hops
> yeast

BARLEY

Barley is a wheat-like cereal grain. It is important because it provides starch which is converted to maltose during the malting and mashing processes. Later, the yeast converts the maltose to alcohol and carbon dioxide. The barley also provides flavor and color. Indirectly, it provides head, carbonation, and body to the beer. So, you can see barley is a key element in beer.

Two types of barley are used in making beer: six-row and two-row. Six-row gives a higher yield and is therefore less expensive; however, the two-row is prized by craft brewers for its superior flavor.

barley

WATER

Even though water is the main ingredient in beer, it is the least important in its effect on the finished product. You can't make a world class beer on the merits of the water--that's where the barley, hops and yeast come in (not to mention the brewer's art). However, to make good beer, the water must be pure. The hardness or softness of the water can be important in several styles. A European Pilsner, for example, should be brewed using relatively soft water. But you don't have to go to Bohemia to obtain soft water--you can treat your local water.

HOPS

Hops are cones which grow on the hop vine (*humulus lupulus*, the Latin botanical name). Only cones from the female vine are used in making beer. Hops were originally used to help preserve beer against spoilage and and to provide bitterness as a counterbalance to the sweet maltiness. Hops can also provide a wonderful bouquet to the beer. There are dozens of hop varieties and most beer is made with a blend of hops. The major American beer brands typically have very small amounts of hops in them.

hops

Breweries may use hops in three forms: fresh, whole hops; pelletized hops; and liquid hop extract. The whole hops are most desirable for their freshness, but they are more bulky to store and are perishable.

YEAST

Yeast is a type of microscopic fungus. During fermentation the yeast consumes the maltose, converting it to alcohol and carbon dioxide. The many varieties of yeast used in brewing fall into two categories: *saccharomyces uvarum* (bottom fermenting) and *saccharomyces cerevisiae* (top fermenting). Each variety, or species, of yeast imparts its own distinct characteristic to the beer's flavor. Two beers, brewed with precisely the same ingredients and in the same manner, but with different varieties of yeast, can taste very different. Because of this, and because there is wild yeast present in the air around us, brewers take great care to protect their beer against contaminating yeast.

At one time all beers where brewed with top-fermenting yeast. Top-fermenting yeast float to the top of the beer and work best at warm temperatures, typically 59-77°F (15-25°C). Ales (see chapter on beer styles) are almost always made with top-fermenting yeast.

Bottom-fermenting yeast sink to the bottom of the beer and work best at colder temperatures, typically 41-54°F (5-12°C). It was on the European continent, where beers were lagered (stored) at very cold temperatures for several months, where bottom-fermenting yeast was first recognized and cultured. All lagers are made with bottom-fermenting yeast.

OTHER INGREDIENTS

Other ingredients used in making beer include: adjuncts, additives, herbs, spices, and fruit.

An adjunct is an unmalted grain, including wheat, corn, rice, or oats, used in addition to the malted barley. In the United States adjuncts have been used to lighten the flavor and body of the beer.

Additives are chemicals, synthetic or natural, added to beer during brewing, packaging, or storing for a variety of reasons. Various sugars, such as lactose and sucrose, which are non-fermentable, are sometimes added to provide body and sweetness. Various types of clarifying aids are used, including Irish moss, isinglass, papain, and polyclar. Enzymes are sometimes added to give beer body and aid in head retention. Burton water salts are sometimes added in order to duplicate the hard water found in Burton-upon-Trent, England, a brewing town famous for its pale ales. Heading liquids are sometimes used to promote foaming action.

A variety of herbs, spices, and fruit have been used in making beer over the years. These include cinnamon, ginger, cherries, raspberries, coriander, peppers, licorice, and spruce. Brewpubs are likely to experiment with these different ingredients.

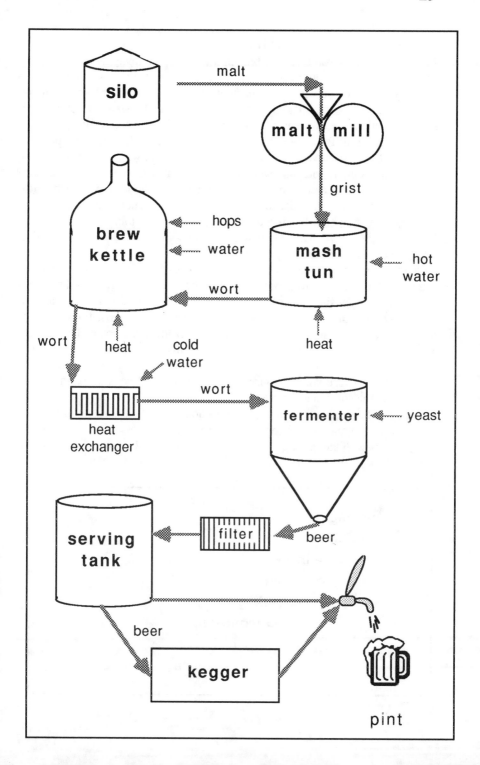

The Process

When you visit a microbrewery or brewpub you will see many tanks, hoses, and other unfamiliar contraptions in the brewing area. The following explanation is designed to provide you with the fundamentals of the brewing process so that you can make some sense of what you are looking at. Many brewpubs label the various tanks, which makes it easier to understand what's going on. But, to make things confusing, different brewpubs use different names for the same piece of equipment. The alternative names are provided in the text which follows.

If you are going to tour a brewery at a time other than when the regular tours are conducted, always call in advance. In fact, it's not a bad idea to let them know your coming even for a regular tour. Brewing staff are usually happy to accommodate you if they can, but it may be difficult to fit a tour into the brewing schedule. Please realize that the brewing staff are doing you a favor in taking time out from their busy schedule to show you around.

One thing you won't see at a brewpub are fields of barley, like you would see a vineyard at a winery. This is because the orientation of wineries and breweries are toward the opposite ends of the process. Wineries are oriented toward the beginning of the process: the growing of the grapes; whereas, breweries are oriented toward the other end: the consumption of the beer. Logically, wineries exist where the grapes grow best. And also logically, breweries are situated near the consumer. For this reason, breweries will never grow their own raw ingredients nearby because you can't grow enough barley and hops in the cities and towns, where the consumers are located.

Because of the space required, brewpubs don't malt their barley either. So, in understanding the making of beer, remember that the process within the brewery usually begins with the milling of the malted barley (see chart on previous page).

The following are the major steps in making beer, listed in sequence:

-> malting
    -> roasting
        -> milling
            -> mashing
                -> boiling
                    -> fermenting
                        -> maturing
                            -> kegging, bottling

MALTING

Malting involves sprouting (or germinating) the barley in order to produce enzymes, which in turn convert some of the starch into fermentable sugars. The barley grains are sorted by size, soaked in water, removed and then spread out and allowed to sprout for about a week.

ROASTING

The malt is next dried and roasted in order to arrest the sprouts. The longer they are roasted in the **kiln,** the darker and more caramelized the malt will become. This will affect the color and flavor of the beer. The malt is then sieved to remove the sprouts.

MILLING

Here is where the process typically begins at a microbrewery. Malt is taken from the **malt silo** and milled (or ground) in a **roller mill** to produce grist. Milling facilitates the extraction of sugars in the next stage. The silo is usually located outside and to the rear of the brewery.

MASHING

Next, the grist is transferred to the **mash tun** (or **lauter tun**) where it is soaked and stirred in hot water of about 150°F (66°C) for one to two hours. The slurry of hot water and malt is called "mash." Mashing converts more of the starch to sugar and extracts the sugar and other solubles from the grist. At higher temperatures less starch is converted to simple sugars, which makes a sweeter, fuller-bodied beer. At lower temperatures more starch is converted to simple sug-

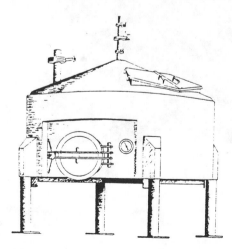

The Mash Tun

photo by Peter Vanderwarker

Jim Koch, at the Boston Beer Company brewery

ars, which produces a drier, light-bodied beer.

The mash tun is drained of solubles and the remaining sediment is sparged (sprayed) with hot water in order to extract as many solubles as possible. The sweet liquid which drains out through strainer plates in the bottom of the mash tun is called wort (rhymes with dirt).

The hot water for the mash is usually, but not always, stored in hot water tanks, called hot "**liquor tanks**" by brewers. Some brewpubs heat the water for the mash in the brew kettle and then transfer it to the mash tun.

Some brewpubs do not mill or mash their own grains. Instead, they use malt extract, a molasses-like substance, which they put directly into the brew kettle.

BOILING

The wort is transferred to the **brew kettle** (or **copper**) where it is boiled with the hops for about 1-2 hours. Bittering hops are added at the beginning of the boil. Flavoring hops may be added at any time, and aroma hops are added near the end of the boil. Some breweries dry hop their beer for extra aroma. In dry hopping, the hops are added after the boil is finished. The wort is transferred to the **whirlpool** where unwanted protein, hops, and other solids are separated through centrifugal force. Next the wort is forced to cool rapidly through a **heat exchanger** (or **cooler** or **wort chiller**).

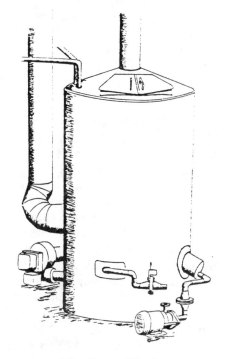

The Brew Kettle

FERMENTING

When the wort has cooled, it is transferred to a **fermentation tank** (also called **uni-tank**, **CIP tank** (CIP = clean in place), or **primary**) and the yeast is pitched (added) to the brew. The wort is briefly stirred in order to provide oxygen to the yeast.

Most microbreweries use closed fermentation tanks; however, some use open fermentation vessels, where you can actually see the beer fermenting. At this stage you can see a great deal of foam at the top of the beer. What you can't see is the sediment (called "trub," rhymes with tube) forming at the bottom of the tank and the carbon dioxide being released into the air.

The Fermentation Tanks

MATURING

When primary fermentation is complete, usually within a few days to a week, the beer (now referred to as "green" beer) is filtered, usually with diatomaceous earth. The latter is made up of microscopic skeletal remains of marine animals and does a very good job of filtering. Next the green beer is transferred to a **conditioning tank** (also called **bright beer tank, serving tank, holding tank, finishing tank,** or **secondary**). Here the beer continues to ferment, but at a much reduced rate. The beer clarifies and the flavors mature and blend. Conditioning tanks are closed; thus, as the beer ferments and the carbon dioxide can no longer escape, the beer becomes naturally carbonated. Conditioning may take anywhere from a few days to several months.

At this point the beer may be piped directly to the tap handles in the pub. Natural, fresh beer dispensed in this manner is known as "real" beer.

KEGGING, BOTTLING

An alternative way to package the beer is to put it into metal **kegs**. This way it can be tapped on premise or shipped to another bar or restaurant. Kegging is generally done by adding carbon dioxide under pressure to the keg. In a few cases kegged beer is pasteurized. Real beer does not use additional carbon dioxide and a wooden peg is placed in the bung, allowing the beer to continue to ferment and condition in the keg. This is sometimes called "cask" beer.

In addition, many microbreweries bottle their beers, a more expensive and time-consuming way to package the beer than kegging. Much of this bottled beer is pasteurized. However, some microbreweries do not pasteurize their bottled beer. This beer still has live yeast in it and is said to be "bottle conditioned." Cask beer and bottle-conditioned beer is much more delicate and perishable than pasteurized and kegged beer.

Most brewpubs offer their beers in bottles to customers to take home. Usually these bottles have been hand-filled and capped, a very labor-intensive process. As these beers have not been pasteurized, I recommend that they be consumed within a few days.

Some brewpubs also will fill buckets, jugs, or what have you, for take out. This beer should be consumed as soon as you get home (but not on the way).

photo by Daniel J. Wigg

Goose Island Brewing, Chicago, Illinois

Beer Vocabulary

additive - chemicals such as enzymes, preservatives, and antioxidants which are added to simplify the brewing process or prolong shelf life.

adjunct - fermentable, unmalted grain, including wheat, corn, rice, or oats, used in addition to the malted barley. In the United States the larger breweries have used adjuncts extensively to lighten the flavor and body of the beer.

alcohol - an intoxicant created through the fermentation process. Alcohol content is expressed as a percentage of the volume or weight of the beer.

all-grain - an adjective describing the brewing process in which the brewer begins with grist, as opposed to using malt extract.
made with malted barley and without adjuncts.

all-malt - an adjective describing beer made with malted barley and without adjuncts.

attenuation - the degree to which the beer has fermented, also stated as the reduction in the wort's specific gravity. Other things being equal, the higher the level of attenuation, the drier, more alcoholic, and lighter bodied the beer becomes.

Balling - a measure of beer's density, devised by Carl Joseph Napoleon Balling in 1843. To convert Balling to specific gravity, take the Balling measure, multiply it by .004, and then add 1.

barley - a cereal grain used in making beer.

barrel - 31 gallons. In Great Britain it is 36 Imperial gallons (43.2 U.S. gallons).

beer - a fermented beverage made from malted cereal grain.

body - the thickness of beer as perceived by its mouthfeel. The density and level of carbonation can affect this mouthfeel.

bottle conditioned - unpasteurized beer, naturally carbonated in the bottle.

breweriana - beer-related memorabilia.

brewhouse - the equipment used to make beer.

brew kettle - the vessel in which wort from the mash is boiled with hops. Also called a copper.

brewpub - an establishment which brews beers and sells it for consumption on premise.

bright beer tank - see under conditioning tank.

bung - the stopper in the hole in a keg or cask of beer through which the keg or cask is filled and emptied. The hole is also referred to as a bung or bunghole. Real beer must use a wooden bung, also called a spile.

carbon dioxide - a gas created from the the fermentation process. Carbon dioxide gives beer its effervescence.

cask - a closed, barrel-shaped container for beer. They come in various sizes and are now usually made of metal. The bung in a cask must be made of wood, which allows the beer pressure to be released from the fermenting beer and to naturally carbonate itself.

conditioning tank - a vessel in which beer is placed after primary fermentation where the beer matures, clarifies, and is naturally carbonated through secondary fermentation. Also called bright beer tank, serving tank, and secondary.

contract beer - beer made by one brewery and then marketed by a company calling itself a brewery. The latter uses the brewing facilities of the former.

copper - see under brew kettle.

dextrin - complex, unfermentable carbohydrate in the malt. Dextrin contributes to the finishing gravity, body, and sweetness of the beer.

fermentation - the conversion of sugar into alcohol and carbon dioxide gas, through the action of yeast.

finishing gravity see under specific gravity.

gravity see under specific gravity.

grist - malt which has been ground.

guest beer - a beer offered by a pub which is not brewed at the pub or at the parent brewery.

hand pump - a device for dispensing draft beer using a pump operated by hand. The use of a hand pump allows cask-conditioned beer to be served without the use of pressurized carbon dioxide to force it up hill.

hard cider - a fermented beverage made from apples.

hops - seed cones which grow on the hop vine (*humulus lupulus*, the Latin botanical name). Only cones from the female vine are used in making beer.

house beer - a beer brewed in the pub or at the parent brewery.

keg - a closed, metal, barrel-shaped container for beer. It is usually pressurized and has a capacity of 15.5 gallons (1/2 barrel). A half keg (7.75 gallons) is referred to as a "pony keg."

krausen - the foam which appears on top of fermenting beer.

krausening - the process of conditioning beer by adding unfermented wort to fully fermented beer before kegging or bottling.

lauter tun - see mash tun.

liquor tank - a tank used to store water (sometimes referred to by brewers as "liquor") for the brewing process. They may store either hot or cold water .

malt - barley which has been soaked in water, allowed to sprout, and then dried.

maltose - a water-soluble, fermentable sugar contained in malt.

mash tun - a tank where grist is soaked in water and heated in order to convert the starch to sugar and extract the sugar and other solubles from the grist.

mead - a fermented beverage made from honey.

microbrewery - a brewery producing small amounts of beer. The upper limit of annual production has been variously set at 10,000, 15,000, and 20,000 barrels.

original gravity - see under specific gravity.

pasteurize - the application of heat to bottled, canned, or kegged beer in order to arrest the activity of micro-organisms, including yeast and bacteria. Pasteurization was first developed by the French scientist Louis Pasteur, who conducted several studies on the pasteurization of beer. Pasteurization may be either flash pasteurization (usually for kegs) where the beer is held at a high temperature for less than a minute and then rapidly cooled, or tunnel pasteurization (usually for bottles) where the bottles go through a tunnel of hot water for up to an hour.

pitch - to add yeast to wort.

Plato - a measure of beer's density, first devised by Carl Joseph Napoleon Balling and later corrected by Dr. Plato. One degree Plato is equal to 0.97 degrees Balling. The Plato measure is prevalent in Germany.

pony keg see under keg.

pub - an establishment serving beer and sometimes other alcoholic beverages for consumption on premise. A pub usually serves food as well. The term originated in England and is the shortened form for "public house."

publican - The owner or manager of a pub (not to be confused with a REpublican).

Reinheitsgebot - German purity law. In 1516 William VI, Elector of Bavaria, declared that only water, malted barley, and hops could be used to make beer. Yeast was not included in the ingredients, but taken for granted. The purity law was amended later to allow malted wheat. It was so important to the Bavarians that they made the continuance of the purity law a condition to their joining the German Republic in 1919. The purity law was struck down in 1987 by the European Court for being protectionist in nature.

room temperature - the temperature of the surrounding air where the beer is stored, typically around 55°F (13°C). "Room temperature" is actually a misnomer; people are referring to "cellar" temperature. Beer served at actual pub room temperature would be unappetizing.

seasonal beer - a beer brewed at a particular time of the year, such as bock or winter warmer.

session beer Any beer of moderate to low alcoholic strength, that can be consumed during a long "session" in a bar.

sparge - to spray grist with hot water in order to remove soluble sugars (maltose). This takes place at the end of the mash.

specific gravity (s.g.) - a measure of beer's density in relation to the density of water, which is given a value of 1 at 39.2°F (4°C). When fermentation begins the wort's density is measured--this is called original gravity (o.g.) The o.g. is always higher than 1 because of the solubles, such as maltose, which are suspended in it. As the yeast converts the maltose into alcohol the gravity drops, alcohol being lighter than water. When the brewers are ready to serve, bottle, or keg their beer, they take a final gravity reading, known as the finishing gravity (f.g.).

wort - the sweet liquid which is created from the mashing and boiling process. When the wort is cooled and fermented, it is called beer.

wort chiller - see under heat exchanger.

yeast - a micro-organism of the fungus family. During the fermentation of beer, the yeast consume maltose and in the process create alcohol and carbon dioxide.

zymurgy - the science or study of fermentation.

Beer Styles

Variety has been a key element in the American beer renaissance. It was not too long ago that our choices among American-brewed beers were American Pilsner, American Pilsner, and American Pilsner. With these boring, watered-down choices it was only a matter of time before some Americans enthusiastically turned to the styles being revived by craft breweries and brewpubs.

As you visit brewpubs you will experience an amazing variety of beer styles. These styles can be confusing. For one thing, the variety is so great. For another, brewers may call their beer just about anything they want to. And if the marketing people are given a free hand in choosing a beer name, heaven help us. The names they use may not reveal anything about their styles. One brewery may call its dark beer a porter; while another may call its dark beer, which is virtually identical to the other's, a stout. Or a brewery may identify its brand simply as a "lager" or an "ale." One major brewery's advertising department was calling its beer a "stout lager," which is a contradiction in terms.

There are two basic families of beers: ale and lager. The difference between ale and lager is more important to the brewer than it is to the taster. One of the questions most often asked is, "What is the difference between ale and lager?" Many authorities have tried to characterize the differences in terms of taste and aroma. I maintain that all such attempts are doomed to failure because the diversity in taste and aroma within each family is so great. There is simply no commonality in taste within either family. So, it is possible to describe the difference between a Pilsner and a bitter, but it is not possible to do the same for ale and lager.

Ales

Ales are made with a yeast which floats to the top of the beer and which works at warmer temperatures than lagers. The brewing process is shorter for an ale than it is for a lager. For this reason many brewpubs make ales. Ales are most prevalent in the British Isles, although in recent decades Germany has experienced a renaissance of its traditional top-fermented styles (weizen, alt, Kölsch).

Ales are frequently served at temperatures which are much too cold to allow one to appreciate the flavor. Americans tend to like their beers cold and it is not uncommon to see an ale served at 35° in a frosted mug. This is a waste of good beer. If you really want to cool off, why not freeze the beer and serve it as a popsicle. If your beer is served too cold, try warming it up with the palms of your hands or placing it on a radiator. Even a microwave warm-up would be acceptable. Don't be embarrassed, the bartender might even get the message.

Lagers

Lagers are brewed with a yeast which sinks to the bottom of the beer and are fermented and served at cooler temperatures than ales. The word "lager" comes from the German, and means "to store." After the initial fermentation they are stored, or aged, for several weeks or months at very cold temperatures. The lagering or aging tends to give the lager a smoother, more refined taste. Lagers are more common on the European Continent.

Lagers made in brewpubs are often not aged as long as they should be because of the high demand for beer. The brewer is faced with the dilemma of serving lager before its time or serving no beer at all. Running out of beer would, of course, be a disaster from which the brewery might never recover.

OUTLINE OF BEER STYLES

ales

alt
barley wine
bitter
blonde ale
brown ale
Kölsch
light ale
mild
old ale
pale ale
porter
Scotch ale
stock ale
stout
Trappist ale
wheat beer

lagers

bock
Dortmunder
dunkel
helles
light beer
Münchner
Oktoberfest
Pilsner
Vienna

Hybrids, specialty beers, and misnomers

amber beer
Christmas ale
cream ale
dry beer
fruit beer
herb beer
Irish red
lambic

light ale
malt liquor
non-alcoholic beer
premium and super premium
rauchbier (smoked beer)
session beer
steam beer (California common)
winter warmer

Following are descriptions of the major styles, defined in fairly general terms, along with examples of some of the best and/or most available brands produced domestically and abroad.

abbey ale See under Trappist ale.

alt or altbier. This is a dark ale-style originating in Germany before the art of brewing lager developed. It is still popular in Dusseldorf and a few other locales. Altbier comes from the German, meaning "old beer," i.e., beer brewed before lager. *Examples: Pinkus Müller Altbier, St. Stan's Alt (dark and amber), Alaskan Amber Beer, and Widmer Alt.*

amber beer This is a term used frequently in brewpubs and craft breweries to describe beers which are tawny or copper in color. They may be ales or lagers. They tend to be fuller bodied and maltier than their golden colored counterparts. *Examples: Boont Amber (Anderson Valley), Bridalveil Ale (Butterfield), Samuel Adams Boston Lager, Albion Amber Ale (Marin), and Red Tail Ale (Mendocino).*

barley wine A very potent ale, usually full-bodied, dark, and bitter-sweet. Its strength is typically between 6% and 11% alcohol by volume (the "wine" implies that it is as strong as wine). *Examples: Big Foot (Sierra Nevada), Old Wooly (Big Time), Old Foghorn (Anchor), and Old Nick (Young).*

bitter A well-hopped, relatively bitter-tasting ale common to England. The term originated to distinguish the "old" unhopped ales from hopped ales. Bitter is usually served on draft and is amber-to-copper in color. There are various subcategories of bitter depending on their strength. These include **ordinary**, **special**, and **Extra Special Bitter (ESB)** *Examples: Sierra Nevada Draught, London Pride (Fullers), Redhook ESB, Liberty Ale (Anchor), Fullers ESB, and Portland Ale.*

blonde ale A pale, light-bodied ale. Also called **golden ale**. *Examples: Full Sail Golden Ale (Hood River) and Prime Time Pale Ale (Big Time), 3 Monts (Saint Sylvestre).*

bock or bockbier. This style means different things to different people. In Germany it means a strong lager, at least 6.25% alcohol by volume. In America the name "bock" has been traditionally applied to dark lagers, at least until Sierra Nevada came out with its Pale Bock in 1990. There is an old wives' tale that bock beer is dark because it is made in the spring when the brewery cleans the dregs out of the brew kettles. There is absolutely no truth in this and anyone understanding the importance of cleanliness in the brewing process will know that brew kettles are cleaned after every batch. There are two theories as to the origin of the name. One is that it is a corruption of "Einbeck," a German city which was once an important brewing center, and where the style may have originated. The other theory is that it is a corruption of the German term ziegenbock or "billy goat." *Examples: Widmer Bock and Bock Octoberfest (Stoudt).*

There are many kinds of bocks, including **pale bock** *(examples: Einbecker Ür Bock and Sierra Nevada Pale Bock);* **Doppelbock** [also called double bock or dopplebock] a strong, malty version *(examples: Aass Bock, Ayinger Celebrator, Bach's Boch [Eugene], Samuel Adams Double Bock [Boston Beer], Virginia Native [Virginia Brewing], Paulaner Salvator, Augustiner Maximator, and Dusseldorfer Doppelbock [Weinkeller]);* **Maibock** *(example: Ayinger Maibock)* a pale bock meant to be consumed in May; **eisbock**, an extra strong bock finished by freezing the beer and removing some of the water *(examples: Kulminator Urtyp Hell [EKU 28] and Samichlaus [Hurlimann]),* and **weizenbock** (examples: *Rubicon Dunkel Weizen*), a dark, strong wheat beer. Doppelbocks frequently end with the suffix "ator" and are easy to identify for this reason. The Paulaner Brewery in Munich started the trend of using the -ator suffix, with its Salvator.

brown ale A dark brown ale. There are three subgroups, based on geographic regions: those produced in southern England, which are relatively low in alcohol and hop bitterness, and sweet; those produced in northeast England, which are drier, but still weak and low in hop bitterness; and those produced in Belgium, which are stronger and more complex. English brown ales are equivalent to the bottled versions of mild ales. *Examples: Grant's Celtic Ale, Pacific Crest Ale (Hart), Tied House Dark, Corsendonk Monk's Brown Ale, Newcastle Brown Ale, Samuel Smith's Nut Brown Ale, Goudenband (Liefmans), and Downtown Brown (Triple Rock), Brooklyn Brown, Pete's Wicked Ale.*

California common A beer made with lager yeast, but brewed at ale temperatures. The style is typified by an amber hue, medium body, and hoppy character. For years it was known as steam beer, but since Anchor Brewing of

San Francisco trademarked the name, the term California common was coined to identify the style in brewing competitions. This is the only beer style indigenous to the United States. California common beer originated in 19th Century California, where brewers had access to lager yeasts but had no means to keep the beer at the proper temperature. At least two theories persist as to the origin of the name. One is that excessive amounts of pressure built up in the wooden casks and when they were tapped they made a loud hissing noise, like steam. The other is that steam power was used in the early California breweries, hence the name "steam beer." *Example: Anchor Steam Beer.*

Christmas beer A beer brewed for the yuletide (in Germany, fest bier). It is also called holiday beer. It is often dark and relatively high in alcohol, but styles vary widely. Many breweries put herbs and spices in their Christmas beer. *Examples: Our Special Ale (Anchor), Celebration Ale (Sierra Nevada), Noche Buena (Moctezuma), and Aass Jule Øl.*

cream ale A pale, light bodied ale which is lagered at cold temperatures or mixed with lager. Sometimes called "lagale." *Example: Little Kings (Hudepohl-Schoenling) and Genesee Cream Ale.*

doppelbock See under bock.

Dortmunder A pale lager, with more body than a Pilsner, and less dry as well. Sometimes called "export." *Examples: Export (Gordon Biersch), Dortmunder (Great Lakes), and DAB Original.*

dry beer A beer made by a special process, using enzymal additives in the mash, in which the yeast converts more of the malt sugars into alcohol than normal, making it drier tasting. In Japan, where the first modern dry beers became popular, they tend to be more potent than their counterpart lagers. In the U.S., dry beers tend to be of normal strength, but the breweries use lower hopping rates, rendering them almost tasteless. This is not the kind of beer you would expect to find in a brewpub. *Examples: Asahi Super Dry, Michelob Dry, Bud Dry, and Rainier Dry.*

dunkel (also, dunkle, dunkler, Munich [or Munchner] dunkel, and dunkles) From the German for "dark." Any dark lager of average strength. Many bocks are dark, but are stronger than dunkels. *Examples: Hübsch Brau Dunkel (Sudwerk Privatbrauerei), Frankenmuth Old German Style Dark, Beck's Dark, and Gartenbrau Dark (Capital).*

export See under Dortmunder.

framboise See under fruit beer.

fruit beer Beer with fruit in it, such as cherries, raspberries, or blueberries. Fruit beer has been brewed over the millenia, but the tradition was kept alive in Belgium. Its popularity has spread to the U.S. in recent years. *Examples: Lindeman's Kriek, Raspberry Trail Ale (Marin), Ruby Tuesday*

(McMenamin's), and Bell's Cherry Stout (Kalamazoo).

golden ale See under blonde ale.

helles Also called "Munich [or Munchner] helles." A pale lager. From the German for "pale." A helles tends to be maltier, less dry, and less hoppy than a Pilsner. *Examples: Penn Light Lager (Pennsylvania Brewing), Manhattan Gold Lager, Miller High Life, and Hopfen Helles (Weeping Radish).*

herb beer Any ale or lager with herbs or spices in it. Many Christmas ales have herbs in them. Common spices used are ginger, nutmeg, and cinnamon. *Examples: Our Special Ale (Anchor), Grants Spiced Ale, Hoppy Holidaze (Marin), and McGuire's Christmas Ale.*

imperial stout See under stout.

Irish red A reddish colored ale, originating from Ireland. *Example: Winchester Red.*

The Great Hall at Oldenberg Brewing
Ft. Mitchell, Kentucky

Irish stout See under stout.

Kölsch A type of blonde ale brewed in and around Cologne, Germany. It tends to be delicate, dry, and fruity. The word "Kölsch" originated from "Cologne." *Example: Küppers Kölsch.*

kriek See under fruit beer.

lager ale (or lagale) See under cream ale.

lambic A well-carbonated, spontaneously-fermented wheat ale, very popular in Belgium. There are several varieties, including fruit lambic (**kriek**-made with cherries, **framboise**-made with raspberries), **Faro** (a sweet version), and **Gueuze** (a blend of mature and young lambics). *Example: Lindemans.*

light ale Meaning varies: 1. the bottled equivalent of a draft ordinary bitter; 2. a low-gravity ale, 3. a low-calorie ale. *Examples: Poleeko Gold (Anderson Valley), Baltic Light (Gorky's), and Grant's Celtic Ale.*

light beer 1. A low-calorie, low-gravity beer. *Examples: Bud Light, Lite (Miller), Coors Light, Boulder Sport, and Boston Lightship.* 2. A pale-colored lager, such as a helles or Dortmunder. *Example: Beck's Light.*

Maibock See under bock.

malt liquor An American tax term for a strong beer. In some states, law requires that beers above a certain alcoholic strength must be labelled as malt liquors. Malt liquors tend to lack malt and hop character. *Examples: Colt 45, Schlitz Malt Liquor, and St. Ides (McKenzie River).*

Märzenbier See under Oktoberfest.

mild ale A lightly hopped ale. They are also frequently dark in color and low in alcohol. *Examples: Grant's Celtic Ale, Newcastle Brown Ale.*

milk stout See under stout.

non-alcoholic beer Also called alcohol-free beer and near beer. Any beer with less than .5% alcohol by weight. Reformed alcoholics should avoid such beers because they still have enough alcohol in them to put them back off the wagon. *Examples: Kalibur, Mousse, and O'Douls.*

Oktoberfest or Märzenbier. Originally, a beer brewed in Germany in March (hence, Märzenbier) and laid down for consumption during the summer and fall. Ceremoniously drunk-up in late September and early October. Oktoberfest is amber in color, medium-to-strong in potency, and malty. Similar to Vienna, but more robust. *Examples: Adler Brau Oktoberfest (Appleton), Spaten Oktoberfest (Ur Märzen), Paulaner Oktoberfest, Samuel Adams Octoberfest, Market Street Oktoberfest (Bohannon), Helenboch Octoberfest, and Octoberfest (Sudwerk Privatbrauerei).*

old ale A medium-strong ale, usually dark in color, lightly to moderately hopped, and full bodied. *Examples: Old Peculier (Theakston), Jubelale (Deschutes Brewing), Eye of the Hawk (Mendocino), and Independence Ale (Kelmers Brewhouse).*

pale ale A copper-colored ale; a term frequently used to describe a brewer's premium bitter, usually in the bottled form. In recent years the term pale ale has frequently been used to describe draft bitter. The name is seemingly a misnomer, since there is nothing "pale" about pale ale. It was originally used to distinguish it from porter, a very dark ale. It is sometime referred to as **Burton ale**, because it originated in the town of Burton-upon-Trent, England. A slightly stronger and hoppier version is known as **India Pale Ale** or **IPA**. It acquired this name because it was originally brewed for export to India. *Examples: Bass, Sierra Nevada Pale Ale, Ballantine India Pale, Red Hook ESB, Geary's Pale Ale, Catamount Gold, Liberty Ale (Anchor), and Rubicon IPA.*

pale bock See under bock.

Pils See under Pilsner.

Pilsner (also spelled Pilsener and frequently referred to as *Pils*) A dry, golden lager, originating in Pilsen, Czechoslovakia. European-style Pilsners tend to be dry and crisp, highly hopped, and have a flowery aroma. Most American premium beers (i.e., from the big brewers) are technically in the Pilsner style, but, in character, are mere shadows of their European counterparts. They are paler in color, less hoppy and malty, and have less body. The major American breweries usually substitute corn or rice for a significant portion of the malt, which weakens the malt character. *Examples: European Pilsner--Pilsner Urquell, Grolsch, Beck's Light, St. Pauli Girl, German Pils (Sudwerk Privatbrauerei), Baderbrau (Pavichevich), August Schell Pilsner, Capital Gartenbrau Lager, Stella Artois, and Heineken; American Pilsner--Budweiser (Anheuser-Busch), Coors, Stroh, Corona Extra (Modelo), Fosters (Carlton), Molson, Moosehead, Carta Blanca (Cuautemoc), and Labatt's.*

porter A very dark-to-black ale. Porter originated in 18th-Century London and was first popular among porters (hence, its name). It is traditionally malty and bitter. Many have a dry coffee taste as well. The stronger and more bitter varieties later became known as stouts, because (it is said) they were appreciated by the "stoutest" of the London porters. *Examples: Coal Creek Porter (Big Time), Samuel Smith's Taddy Porter, Sierra Nevada Porter, Anchor Porter (bottom fermented), Black Rock Porter (Triple Rock), Blackhook (Redhook), and Boulder Porter.*

premium and **super premium** 1. These are price categories used by large American breweries. Premium is usually in the middle price range and super premium is higher priced. These names imply quality, but have been so misused, microbrewers avoid using them. 2. Beer of high quality.

rauch (smoked) or rauchbier. Beer made with smoked malts. The classic examples come from Franconia, near Bamberg, Germany. *Examples: Alaskan Smoked Porter, Kaiserdom Rauchbier, and Rauch (Oregon Brewing).*

Scotch ale A strong, amber-to-dark, malty, full-bodied ale, originally from Scotland. Also known as "wee heavy." It has also been brewed in Belgium for many years. *Examples: Grant's Scottish Ale, MacAndrew's Scotch Ale (Caledonia), McEwan's Scotch Ale, Our Holiday Ale (Sun Valley Brewing) and Belhaven Scottish Ale.*

spiced ale See under herb beer.

steam beer See under California common.

stock ale (or stock beer) A strong ale originally brewed to be stored for a long period of time. *Example: Boston Stock Ale.*

stout A very dark-to-black, full-bodied ale; a stronger variety of porter. Two main subcategories exist: **dry stout** (also known as **Irish stout**) and **sweet stout** (sometimes called **milk stout**, because it has lactose [milk sugar] added to it), more common to England. In addition there is **imperial stout** (also known as Russian imperial stout), **oatmeal stout**, and **cream stout**. Imperial stout was originally brewed in England and exported to Catherine the Great's court in St. Petersburg. Cream stout is not really considered a style; this term is used in referring to its creamy mouthfeel. *Examples: Guinness Extra Stout, Mackeson's Triple Stout, Barney Flats Oatmeal Stout (Anderson Valley Brewing), San Quentin's Break Out Stout (Marin), Sierra Nevada Stout, Boulder Stout, Grant's Russian Imperial Stout, Samuel Smith's Oatmeal Stout, Sheaf Stout (Tooth & Co.), and Killer Whale Stout (Pacific Coast Brewing).*

strong ale See under old ale.

Trappist ale An ale style originally brewed by Belgian and Dutch Trappist monks. A true Trappist ale should be relatively strong, use candy sugar in the brewing process, and be bottle conditioned. They tend to be assertive and complex. Some are full bodied, with a rich and rounded palate; others are tart and fruity. Stronger versions of the same brand are frequently referred to as "double" or "triple." Also known as abbey ale. *Examples: Orval, Chimay.*

Vienna A reddish-amber lager; usually malty and moderately hopped. The style originated in Vienna in the 19th Century. *Example: Dos Equis.*

wee heavy See under Scotch ale.

wheat beer Any beer using malted wheat. There are many styles. **Berliner Weisse** is an unfiltered, tart, low-alcohol, light-bodied, well-carbonated beer, originally from Berlin. It is frequently served with fruit syrup. *Example: Berliner Weisse (Schultheiss).* Other varieties originating from southern Germany are variously called **weizenbier, weisse,** or **weissbier.** *Examples: Anchor Wheat, Spaten Club-Weisse, August Schell Weiss Beer, and Pyramid Wheaten Ale.* These beers are of a more conventional alcohol strength and body, but are also tart and fruity. They are frequently served with a twist of lemon. Wheat malt content varies from 50%-80%. Bottle-conditioned wheat beers are usually called **hefe-weizen** *(examples: HefeWeiss [Gordon Biersch] and Weizen [Stoudt Brewing]).* Other styles include **dunkelweizen** (dark wheat) and **weizenbock,** or wheat bock, *(examples: Miwok Weizen Bock [Marin].* Weis means "white" in German, and refers to the very pale color of the beer. Weizen means "wheat" in German. Wheat beers are generally brewed with ale yeasts. **Witbier** is a Belgian version of wheat beer with an orangey character and a honeyish aroma *(Examples: Wittekop Biere Blanche, Hoegarden Biere Blanche).*

white beer See under wheat beer.

witbier See under wheat beer.

winter warmer A beer brewed for consumption in winter, frequently dark, malty, and fairly high in alcohol, but there are some that are light colored and emphasize hops instead. *Examples: Youngs Winter Warmer, Wassail Winter Ale (Hood River)and T.W. Fisher's Winter Warmer.* See also under Christmas beer.

Beer Festivals

One enjoyable upshot of the North American beer renaissance has been the rebirth of beer festivals. They provide an opportunity for beer lovers to try different brands of beer from the many craft, regional, and foreign breweries.The first to get started was the Great American Beer Festival in 1982 in Boulder (now held in Denver), followed the next year by the KQED International Beer and Food Festival in San Francisco. Each year brings more festivals. Although they predominate in the west some very successful festivals have begun in the East during the last couple of years.

Provided below is a directory of the most prominent of these festivals in the East and Canada, presented in the order in which they take place during the year.

American Institute of Wine and Food
Beer & Food Fest
When: March (always on a Monday evening)
Location: New York, New York
Attendance: 1,200
Format: sampling of beer and food of 30 breweries paired with 30 New York City restaurants
Entrance fee: $20 for members ($30 for nonmembers)
Contact: AIWF, tel. (212) 447-0456

Blessing of the Bock
When: March (closest weekend to St. Joseph's Day (March 19)
Location: Milwaukee, Wisconsin
Attendance: 600
Format: dinner, beer tasting, and blessing of the bock Saturday night; beer fest with food on Sunday (about 15 breweries represented)
Entrance fee: $20 for each event
Contact: Lakefront Brewing, tel. (414) 372-8800

Beer Camp
When: Friday - Sunday in March and September
Location: Oldenberg Brewery, Ft. Mitchell, Kentucky
Attendance: 100-200
Format: homebrew demo, hospitality suite with 100-150 craft brewed beers, beer dinner, tour of Cincinnati's old bars, and more
Entrance fee: about $295 per person, double occupancy
Contact: Oldenberg Brewery, tel. (800) 354-9793

Chicago Beer Society All American Beer Tasting
When: late April/early May
Location: Chicago, Illinois
Attendance: 250-300

Format:	dinner and tasting of 10-12 craft or regional brewery beers at a Chicago restaurant; participants vote on their favorite beers
Entrance fee:	about $30
Contact:	Chicago Beer Society, tel. (708) 973-0240

Boston Brewers Festival

When:	May 1
Location:	World Trade Center, Boston, Massachusetts
Attendance:	5,000
Format:	sampling of beers from about 60 breweries; live music
Entrance fee:	$20
Contact:	Jonathan Tremblay, tel. (617) 547-2233

Great Taste of the Midwest

When:	August
Location:	Madison, Wisconsin, Olin Terrace
Attendance:	1,000
Format:	2-oz. tastings of beers from 30+ Midwest breweries; fee for food
Entrance fee:	$12
Contact:	Madison Homebrewers & Tasters, tel. (608) 244-4142

CAMRA Victoria Microbrewery Festival

When:	October
Location:	Victoria, B.C., Victoria Conference Center
Attendance:	?
Format:	beer samples from British Columbian breweries, as well as breweries from other parts of Canada and Oregon and Washington; eats and music too
Entrance fee:	?
Contact:	CAMRA Victoria, Box 30101, Saanich Centre Postal Outlet, Victoria, BC V8X 5E1

Chicago Beer Society International Beer Tasting

When:	in the fall, usually the weekend before Thanksgiving
Location:	Chicago, Illinois
Attendance:	250-300
Format:	dinner and tasting of 10-12 imported beers at a Chicago restaurant; participants vote on their favorite beers
Entrance fee:	about $30
Contact:	Chicago Beer Society, tel. (708) 973-0240

Great Eastern U.S. Invitational Microbrewery Beer Festival

When:	early June
Location:	Stoudt's Brewery, Adamstown, Pennsylvania
Attendance:	1,000
Format:	sampling of beers from about 25 craft breweries; food & live music
Entrance fee:	$20
Contact:	Stoudt Brewery, tel. (215) 484-4387

Drinking and Driving

Many of those using this guide will be drinking and then driving under the influence of alcohol. It is important for your own safety and of others that you know your limits. Although most states have a legal limit of .1% blood alcohol for driving under the influence, much smaller amounts of alcohol can impair your driving ability. If possible, walk home, take public transportation, or travel with a designated driver. Further, it is important to remember you can be convicted for driving under the influence even if your blood alcohol level is lower than the legal state limit. If the arresting officer thinks your driving is impaired, a blood alcohol level of less than the legal limit may not save you from being convicted.

Legal Limits

In 45 of the 50 states, a blood alcohol level of .1% is grounds for automatic arrest for driving under the influence, regardless of how well you were driving at the time you were stopped. In California, Maine, Oregon, Utah, and Vermont the level is .08%.

Blood Alcohol Charts

The blood alcohol charts on the following pages are provided as a guide for those who may drink or drive. They are not sufficiently accurate to be used as legal evidence.

The charts allow for three important variables which affect blood alcohol level: body weight, number of beers consumed, and the length of time during which the beer is consumed. Unfortunately, there are several other factors which are not shown. The most obvious is the alcohol percentage of the beer. When I asked several agencies who distribute blood alcohol charts what percent beer was used for the chart, I received the explanation that these were for a beer of average strength. However, none of the agencies in question were able to identify the average strength of beer.

In addition, different individuals' bodies may be able to handle alcohol in different ways. Things such as gender, psychological factors, food in the digestive system at the time of alcoholic consumption, the use of medicine, and the ability of the liver to handle alcohol all have a bearing on blood alcohol levels. So, even though the charts may show that you would have a blood alcohol level less than the legal limit, due to the above mentioned factors you might actually be in violation of the law.

Alcohol Labeling

One of the biggest problems facing the responsible beer drinker is a federal law prohibiting the posting of the alcoholic content of beer on the container. Obviously, a bottle of Sierra Nevada Big Foot is going to get you drunker than a bottle of Grant's Celtic Ale. But the law forbids the brewery from warning the consumer about this important information. I think this law is an obvious violation of the First Amendment's guarantee of free speech and is also an obstruction to the responsible consumption of beer.

Blood-Alcohol Charts

Person weighing 100 pounds

number of hours

no. of 12-oz. beers	1	2	3	4
1	.03	-	-	-
2	.06	.04	.02	-
3	.10	.08	.07	.05
4	.13	.12	.10	.09
5	.17	.16	.14	.13
6	.21	.19	.18	.16
7	.25	.23	.22	.20
8	.28	.27	.25	.24

Person weighing 120 pounds

number of hours

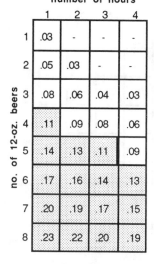

no. of 12-oz. beers	1	2	3	4
1	.03	-	-	-
2	.05	.03	-	-
3	.08	.06	.04	.03
4	.11	.09	.08	.06
5	.14	.13	.11	.09
6	.17	.16	.14	.13
7	.20	.19	.17	.15
8	.23	.22	.20	.19

Person weighing 140 pounds

number of hours

no. of 12-oz. beers	1	2	3	4
1	.02	-	-	-
2	.05	.02	-	-
3	.07	.05	.03	.02
4	.09	.08	.06	.04
5	.12	.10	.09	.07
6	.15	.13	.12	.10
7	.17	.16	.14	.13
8	.20	.18	.17	.15

Blood-Alcohol Charts

Person weighing 160 pounds

number of hours

no. of 12-oz. beers	1	2	3	4
1	.02	-	-	-
2	.04	.02	-	-
3	.06	.04	.02	.01
4	.08	.06	.04	.03
5	.10	.09	.07	.06
6	.13	.11	.09	.08
7	.15	.13	.12	.10
8	.17	.16	.14	.13

Person weighing 180 pounds

number of hours

no. of 12-oz. beers	1	2	3	4
1	.01	-	-	-
2	.04	.01	-	-
3	.05	.03	.02	-
4	.07	.05	.04	.02
5	.09	.07	.06	.04
6	.11	.09	.08	.06
7	.13	.12	.10	.09
8	.15	.14	.12	.11

Person weighing 200 pounds

number of hours

no. of 12-oz. beers	1	2	3	4
1	-	-	-	-
2	.04	-	-	-
3	.05	.03	.01	-
4	.06	.04	.03	.01
5	.08	.06	.04	.03
6	.10	.08	.07	.05
7	.12	.10	.09	.07
8	.13	.12	.10	.09

Person weighing 220 pounds

number of hours

no. of 12-oz. beers	1	2	3	4
1	-	-	-	-
2	.03	-	-	-
3	.04	.01	-	-
4	.06	.03	.01	-
5	.07	.05	.03	.01
6	.09	.07	.06	.04
7	.11	.08	.07	.05
8	.12	.10	.08	.06

U.S. Brewpub - Craft Brewery Count by State

April 1993

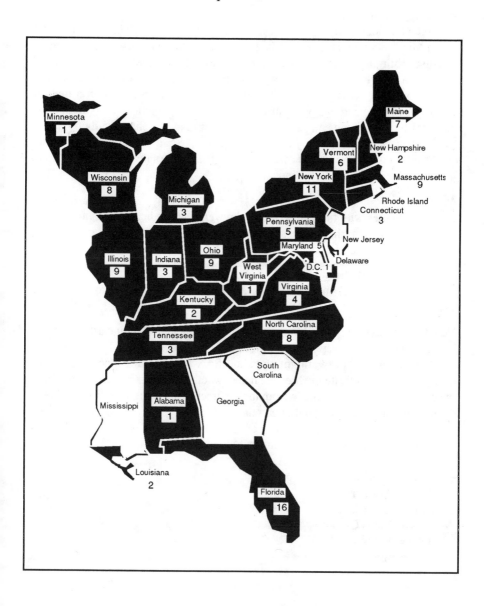

GUIDE TO THE GUIDE

Scope

On Tap covers brewpubs and craft breweries which you can visit. If you cannot visit it, it is not in the guide.

Arrangement

On Tap is divided into two volumes. This volume covers the United States east of the Mississippi River and Canada. Louisiana is covered in the eastern section, because both breweries in that state are located east of the Mississippi. Minnesota is divided between the two volumes. Each book is arranged alphabetically by state or province. Each state/provincial section begins with a map of the state/province and in several instances, a map for a major metropolitan area, followed by a one-page entry for each brewery, arranged alphabetically by name. Many breweries are known by two or more names. So, if you don't find a brewery listed by the name you know, check under the alternate name. If you don't know an alternate, look in the index.

Maps

Towns and cities with brewpubs or craft breweries are indicated with a solid dot or area. In addition, their names are outlined with a white box. For reference, other important cities are indicated with a hollow dot or area.

Individual entries

In each entry, brewpubs are indicated in boldface. Craft breweries are indicated in shadowed letters.

New information is provided in this edition. This includes credit cards accepted, handicapped access, fireplaces, the availability of wines and hard liquor, availability of rooms for an overnight stay, and FAX numbers for placing take-out orders. Also, we indicate the brewers name, whether the beer is cask conditioned or served under pressure, made from malt extract or all grain, filtration, and production during 1992 expressed in barrels.

Abbreviations for credit cards are as follows:

AE = American Express
CA = Mastercard
CB = Carte Blanche
DC = Diners Club
DS = Discover
VI = Visa

SAMPLE ENTRY

The entries are intended to be as self-explanatory as possible. The following is provided to assist in ease of interpretation.

Pint-Size Pub 1234 Main Street Sonoma 90000	**Bold face text** indicates this is a brewpub. Shadowed text indicates a craft brewery.
☎ (415) 292-BEER	Telephone for the pub, the business phone may be different.
🕐 11 am - midnight daily	These are the pub hours, in some cases the restaurant hours may differ.
🍺 Gold (1.042, Pilsner) Peggy's Porter (1.048) Seasonal: Oktoberfest (1.052) **Brewer:** Droopie the Brewer 500 barrels. Beer to go in kegs. Three draft beers; 27 bottled beers	Beer brewed on premise. Original gravity, when available, is indicated in parentheses. If the name does not reveal the style, the style or season (according to the brewer) may be indicated in parentheses. Brewers' name; production in 1992; beer to go; beer sold, but not brewed on premise.
🍴 Pub grub	Types of food served
♪ live music Friday night	The music symbol refers to live or background music and/or juke box.
EVENTS: Oktoberfest	
📺 2 and a dish	Television
🌷	Beer garden or an open-air/outdoor drinking or dining area
🎯 darts, shuffleboard	Games offered
🚭 🚗 $$$ CA, VI 🛏 ♿ 🔥	Non-smoking area or non-smoking pub Off-street parking credit cards accepted rooms for overnight stay handicapped access fireplace

Alabama

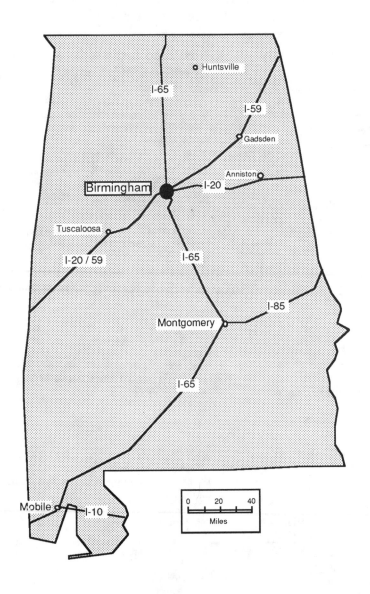

Birmingham Brewing

3118 3rd Avenue South
Birmingham
35233

📞 (205) 326-6677

Located in a historical light industrial area known as the Lakeview District.

Red Mountain Red Ale (1.050, American amber)
Red Mountain Golden Lager (1.046, American premium lager)
Red Mountain Golden Ale (1.046, American pale ale)

Brewer: John Zanteson

Brewer John Zanteson plans to brew at least three seasonals, including Red Mountain Wheat (1.044, American wheat), Red Mountain Holiday Ale (1.050, brown ale), and Red Mountain Fest Beer (1.054, Märzen-Oktoberfest). Zanteson brews 30-barrel batches with a full mash. Birmingham Brewing is now distributing their three beers in 12-oz. bottles and kegs in Alabama and Georgia.

Tours are available; please call several days in advance. They are not allowed to sell beer on premise.

CEO Ben Hogan says Birmingham Brewing is the first brewery to operate in the city since the county went dry in 1908. In 1907 there existed a Birmingham Brewing Co. which produced 40,000 barrels annually. In May 1908 county officials emptied 300 barrels of beer into the streets of Birmingham.

Opened May 1992.

Connecticut

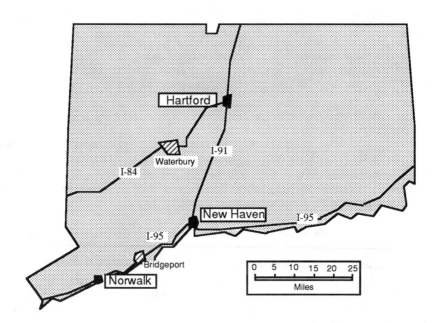

Hartford Brewery

35 Pearl Street
Hartford
06103

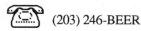 (203) 246-BEER

Located in the downtown financial district, near the old State House.

Bar: Mon - Thurs: 11:30 am - 1 am; Fri: 11:30 am - 2 am; Sat: noon - 2 am
Sun: 4 pm - 1 am
Kitchen: Sun - Thurs: 'til 9:00 pm; Fri - Sat: ' til 10:00 pm

Arch Amber (1.048, amber ale)
Pitbull Gold (1.042, golden ale)
I.P.A. (ale)
Dunkelweiss (ale)
Bacchus (old ale)
Bitter (ale)

Seasonal:
  wheat beer
  mild ale
  pale ale
  stout
  porter
  Kolsch
  alt
  Scotch ale

Brewers: Les Sinnock and Phil Hopkins
Beer is all grain, cask conditioned, unfiltered; 550 barrels.
Good selection of imported beers; five house beers on tap.

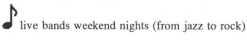

The food is described as being gourmet deli. Menu items include nachos, pastas, chicken, quesadilla, ploughman's lunch, Brewery Chili, hamburgers, Pitbull Steamed Bratwurst, soups, clam chowder, salads, and homemade desserts. Sandwiches include reuben, corned beef, smoked turkey, and club. Wine and full bar available.

The brewery is housed in an old Friendly's Ice Cream Restaurant with an exterior described as being "brutal, early seventies functional" in style. The interior design is eclectic, with two tiled-floor rooms. The brew kettle is behind the bar and the fermentation tanks are in the back. Brewer/partner Les Sinnock has studied brewing for nine years in England, Belgium, and Africa. He did an apprenticeship at Geary's in Portland, Maine, and has visited some 50 microbreweries and brewpubs in the U.S. Opened August 1991.

♪ live bands weekend nights (from jazz to rock)

 darts (dart leagues on Wed), chess, backgammon, pool, pinball, and a multitude of board games

  (pay)

$$$ CA, VI

New England Brewing

 (203) 866-1339

25 Commerce Street
Norwalk
06850

Next to the Classic Ice Co. and the Norwalk Garden Center.

 Atlantic Amber (1.048, steam)
Gold Stock Ale (1.058)
Seasonal:
    Oatmeal Stout (1.052)
    Holiday Ale (1.054, spiced ale)
    Light Lager (1.038)

Brewer: Phil Markowski
Beer is all grain, filtered; 3,000 barrels. Beer is distributed in kegs and bottles.

<u>Beer is available for sampling only on tours.</u>
Tours are by appointment, reservations required 2-3 days in advance. Best time to call: Mon - Fri: 9 am - 7 pm. Their plans call for a conversion to being a combination microbrewery and brewpub.

New England Brewing Co. was a historic kname borrowed from Connecticut's brewing past. The original New England Brewing Co. was founded in Hartford in 1897, and located at 503-529 Windsor Street. With an annual capacity of 200,000 barrels, it was one of the largest breweries in the state. Like most breweries, it closed during Prohibition and reopened in 1936. At this time, the popular star of stage, screen, and radio, J. Harold Murray ran the company. It was purchased by Largay Brewing Co. of Waterbury in 1940. It finally closed in 1940.

New Haven Brewing

458 Grand Avenue
New Haven
06513

 (203) 772-2739

Elm City Connecticut Ale (1.047)
Elm City Golden Ale (1.042)
Blackwell Stout (1.051)
Mr. Mike's Light Ale (92 calories, wheat based)

Brewer: Blair Potts
Beer is all grain, filtered; 4,500 barrels. A barley wine is planned for the near future. Beers are distributed in bottles and kegs.

Beer is available in the tasting room only during tours.
Tours are available by reservation--just call and set up a time. They do not sell any beer on premise. They opened in September 1989. Blackwell Stout is named after the brewhouse watch dog and mascot.

Washington, D.C.

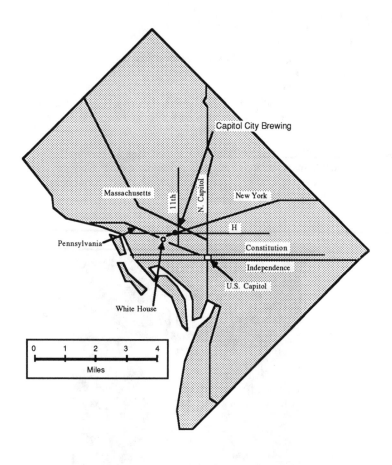

Capitol City Brewing

1100 New York Avenue, NW
Washington
20005

 (202) 628-2222

Located at the corner of New York and H, across the street from the Washington Convention Center and the Hyatt Hotel, one block from the Metro Center subway stop.

 11 am - 2 am daily (breakfast served Mon - Fri from 7 am)

Bitter
Pale Ale
Nut Brown Ale
Porter
Alt
Kolsch

They have several other micro-brewed beers on tap and a limited bottle selection.

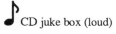 **braumeister:** Martin Virga
Beer is all grain, served under pressure, filtered, 540 hectoliters.

 Many grilled items, appetizers, soups, salads, sandwiches, and desserts. Bratwurst steamed in beer, pale ale chili, burgers, sausages and baby back ribs are their specialties. Wine and full bar available.

The brewery is housed on the ground floor of a new office building adjacent to the old art deco Greyhound bus terminal. It has 22-foot ceilings and 20-foot high display windows looking onto the street. It is laid out in cavernous room with two antique copper brew kettles in the center, surrounded by an oval bar. The seating capacity is 240 and most of the seats are in booths around the exterior wall. Opened August 19, 1992 and began serving their own beer in September. This is the first brewery to operate in Washington since the Christian Heurich Brewing Co. closed in 1956.

♪ CD juke box (loud)   cable

 (garage in the office building)

 $$$ AE, CA, CB, DC, DS, VI

Florida

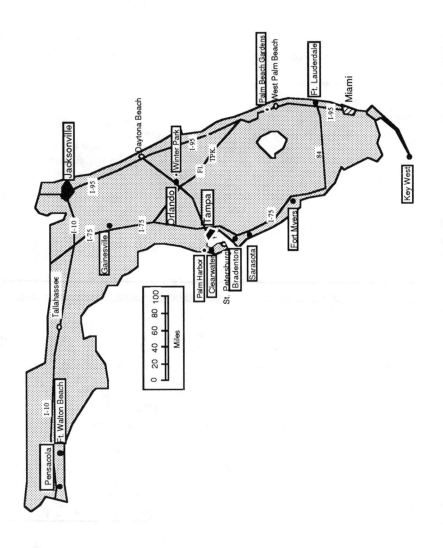

Hops Grill & Brewery

18825 U.S. Highway 19 North
Clearwater
34624

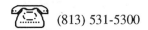 (813) 531-5300

 Mon - Thurs: 11:30 am - 11 pm; Fri - Sat: 11:30 am - midnight
Sun: 11:30 am - 10 pm

 Hops Extra Pale Ale
Hammerhead Red (amber ale)
Hops Golden Lager
Seasonal:
   Anniversary Ale

Brewer: Tom Netolicky

 A 400-seat restaurant that offers American cuisine. They serve their own cut beef, smoked meats, and homemade pasta. Entrees include fresh seafood, smoked ribs, and shrimp cooked in Hammerhead Red and beer cheese.

This is a large restaurant with a completely open interior, featuring an open grill, bar, and brewery operation. They opened in November 1989.

 $$$ AE, CA, CB, DS, VI

Hops Grill & Bar

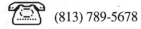 (813) 789-5678

33086 U.S. Highway 19 N.
Palm Harbor
34684

 Mon - Thurs: 11:30 am - 11 pm; Fri - Sat: 11:30 am - midnight
Sun: 11:30 am - 10 pm

Clearwater Light	Seasonal:
Hammerhead Red	Hop's Extra Pale Ale
Hop's Golden Lager	Anniversary Ale

 The restaurant offers American cuisine and features Iowa corn-fed beef, smoked meats, fresh pasta rolled and cut in-house, fresh fish, and burgers made with freshly ground chuck. All soups, salad dressings and sauces are made from scratch daily. Wine and full bar, lunch specials, and happy hour daily 3-7.

This is a large restaurant with a seating capacity of 250 and a completely open interior, featuring a display kitchen, bar, and an observation brewery. Opened May 1992.

 live music on occasion

$$$ AE, CA, CB, DS, VI

Hops Grill & Bar

14303 N. Dale Mabry Highway
Tampa
33618

 (813) 264-0522

 Mon - Thurs: 11:30 am - 11 pm; Fri - Sat: 11:30 am - midnight
Sun: 11:30 am - 11 pm

 Clearwater Light
Hammerhead Red
Hop's Golden Lager

Seasonal:
  Hop's Extra Pale Ale
  Anniversary Ale

Brewer: Tom Netolicky

 The restaurant offers American cuisine and features Iowa corn-fed beef, smoked meats, fresh pasta rolled and cut in-house, fresh fish, and burgers made with freshly ground chuck. All soups, salad dressings and sauces are made from scratch daily. Wine and full bar, lunch specials, and happy hour daily 3-7.

This is a large restaurant with a seating capacity of 250 and a completely open interior, featuring a display kitchen, bar, and an observation brewery. Opened April 1991.

 live music on occasion

$$$ AE, CA, CB, DS, VI

Hops Grill & Bar

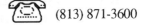 (813) 871-3600

327 N. Dale Mabry Highway
Tampa
33609

 Mon - Thurs: 11:30 am - 11 pm; Fri - Sat: 11:30 am - midnight;
Sun: 11:30 am - 10 pm

 Clearwater Light
Hop's Golden Lager
Hammerhead Red.

 The restaurant offers American cuisine and features Iowa corn-fed beef, smoked meats, fresh pasta rolled and cut in-house, fresh fish, and burgers made with freshly ground chuck. All soups, salad dressings and sauces are made from scratch daily. Wine and full bar, lunch specials, and happy hour daily 3-7.

This is a large restaurant with a seating capacity of 250 and a completely open interior, featuring a display kitchen, bar, and an observation brewery. Opened November 9, 1992.

 live music on occasion

 AE, CA, CB, DS, VI

Irish Times Pub & Brewery

9920 Alt. A1A, Ste. 810
Palm Beach Gardens
33410  (407) 624-1504

From I-95, take exit 56 (PGA Blvd.). Located in the Promenade Plaza mall, next to the movie theater.

 11:30 am - 2 am daily

Irish Times Red Ale
Irish Times Pale Ale
Irish Times Lite

Seasonal:
  Dry Pale
  Trappist Ale
  Raspberry Beer
  Octoberfest

Brewer: Flip Gary
Also on draft: Guinness Stout, Harp, and Murphy's Stout
In bottles: Bud, Miller Lite, Coors Light, Amstel

 They have a full menu, with a strong emphasis on Irish pub grub, such as Irish stew, corned beef & cabbage, beef & Guinness stew, potato-leek soup, bangers & mash, fish 'n chips, mussels, and shepherd's pie (their most popular item). In addition they have appetizers, soups, salads, burgers, and entrees such as fresh smoked salmon and steaks. About ten wines served; full bar.

The Irish theme permeates this pub, with lots of green, light brown wood, and brass. Photographs of the Irish countryside, patriots, and writers are featured on the walls. There are several beautiful antiques in the loft. The bar is slightly elevated from the dining area. The brewhouse is behind glass, next to the bar. The Palm Beach Draftsmen (local homebrew & beer appreciation club) meet here on a regular basis. Irish Times opened January 4, 1991.

♪ Wed - Sat: Irish folk music (groups brought from Ireland); Irish CDs at other times in the evening; radio during lunch

📺 3 (big screen brought out for special events)

EVENTS: St. Patrick's Day and in September, Half Way to St. Patrick's Day.

 darts   partial handicapped access

$$$ AE, CA, VI

Kelly's Caribbean Bar, Grill, & Brewery

301 Whitehead Street
Key West
33040

 (305) 293-8484

Located at the corner of Whitehead and Caroline, on the Key West Marina.

 11:00 am - 2:00 am daily

Havana Red Ale (red ale)   Paradiso Caribe (fruit beer)
Key West Golden Ale (mild ale)   Southern Clipper (non-alcoholic)

Brewer: Stephan Scheinder
Beer is all grain, served under pressure, filtered. Six beers on draft.

 The restaurant offers both a lunch and dinner menu featuring Caribbean influenced appetizers, salads, and entrees. Appetizers include the Key West Classic Conch Fritters, fried coconut shrimp with pineapple dipping sauce, island vegetable and meat patties, and gaspacho. Entrees include many island favorites including curried vegetable roti, angel hair pasta with shrimp and lime, pan fried fresh fish with papaya and toasted coconut, grilled shrimp in a special curry blend, and a tropically marinated, grilled Delmonico steak. Twenty-three wines available; full bar.

This Key West bar & grill, located in a late 1800s historic wooden house, is owned and operated by actress Kelly McGillis, star of such movies as *Top Gun*, *Witness*, and *The Accused* . She and her husband, Fred Tillman, supervised the renovations of the house and can usually be found around the restaurant. The house itself is the former Pan Am building. The restaurant is decorated with Caribbean influence and aeronautical memorabilia. Tours are available upon request. Opened January 16, 1993; began brewing in March of the same year.

♪ live music after 10 pm (variety); background music   4

 free parking;
bike & scooter parking

 AE, CA, DC, VI

McGuire's Irish Pub & Brewery

600 E. Gregory Street
Pensacola
32501

 (904) 433-6789

On hwy. 98 (Gregory St.) between the Bay Bridge & the Civic Center.
Look for the double-decker bus.

 11 am - 2 am daily

McGuire's Irish Red Ale (1.048)   McGuire's Stout (1.060, ale)
McGuire's Porter (1.052)   McGuire's Lite (1.038, ale)

Brewer: Steve Fried

Beer is all grain, served under pressure, filtered, 800 barrels. 2 draft beers, many domestic bottled beers, imported bottled beers include Fosters, Guinness, & Bass. Bottled McGuire's Irish Old Style Ale also available (sold in the southeast U.S.).

The restaurant offers American pub fare: snacks (try the onion rings), great burgers--30 kinds, U.S.D.A. prime steaks, kosher sandwiches (pastrami on rye), and seafood. Check out the Irish favorites and the 18¢ Senate Bean Soup, as they say in the ads, some restrictions do apply! The Alka Seltzer Award is given to anyone eating 3 burgers or kosher sandwiches. Succeed and you get a free T-shirt and tablet! Root beer also brewed on premise.

A decidedly Irish bar and restaurant located in Pensacola's original firehouse. It is filled with collectables and antiques with over 45,000 dollar bills signed by "Irishmen" of all nationalities lining the ceilings and walls. A "mug club" has over 2,000 mugs hanging over the bar. You too can join and let your mug wait for you! Pub motto: "Cead Mile Failte," translated from the Gaelic means "a hundred thousand welcomes." Brewery tours are available when brewmaster is on premises or with 48 hours notice for groups. The brewing system was added in 1988. One of Florida's top 100 restaurants. The Escamba Bay Home Brewers meet here on a regular basis.

♪ live music nightly - Irish traditional sing-a long and soft rock n' roll

EVENTS: St. Patrick's Day 5K Run (Sat. closest to March 17), McGuire's Sportfishing Tournament (mid-October). Mon.: Irish Ale Nite, Tues.: McGuire's Peristroika Nite, Wed.: Mug Club Nite, Thurs,: Wetback Nite, Fri.: P.O.E.T.S. Blarney Hour 4-6 pm, Sat.: Irishmen's Nite Out, Sun: Emory Chenoweth Nite

 - features internat. sporting events

     AE, CA, DC, DS, VI

Market Street Pub

120 Southwest First Avenue
Gainesville
32601

 (904) 377-2927

Located in downtown Gainesville, at the corner of SW 1st Ave. and SW 2nd Street.

 Mon - Thurs: 11 am - 1 am; Fri - Sat: 11 am - 2 am; Sun: 1 am - 9 pm

 Kooka Brew (spiced ale)
Gainesville Gold (golden ale)
Downtown Brown (amber ale)

Brewer: Ed Cooper
Several draft beers and imported &
domestic bottled beers (many English)

Seasonal:
Light Pilsner
Brewmaster's Choice (varies
with the season)
Wheat Bier
Oktoberfest
Winter Special

The restaurant features their own homemade sausage--four different kinds--and handcrafted meats that they feature in their own original recipes. They offer a selection of burgers, a half dozen salads, sandwiches and fish 'n chips. Other entrees include their own sauerbraten, corned beef; and chicken, crab, and tuna gyros. Try their French fries, special soups, or chili. About six wines; full bar.

They are located on the site of a hundred-year old grocery store in downtown Gainesville. It is in the style of a typical British country pub with red mahogany panels, oak flooring, frosted glass and exposed brick walls. It has a main dining room, a side room, and a dart room. Seats 120. Opened in 1989.

♪ live music Thurs. - Sat. (acoustic jazz, bluegrass, cajun, folk & easy   listening)

EVENTS: Oktoberfest (last weekend in Sept.), Island Night (spring), Halloween and New Year's Eve Party.

 darts

$$$ CA, VI, DS,

Mill Bakery, Eatery, & Brewery

11491 Cleveland Avenue
Fort Myers
33907

 (813) 939-2739

Located just south of Page Field (the old airport), on Route 41, on the edge of town.

 11 am - 2 am daily

Seminole Light
K Rock Red
Magic Brew (nut brown ale))

Joe & Stan (named after two local
radio personalities)
Scottish Ale (1.050)

Brewer: Edward Collins
Six guest beers are available as well.

 The menu is for those people seeking healthy, nutritious alternatives in their diet. A wide selection of homemade breads, sandwiches, pizza, soups and salads are offered, all with American Heart Association approval and recommendation. The emphasis is on high-fiber foods. They have several fish dishes and Birmingham Chicken is their most popular dish. Wine and mixed drinks are available. Don't forget to check out the bakery.

The Mill is located in a former Western Sizzlin' Steak House and has a working mill out front. It opened as Kidder's Brewery on Easter Sunday 1991; closed and was bought and reopened as The Mill April 1, 1993.

 live music Thurs - Sat; mostly reggae and rock   2

Mill Bakery, Eatery, & Brewery
Beach Brewing

5905 S. Kirkman Road
Orlando
32819

(407) 345-8802 - brewery
(407) 345-4833 - The Mill

Located in the Holiday Inn across the street from Universal Studios.

 7 am - 2 am daily (no beer sales before noon on Sunday)

Knight Light
Beach Blonde
Red Rock
Magic Brew (nut brown ale)

Brewer: Brian Baldasono

Beach Brewing's beers are also sold at several Florida bars and restaurants. Red Stripe served on reggae night.

 The menu is for those people seeking healthy, nutritious alternatives in their diet. A wide selection of homemade breads, sandwiches, pizza, soups and salads are offered, all with American Heart Association approval and recommendation. The emphasis is on high-fiber foods. Wine and mixed drinks are available. Don't forget to check out the bakery.

This brewpub is unusual because it is the only one with a beach volleyball court with a window onto the brewery. Owner Angela Ranson says the brewery sponsors a rollerblade hockey league which plays in the parking lot. Opened July 1992.

 wide variety of live music, with a different theme nightly, ranging from progressive, acoustic, jazz, reggae, salsa, blues, and country. Other times they have music piped in with a video link up.

 beer garden with a beach (hence the name) and swimming pool

beach volleyball, rollerblading

 10 TV sets

Mill Bakery, Eatery & Brewery

330 West Fairbanks
Winter Park
32789

 (407) 644-1544

Located in the New York Plaza, about halfway between I-4 and Rollins College.

 6:30 am - 2 am daily

Harvest Light (Pilsner)
Seminole Gold (Pilsner)
Magic Brew (amber lager)
Rollins Rock (golden Pilsner)

Seasonal:
  Wheatfield Dry (weizen)
  Traditional Pilsner
  Holiday Ale (Christmas brew)

Brewer: John Stewart
Gatortail Ale (dark, made under contract)

 The Mill reflects the health and fitness craze of the nineties. The menu offers sandwiches, soups, salads (100-item salad bar), and pizzas, many of which are formulated according to the American Heart Association guidelines and all are analyzed for nutritional content. They also offer fine cakes, cheesecakes, pies, and an array of pastries, and home-baked breads and muffins. A breakfast buffet is served on weekends. Something for everyone! Wine and mixed drinks available.

The Mill has a country, rustic interior with wooden floors, tables, and walls and is filled with plants, baskets, and framed, early-20th century beer advertisements and other memorabilia. The brewhouse is visible from the mezzanine lounge-dart room. It has a pond and mill wheel outside. A neighborhood gathering place for a snack, lunch, or a good brew.

♪ live music on Wed. - Sat. nights (acoustic rock, open mike on Wed.);
background music - moderate (contemporary)

  darts

Ragtime Tavern & Grill

207 Atlantic Boulevard
Atlantic Beach (Jacksonville)
32233

 (904) 241-7877

Located in Jacksonville's beach community (Atlantic Beach), where Atlantic Blvd. meets the Atlantic Ocean.

 11 am - 2 am daily

Redbrick Ale (1.047, Irish ale)
A Strange Stout (1.050)
Westbury Wheat (1.044)
Dolphin's Breath Lager (1.048)
Seasonal:
  Octoberfest
  Holiday Ale

Seasonal (cont'd):
  Best Bitters
  Bock
  Almond Ale
  Rainlager
  Maddies Marzen
  Loggerhead Light

Brewer: Scot Morton
There are 40 other brands available in bottles.

 Ragtime features fresh, Florida seafood with a Cajun and Creole twist, such as bayou bouillabaisse, grilled Cajun shrimp, and gumbo. They also have soups, salads, desserts, and an extensive list of finger and hand foods. They offer 80 wines and a full bar.

It was originally opened in 1983 by brothers Tom and Bill Morton as a tavern and restaurant. Ragtime expanded into a vacant store next door where the brewhouse and Tap Room are located. It is located in the oldest commercial building in Atlantic Beach. The interior is split level, with an exposed kitchen and brewery. The walls are made of antique brick, with oak paneling, molding, and mill work. The Northeast Florida Society of Brewers (the S.O.B.s) meets here the 2nd Sunday of the month. Scot Morton is brewer in the 12 hectoliter brewhouse. All beer is on tap - no bottling or kegging. They began serving their own beer on September 30, 1991.

♪ live jazz Thurs. - Sun. evenings

EVENTS: Mardi Gras with a costume contest, a parade, and other festivities

 $$$ AE, CB, DC, DS, CA, VI

Riverwalk Brewery

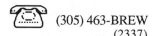

111 SW 2nd Avenue
Fort Lauderdale
33301

(305) 463-BREW
(2337)

Located in the Bon Ton Square.

 Mon - Sat: 11 am - midnight; Sun: noon - midnight

 Lauder Light (ale, 3.5% alc.)
Lauder Ale (dunkel)

Brewer: Stephan Scheinder

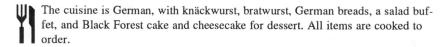

The cuisine is German, with knäckwurst, bratwurst, German breads, a salad buffet, and Black Forest cake and cheesecake for dessert. All items are cooked to order.

This brewpub is German throughout, from its four German owners to its imported brewhouse, with twelve fermentation tanks. The owners sent an architect to Germany to copy a beer hall, and then spent more than $2 million making the conversion. The brewhouse is located in the middle of the German beer hall. It has a medieval, castle-like theme. Opened March 1991.

♪ live music Fri. and Sat. with contemporary music in the beer garden & German background music inside; during the week they have a roving German accordion player.

 $$$ AE, CA, VI

Santa Rosa Bay Brewery

54 Miracle Strip Pkwy
Ft. Walton Beach
32548

 (904) 664 - BREW

 Mon - Thurs: 11 am - midnight; Fri - Sat: 11 am - until; Sun: noon - 10 pm

Red Irish Ale	Seasonal:
Golden Ale	Christmas Ale
Wheat Ale	Summer Dark Wheat

brewer: Theodore F. Bass
Beer is all grain, served under pressure, filtered. 12 bottled beers available, including several domestics.

 Seafood and steak is featured on the menu. Many wines are available; full bar.

This brewpub has an English/Irish theme. Twenty or thirty stained glass windows surround the restaurant. Be sure to notice also the tin ceiling. The F.W.B. Brewers, a homebrew club, meet here on a regular basis. Opened November 1, 1992.

ANNUAL EVENT: Brewfest (Sept 11, 1993)

 Live music Fridays and Saturdays (jazz); background music

 12 sets (wide screens)

 pool-billiards

 free

 $$$ AE, CA, VI

Sarasota Brewing

5872 14th Street West
Bradenton
34207

 (813) 751-1991

Located in a strip mall on West 14th Street, which is also Bradenton's main street, and is also U.S. Highway 41.

 Mon - Sat: 11am - 2 am; Sun: noon - midnight

 Cobra Light (lager)
Presidential Pale Ale
Sequoia Amber Lager

Seasonal:
   Prince Albert Imperial Dark Ale
   Andy's Maibock

Twelve bottled beers, including Anchor Steam, Amstel Light, and Grolsch.

 The menu features sandwiches and burgers, grouper, shrimp, and fillet mignon. The menu is the same as in the Sarasota Brewing in Sarasota. Six wines available at all times; full bar.

This is a brewpub-sports bar featuring sports decor and, count them, 12 televisions, four of which are wide screen. The wooden bar is in the middle of the brewpub, with booths on the walls. The brewhouse is behind the bar. They opened in early March 1991, but held the official opening party on June 14 of the same year.

 live music Mon. (blues) & Thurs. (fifties and sixties)   12

 CA, DC, DS, VI

Sarasota Brewing

6607 Gateway Avenue
Sarasota
34231

 (813) 925-BEER

Behind the Gulf Gate Mall.

  Mon, Fri, Sat: 11 am - 2 am; Tues - Thurs: 11 am - midnight
Sun: noon - midnight

  Cobra Lite (lager)
Presidential Pale Ale
Sequoia Amber Lager
Ja Mill's Honey Mead Beer

Seasonal:
Muristan Weizen
Londonderry Porter

Brewer: Gisele Budel
Eight bottled beers available.

 Try one of the char-grilled steakburgers or order from the sandwich selection - The Shoeless Joe Jackson (BBQ pork) or The Bahamian Grouper Sandwich. Other selections include designer pizzas or a full pound of fried onion slivers (pre-washed in beer, of course).

A neighborhood sports bar housed in "mountain architecture." It is filled with beer and sports memorabilia and has a digital sports ticker. The varnished pine paneling and stone wall interior suggest an alpine ski lodge. It opened in 1989.

live music on Monday (blues); background music (popular)

  video games

🖥 (2 wide-screen monitors)

🚗

Illinois

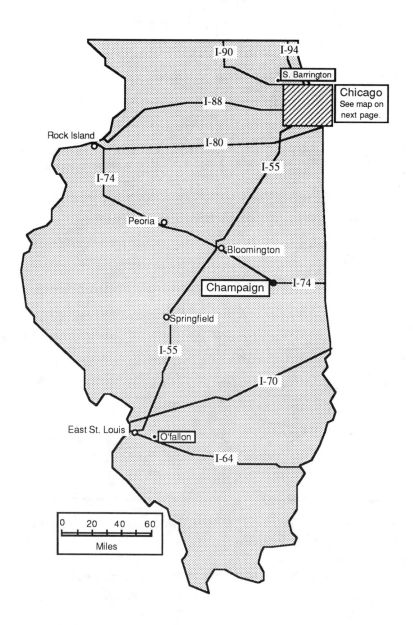

Chicago Area Breweries

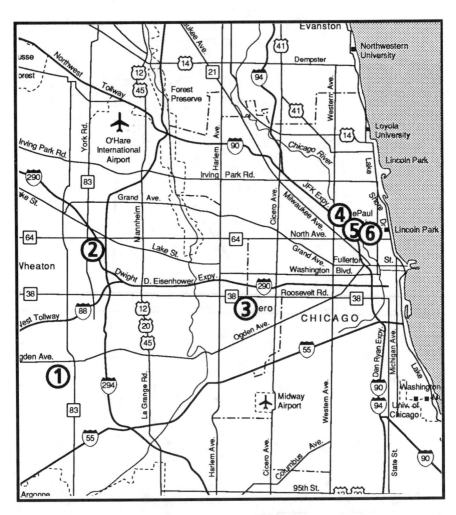

1. **Weinkeller Brewery**
   651 Westmont Drive, Westmont

2. **Pavichevich Brewing**
   383 Romans Road, Elmhurst

3. **Weinkeller Brewery**
   6417 W. Roosevelt Road, Berwyn

4. **Golden Prairie Brewing**
   1820 W. Webster Ave., Chicago

5. **Chicago Brewing**
   1830 North Besly Court, Chicago

6. **Goose Island Brewing**
   1800 N. Clybourn, Chicago

Chicago Brewing

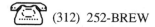 (312) 252-BREW

1830 North Besly Court
Chicago
60622

Just east of the Armitage exit, off I-90/94 (Kennedy Expressway) and
1/2 block west of the intersection of Elston Ave. and Cortland St.

Legacy Lager (1.050)
Legacy Red Ale (Irish ale, 1.050)
Heartland Weiss (1.048)
Big Shoulders Porter (1.054)

Brewer: Greg Moehr
7,500 barrels.

<u>Tasting room for sampling beers on tours.</u>

Tours are given every Saturday at 2:00. Tours include a brief history of beer as well
as details on the brewing process. Free draft beer to adults 21 years of age and older.
Located in the first story of a four story building that was constructed as a pickle factory in the 1920s. Best time to call for directions or more information: Mon. - Fri.:
9 am - 5 pm. Chicago Brewing was founded by the Dinehart family--Stephen, his
wife Jennifer, and brother Craig. They began selling their first beer, Legacy Lager in
July 1990.

Golden Prairie Brewing

 (312) 862-0106

1820 West Webster Avenue
Chicago
60614

Located on the north side, between I-94 and the North Branch of the Chicago River.

 Golden Prairie Ale

Brewer: Ted Furman

Furman was a local homebrewer who took an interest in commercial brewing. He was assistant brewer at Sieben's before it closed its doors in 1990. He wanted to open his own brewery, but didn't have the funds, until a guest at his wedding reception fell in love with his homebrew and put up half the necessary funds to start the brewery. Furman's bride put up the rest. He began brewing three-barrel batches of his Golden Prairie Ale in the fall of 1992. Furman is distributing his beer in kegs and plans to put more brands on the market.

Tours can be arranged; please call in advance.

Goose Island Brewing

1800 North Clybourn
Chicago
60614

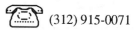 (312) 915-0071

On the north side of town, on the corner of Willow and Marcy, one block west of intersection of Willow, Clybourn, & Marcy.

 Mon - Thurs: 11 am - midnight; Fri - Sat: 11 am - 2 am
Sun: noon - 11 pm

 Golden Goose Pilsner (1.043)
Lincoln Park Lager (1.045)
Honker's Ale (1.049, pale ale)
Seasonal:
  Old Clybourn Porter (1.055)
  Chicago Vice Weizen (1.042)
  Special Brown Ale (1.066)
  Christmas Ale (1.070)
  PMD Mild Ale (1.034)
  Weizen ((1.042)

Seasonal (cont'd):
  RAF Best Bitter (1.062)
  Aviator (1.078, dopplebock)
  Honest Stout (1.068)
  Hop Scotch Ale (1.046, bitter)
  Old Abeerration Barleywine (1.095)
  Oktoberfest (1.056)
  Irish Stout (1.042)
  Russian Imperial Stout (1.090)
  Oatmeal Stout (1.058)

Brewer: Gregory Hall
Beer is all grain, served under pressure, most are filtered; 2,000 barrels.
Beer to go in 64 oz. growlers, kegs, & pony kegs. Additional seasonals brewed.

 The cuisine is home style ethnic with an assortment of dishes that are American, Mexican, English, Belgian, and German. They have a nationally acclaimed chef. Several wines available; full bar.

The brewpub is housed in the old Turtle Wax factory with a brick exterior and a brick, exposed, beams, and wooden floor interior. It has exposed ductwork and features a big old fashioned bar-in-the-round. Authentic English pub atmosphere. It is split-level with separate dining area. Brewery tours every Sunday at 3 (groups of 8+ please call in advance). The Chicago Beer Society meets here on 1st Thurs. of each month. Opened May 1988. Check out the T-shirts, sweat shirts, hats & postcards.

 background music (moderate to loud)    $$$ AE, CA, DC, DS, DI, CB

EVENTS: Last Taste of Summer, Octoberfest, Brewmaster's Dinner, seasonal beer tastings (their beers & commercial beers)

 darts, pool, chess, backgammon

Joe's Brewery

706 South 5th Street
Champaign
61820

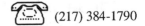 (217) 384-1790

On the University of Illinois campus.

 11 am - 1 am daily

 Young William's Pale Ale (1.064)
Seasonal:
   Brownstone Porter (1.065, winter)
   Aviator Dopplebock (1.100, spring)
   Heffeweizen (1.048, summer)
   Harvest Moon Oatmeal Stout (1.080, fall)
   Old Boneyard Barley Wine (1.100)

Beers made from malt extract; unfiltered.

Also on draft: Miller Lite, Miller Genuine Draft, Bud, Bud Light, Geo. Killian's; eight bottled beers.

Brewer: Bill Morgan
Beer to go: bring your own container.

They feature pub grub, with several kinds of appetizers, burgers, and sandwiches. The Buffalo Wings, nachos, and potato skins are very popular. They also have soups and salads. A few wines on the menu; full bar.

They are located in an old, brownstone book depository. It features an atrium in the front and 10,000 sq. feet divided into three rooms: the bar, a dance club, and a lounge. Originally opened as Chief's in the spring of '91; reopened under new management as Joe's in September '91 and began serving their own beer January 31, 1992. The Midwest homebrew club meets here on 1st Sunday of each month.

♪ live jazz Friday during happy hour (5-7); background music other times (each room has it's own stereo system); CD jukebox; DJ in the dance club

 4 ; big screen in dance club for major sporting events; closed circuit video system in the dance club

breath analyzer (50¢)

electronic darts, 2 pool tables
golf machine

 limited off-street parking

 handicapped access to
main bar, dance floor
and restroom

 $$$ CA, VI

Mill Rose Brewing

45 South Barrington Road
South Barrington
60010
(708) 382-7673

From I-90 take the South Barrington exit; it's just north of I-90.

  Mon - Sat: 11 am - 1 am; Sun: 11 am - 10 pm

Dark Star (lager)
Downtown Brown Ale (1.052)
Country Inn Ale
Prairie Pilsner

W. R. Stout (1.056)
General's Ale (1.056)
Wheat n' Honey (1.056, ale)
Weiss

Brewers: Victor Ecimovich & Tom Sweeney

Beers are made from malt extract. They rotate and at least four are on tap at all times; 175 barrels. Leinenkugel Limited is on tap. Twenty-five bottled beers available.

 As this brewpub is owned by the Rose Packing Co., the emphasis is on the meat dishes. They have a very large menu with everything from chili burgers to rack of lamb with seafood, poultry, venison, and Canadian bacon in between. The rib combos and pork chops are very popular. They also have soups, salads, appetizers, sandwiches, pasta and desserts. Forty-three wines on the menu; full bar.

They are located in an old milk barn. The interior has been refurbished (the cows wouldn't even recognize the place), but it remains rustic in style, with 40-foot ceilings. The dining area seats 210 and the bar 100. They also have a banquet room for 100. The brewhouse is displayed behind glass. Homebrewing classes conducted Tuesday evenings. Opened October 28, 1991.

 background music (style varies)   7 TVs (1 big screen); satellite dish

 patio seats 120 and has 3 fireplaces   2 inside; 3 outside

$$$ AE, CA, DC, DS, VI

Pavichevich Brewing

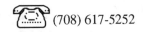 (708) 617-5252

383 Romans Road
Elmhurst
60126

Five miles south of O'Hare Airport. Romans Road is off County Line Road.

 Baderbrau Pilsener (European style)
Baderbrau Bock (European style)

Brewer: Doug Babcook
Beer is all grain, filtered; 6,200 barrels.

<u>Beer is available for sampling only in tasting room during tours.</u>

Tours are held on Saturdays with a reservation of at least 24 hours required. The best time to call is Mon. - Fri. from 8:30 am to 5 pm. Beer is available to go in six-packs and cases (12- oz. bottles) and in 50- liter kegs. Owner Ken Pavichevich says Baderbrau is distributed widely in the Chicago market. Opened in March 1989.

Weinkeller Brewery

6417 W. Roosevelt Road
Berwyn
60402

 (708) 749-2276

On the corner of Roosevelt and Ridgeland, ten minutes from the Loop. Take Eisenhower to the Austin Exit.

 Mon - Thurs: 11:30 am - 1 am; Fri - Sat: 11:30 am - 3 am; Sun: 2 pm - 1 am

Berwyn Brew Pilsner (1.045)
Bavarian Weiss (1.048)
Aberdeen Amber Ale (1.048)
Düsseldorfer Doppelbock (1.074)
Dublin Stout (1.072)
Berliner Weisse (1.042)

Seasonal:
Octoberfest (1.054)
Christmas Ale (1.076)

Brewer: Darin Floyd
24-oz. Champagne bottles, kegs, and pony kegs to go.
Draft beers, over 500 bottled beers, cider on draft.

The cuisine is German - American featuring sauerbraten, schnitzel, pork roast in beer and six different sausages. Many entrees are cooked in beer.

This pub combines a brewery, restaurant, bar, and a full service liquor store. It's interior features a rustic black and white scheme with old metal ceilings. Owner Udo Harttung runs the pub, directs the brewing of the beer, and pumps the beer.

♪ background music (jazz, oldies, classical, and German-moderate)

EVENTS: beer tastings

 darts

Weinkeller Brewery

651 Westmont Drive
Westmont
60559

 (708) 789-2236
FAX your orders to 789-2368

Located just off Ogden Avenue (Rte. 34).

 Mon - Thurs: 11 am - 1 am; Fri - Sat: 11 am - 2 am; Sun: noon - 1 am

Westmont Pilsner (1.045)
Bavarian Weiss (1.046, unfiltered)
Kristall Weiss
Aberdeen Amber Ale (1.048)
Düsseldorfer Doppelbock (1.082)
Weinkeller ESB

Dublin Stout (1.078)
Berliner Weisse (1.042)
Seasonal:
    Octoberfest (1.050)
    Christmas Ale (1.076)

Brewer: Udo Harttung

24- oz. Champagne bottles, 92- oz. refillable carry-kegs, kegs, and pony kegs to go.
Woodpecker Cider; several other bottled beers served.

 The cuisine is German-American featuring sauerbraten, schnitzel, pork roast in beer and six different sausages. Many entrees are cooked in beer. About 35 wines served--sold by the bottle or glass.

The interior is continental in style and has the brewhouse visible behind glass. The step-down bar area seats 80. The L-shaped dining area is in the rear and seats 140. Owner/brewer Udo Harttung runs the pub, brews the beer, pumps the beer and runs his other brewpub in Berwyn too! Opened March 10, 1992.

♪ occasionally they have strolling musicians; background music (jazz, oldies, classical, and German-moderate)

 big-screen, satellite   large beer garden

   partial handicapped access

$$$ AE, CA,CB, DC, DS, VI

Wolfgang's Restaurant & Brewery
O'Fallon Brewing

1711 West Highway 50
O'Fallon
62269

 (618) 632-BREW

Located three blocks west of I-64, on U.S. 50.

 Mon - Thurs: 11 am - 1 am; Fri - Sat: 11 am - 2 am; Sun: 11 - 1 am

Light
Amber
Pilsner

Seasonal:
   Numbskull Amber Lager (1.056)
   Horst's Oktoberfest (1.056)

Brewer: Ben Pierson

 They offer American/continental cuisine with several German dishes.

Wolfgang's is housed in an old car dealership with the brewhouse behind the display windows in the front. Inside it has a rustic German theme and features many antiques. The restaurant/bar is on the first floor and has a beautiful antique, mahogany bar and backbar. The booths around the exterior walls were made from old church pews. The seating capacity is 200. The pub is on the second floor, which has a balcony looking over the restaurant. There is also a banquet room for 200 and a meeting with a fireplace. They opened August 3, 1992.

light classical background music   cable TV in upstairs bar

 handicapped access on first floor only

 $$$ AE, CA, VI

Indiana

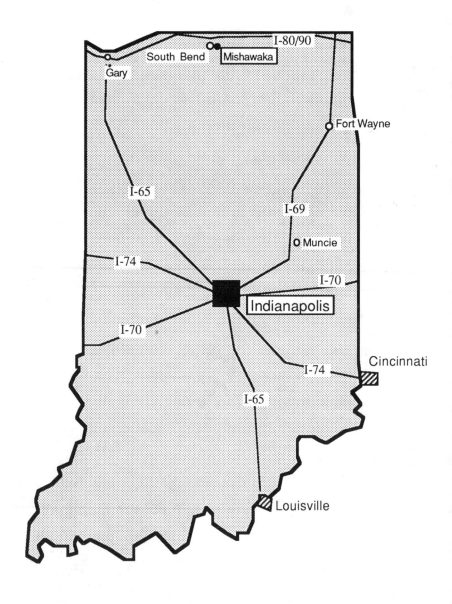

Broad Ripple Brewpub

 (317) 253-2739

840 East 65th Street
Indianapolis
46220

Located in the Broad Ripple entertainment district.

 Mon - Thurs: 11 am - midnight; Fri - Sat: 11 am - 1:30 am; closed Sunday

Red Bird Mild	Seasonal:
Pintail Pale Ale (1.060)	Wee Heavy
E.S.B. (1.049)	Copper Ale
Monon Porter (1.057)	Dry Stout
	Bavarian Wheat
	Kölsch (1.046)

Brewer: John Hill

Other microbrewed beers served include Main Street Pilsner, Main Street Premium
Lager, Oldenburg, Pete's Wicked Ale, and Kalamazoo; 40 bottled beers in all.

 The restaurant offers a full menu with a wide selection of soups, salads, burgers,
sandwiches, and vegetarian items. Steaks are their specialty.

This neighborhood pub features two tin-ceilinged rooms: one is Victorian in style
and the other is "craftsman" style. They have a fireplace and a cozy 10-seat bar.
Opened November 1990.

Background music

Indianapolis Brewing

 (317) 898-1235

3250 N. Post Road, #285
Indianapolis
46226

West of Post Road, facing 33rd Street.

 Duesseldorfer Amber Ale (1.046)
Duesseldorfer Dark Ale (1.055)
Duesseldorfer Pale Ale (1.042)
Seasonal:
  Brick Yard Bock (1.064)
  Oktoberfest (1.046)

Brewer: John Battles
Beers are filtered and all grain; 2,000 barrels.
Six packs and cases available for take out.

<u>Beer available for sampling in tasting room on tours ($1 per person, per state law)</u>. They are also brewing Pike Place India Pale Ale under contract. Best time to call for tours: 7:30 am - 5 pm, Mon. - Fri. Began selling beer in 1989.

INDIANAPOLIS, IND.,
U.S.A.

Mishawaka Brewing

 (219) 256-9993

3703 North Main Street
Mishawaka
46545
Located on far north side of Mishawaka, 3 miles east of the Univ. of Notre Dame.

 Mon - Thurs: 11:30 am - 11 pm; Fri and Sat: 11:30 am - 1 am
Sun: noon - 9 pm

 Mishawaka Gold Lager (1.042)
Lake Effect Pale Ale (1.042)
South Shore Amber Ale (1.047)
Founder's Classic Dry Stout (1.054)
Ankenbrock Weisen (1.043)

Brewers: Tom & Rick Schmidt
Beer to go in 22 oz. bottles. They also serve guest microbrews
and Coor's Light and Coor's Cutter (non-alc.).

 The restaurant has an ample menu, including appetizers, soups, salads, sandwiches, burgers, desserts, English pub favorites (including Lancashire pot pie, fish'n' chips, ploughman's lunch, bangers 'n mash, ham and leek pie, and shepherd's pie), and entrees including baby-back ribs, and chicken. Several wines and wine coolers are served.

Owners Tom Schmidt and John Foster have done a nice job of reshaping a former fitness center into a traditional London pub. The brewpub features a custom-built bar of cherry, bird's-eye maple, and brass, with a backlit etched glass with the Mishawaka logo and the brewery visible through a window, with its copper mash/lauter tun and brew kettle. The restaurant seats 275, with fifty additional seats in the beer garden. A separate club room features a stand-up bar, fireplace, and bristle board darts. They have even created an Anacreontic Society, modeled after the English men's health club (Anacreon was an ancient Greek writer of love poems and drinking songs). The club held weekly meetings at London's Crown and Anchor Pub where they sang "Anacreon in Heaven". Francis Scott Key borrowed the melody when he wrote the Star-Spangled Banner. Mishawaka Brewing is the first brewery to open in that city since the closing of the Kamm and Schellinger Brewery in 1951. House beers are all grain, filtered and served under pressure. Opened October 16, 1992.

  darts

  $$$ AE, CA, VI

Kentucky

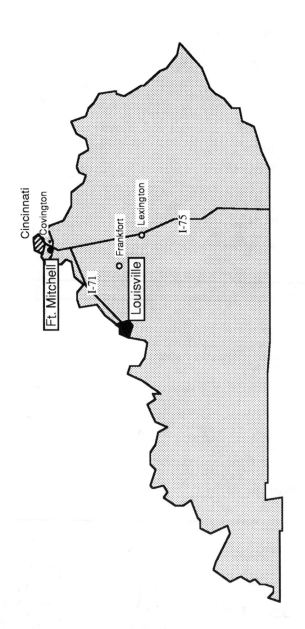

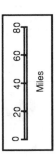

Oldenberg Brewery & Entertainment Complex

I-75 & Buttermilk Pike
Fort Mitchell
41017

 (606) 341-2800
(800) 354-9793

At the Buttermilk exit, just five miles south of Cincinnati, on Interstate 75.

 Tues - Sun: 11 am - 10 pm; closed Monday

 Premium Verum (1.046, light amber lager)   Seasonals:
Oldenburg Blonde (1.035)   Stout
Oldenburg Weiss (1.042)   Outrageous Bock
Vail Ale (1.048)   Oktoberfest
                                                     Winter Ale

Brewer: Ken Schierberg

Beer is all grain, filtered, and served under pressure; 9,135. Bottled and kegged beer is sold to office premise accounts. Beer to go in 12-oz. bottles.

Victuals are offered in their old English brewpub, called J.D. Brew's, located on the upper level and adjacent to the Great Hall balcony. It seats 240 and offers lunch, dinner, and appetizers. Gretchen's Bakery offers a wide selection of strudels, chocolate creations, wonderful cookies, and much more. Food and beer is served in the Beer Garten spring through fall, 11 am-midnight (Sunday-Thursday) and 11 am - 1 am (Friday & Saturday). About 10 wines and full bar.

In addition to J. D. Brew's and the Beer Garten, the complex encompasses the Great Hall (for groups from 100 - 1,500), the Crown Market Gift Shop, the Drawbridge Estate, the American Museum of Brewing History and Arts, and the brewery. The Great Hall is is a magnificent 12,000 sq. ft. facility and is available for public or private events. The Brew-ha-ha Revue provides live entertainment every night but Monday. J.D. Brew's is an authentic English pub which provides a much cozier atmosphere than the Great Hall. Brewery tours are offered every hour beginning at 11:00 am. Tastefully displayed throughout all these areas is the largest breweriana collection in the world, including a beer delivery truck, 125,000+ labels, 45,000+ coasters, 27,000+ bottles, 12,500+ cans, 2,000+ tap knobs, and 600+ books & magazines. The Bloatians (homebrew club) meet here on a regular basis. Opened in 1988.

EVENTS: Beer Camp and Autumn Fest

 backgammon
& chess in J.D. Brew's

 $$$ AE, CA, DC, DS, MA, VI

Silo Brew Pub

630 Barret Avenue
Louisville
40204

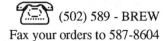 (502) 589 - BREW
Fax your orders to 587-8604

Located in the Phoenix Hill Area (downtown); next to an enormous grain elevator.

 Mon - Thurs: 11:30 am - 1:30 am; Fri - Sat: 11:30 am - 2:30 am
Sun: 4:00 pm - midnight

 Silo Premium Light (1.040, light ale)
Red Rock Ale (1.050, Irish red ale)
River City Raspberry (1.040, fruit beer)
Seasonal:
  Wheat (1.040, American wheat)
  Cream Ale (1.042)

Sixteen bottled beers are available.

Seasonal (cont'd):
  Pale Ale (1.044)
  Dark (1.054, brown ale)
  Porter (1.054)
  Stout (1.068, oatmeal)
  Pale Bock (1.066)
  Hercules Winter Warmer
    (1.068, old ale)

An extensive appetizer list, including a pretzel sampler and beer cheese, provides a complement to any beer selection. With emphasis on innovative, American cuisine, the menu features salads, sandwiches, fish and chicken dinners, and several pasta dishes. Pub specialties include a roasted free-range chicken, a sizzling sausage and peppers dinner, and Wisconsin beer cheese soup. Four brands of wine and full bar available.

This brewpub is housed in a converted warehouse, originally belonging to Ballard Biscuit Company, the predecessor of Pillsbury. The sandblasted brick and natural wood interior consists of 16,000 square feet. A large inside window shows the copper brew kettles. The brewery itself is walled with glass which allows customers to view the brewing process. Brewery tours are also available. Opened October 19, 1992.

Wed: ladies night; Fri-Sat:live music (variety--rock & roll,
  rhythm & blues, jazz, sixties-nineties); background music other times

 7, including a wide screen

 outdoor drinking area

Louisiana

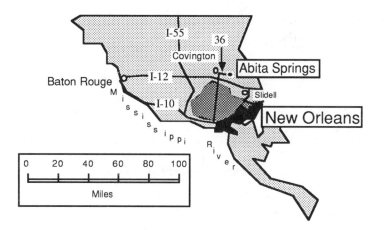

Abita Brewing

 (504) 893-3143

100 Leveson
Abita Springs
70402

Located in the center of town, at the railroad tracks.

 Abita Golden (1.042, lager)
Abita Amber (1.045, lager)
Seasonal:
  Wheat Beer (1.042)
  Mardi Gras Bock (1.054)
  Turbodog (1.060)
  Fall Fest (1.054)

Brewer: Jim Patton
Beer is all grain; 11,000 barrels

Beer is available for sampling only during tours.
Tours are available by appointment only with at least 24 hours notice. Best time to call is Monday - Friday, from 8 - 5. Begun in 1986, this brewery uses the famous waters from Abita Springs. The local Indians claimed the water protected them from Yellow Fever. The beer is marketed in both bottles and on draft.

THE NEW LOUISIANA LAGER
ABITA BREWING CO., INC., ABITA SPRINGS, LA.

Crescent City Brewhouse

 (504) 522-0571

527 Decatur Street
New Orleans
70130

Across the street from the Jax Brewery, near Jackson Square.

 Pub: 11 am - [whenever] daily
Kitchen: Sun - Thurs: 11 am - 11 pm; Fri - Sat: 11 am - midnight

Red Stallion (1.048, Märzen)
Pilsner (1.046)
Black Forest

Seasonal:
Carnival (1.050, dark lager)
Maibock
Oktoberfest
Christmas Bock
Weissbeer

Brewer: Wolfram Koehler
Beer is all grain, served under pressure, filtered and unfiltered (specials); 1,250 barrels. Beer to go in cup sizes up to 34 oz. (It's legal to drink in streets in N.O.!)

 The cuisine is a mix of New Orleans and international, prepared by a New Orleans chef. Selections include Crescent City pizza, oysters, shrimp, catch of the day, shrimp chili, seafood pasta, grilled chicken, and daily specials. Fifteen wines available; full bar.

This pub/restaurant is housed in an old warehouse dating from 1840. They have 17,000 sq. feet on two levels, which includes a full-service restaurant and formal seating for more than 300. The brewhouse is visible behind the bar. The second floor restaurant offers a view of both the serving tanks and the Mississippi River. The decor is New Orleans style and they have a courtyard and balcony. Art exhibits are also displayed (they change regularly). Reservations are recommended on weekends. Half price on all drinks and beer during Happy Hour (Mon - Fri: 5 - 7). Opened January 1, 1991.

♪ live music - weekends (New Orleans jazz) & happy hour

EVENTS: Mardi Gras

 courtyard and balcony

 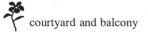 $$$ AE, CA, DC, VI

Maine

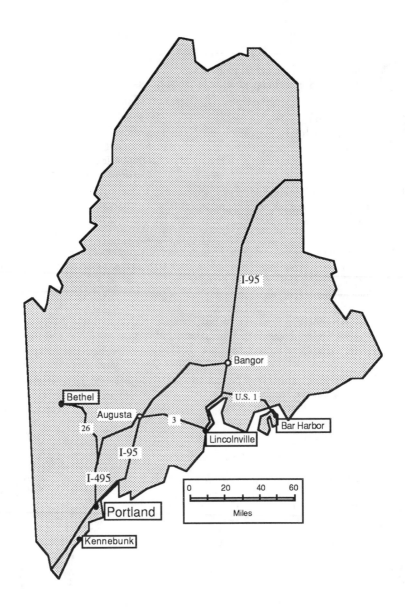

Andrews Brewing

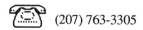 (207) 763-3305

RFD. #1 Box 4975
Lincolnville
04849

Call for directions.

Andrew's Old English Ale (1.050, pale ale)
Andrew's Brown Ale (1.053)
Andrew's Old St. Nick Porter (1.054)

Brewer: Andrew Hazen
Beer is all grain.

On December 23, 1992 Andy Hazen began distributing three beers from his one-barrel brewing system. Hazen began homebrewing about ten years ago. He later became intrigued with the various small breweries which were starting up in Maine.

He started with a pilot brewing system from the Brass Corkscrew in Seattle, Washington. His system consists of two 20-gallon mash tuns, a 50-gallon sparging tank, a brew kettle, and a 52-gallon closed wine fermenter. Hazen has purchased a small hand bottler (fills six bottles at a time) but had not put it into production at press time. The brewery is housed in an outbuilding he built himself, behind his farmhouse.

Currently Hazen kegs all his beer for his three accounts in nearby Belfast and Camden. Maine allows brewers to distribute up to 50,000 gallons without going through a distributor. Hazen uses his pickup truck to do his distributing.

Bar Harbor Brewing

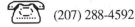 (207) 288-4592

Route 3, Otter Creek
Bar Harbor
04609

From Bar Harbor follow Route 3 south three miles past the Jackson Laboratory on the way to Blackwoods Campground.

Cadillac Mtn. Stout (1.075, Imperial Stout)
Thunder Hole Ale (1.060, brown ale)
Harbor Light Pale Ale (1.043, limited availability at Brewery only)

Brewer: Tod Foster
Beer is made from malt extract with partial mash,
bottle-conditioned, unfiltered; 140 barrels.

In a rural setting, five minutes from downtown Bar Harbor, the Bar Harbor Brewing Company handcrafts bottle-conditioned specialty ales, such as its Cadillac Mtn. Imperial Stout. The craft brewery, adjoining the Foster's house, is a modern day tribute to times past when brewing was a cottage industry.

Free tours and tastings begin in the log cabin by "Alewife Pond" (follow the path from parking area to the left). In season tours: Monday - Friday 3:30 - 5:00. Tours are popular so call ahead, if possible, to ensure space. Off season and weekends by appointment.

You can find Cadillac Mtn. Stout and Thunder Hole Ale in many local restaurants and stores, or at the brewery in hand-bottled 22-ounce, long-neck bottles. Harbor Light Pale Ale is available in limited quantity at the brewery only.

D.L. Geary Brewing

 (207) 878-2337

38 Evergreen Drive
Portland
04103

Located on the west side of town.

 Geary' Pale Ale (1.047)
Seasonal:
Hampshire Special Ale (1.070, strong ale)

Brewer: David Geary
Beer is all grain, filtered; 6,000 barrels.
Beer available to go in six-packs & cases.

<u>Beer available for free sampling in tasting room, on tours only.</u>
Best time to call for reservations: 8 - 4, Monday - Friday. Opened in 1986.

They recently installed a new bottling line and a 50 barrel fermenter.

Gritty McDuff's Brew Pub

 (207) 772-BREW

396 Fore Street
Portland
04101

In Portland's historic Old Port, one block from the waterfront/harbor.

 Mon - Sat: 11 am - 1 am; Sun: noon - 1 am

McDuff's Best Bitter (1.048)
Portland Head Light Pale Ale (1.040)
Black Fly Stout (1.045)
Lion's Pride Brown Ale (1.043)
Sebago Ale (1.035)
Seasonal:
    Halloween Ale (1.076, ESB)
    Christmas Ale (1.064, ESB)

Seasonal (cont'd):
Nuptial Ale (1.042)
IPA (1.050)
Summer Wheat (1.042)
Winter Wheat (1.045)
Old Porter (1.050)
Mild (1.038)

Brewer: Ed Stebbins
Beer is all grain, some cask-conditioned and some served under pressure,
unfiltered; 1,400 barrels. Geary's Pale Ale on draft, Woodpecker Cider on draft.

 The restaurant offers pub grub with fish 'n chips, shepherd's pie, steak 'n kidney
pie, ploughman's lunch (yum), and chicken sweet potato pie gracing the menu.
They offer fresh seafood purchased every day from the waterfront- lobster,
clams, squid, crab, etc. They serve a variety of burgers, sandwiches, nachos, salads,
and vegetarian items. Several wines available; full bar.

Housed in a turn-of-the-century warehouse, this brewpub features a copper bartop,
brick walls, old floor boards, and exposed beams. Their slogan; "If ale and good food
be faults, may God have mercy on the wicked!" (quote from Gritty McDuff, renowned
brewer, pub philosopher, and the pub's namesake himself!) Ask about the Mug Club.
View the brewery by going downstairs. A bright beer tank and new fermentation
room have just been added. Drop by the Brewtique where T-shirts, beer to go, and
brewery-related items are sold. Opened December 1988.

♪ live music on Tuesday evening and Sunday afternoon - blues, folk, Irish
Background music - eclectic

   darts

 (evening only)

 VI,AE

Kennebunkport Brewing
Lobster Deck Restaurant
Federal Jack's Brew Pub

8 Western Avenue #6
Kennebunk
04043

(207) 967-4322 (restaurant)
(207) 967-4311 (brewery)

Located at the end of the Shipyard Shops on the harbor between Kennebunk and
Kennebunkport.

 noon - 1 am daily

Fast Freddie's Ultralight (1.034, light ale)
Goat Island Light (1.042)
Shipyard Export Ale (1.052, Canadian ale)
Taint Town Pale Ale (1.047)
Kennebunkporter (1.048)

Seasonal:
   Winter Ale (1.058)

Brewer: Alan Pugsley

Some of the beers are cask conditioned and unfiltered, others are filtered and
served under pressure; 417 barrels. Beer to go in five litre cans; served on tap
in approximately 20 restaurants throughout southern Maine. Bottled beers:
Geary's Pale Ale, Rolling Rock, Budweiser, and Miller Lite. In addition, there
is a hard cider on draft.

 Light fare, including sandwiches, soups, salads, and, of course, seafood; three
wines, full bar.

The brewery was added to two existing restaurants--the Lobster Deck and Federal
Jack's; they began serving their own beer in June 1992.

 frequently live music on weekends,
including blues, acoustic, and rock & roll

 4 televisions (wide screen)

 darts, pool, foosball,
and backgammon

$$$ CA, VI

Lompoc Cafe & Brewpub
Acadia Brewing

34-36 Rodick Street
Bar Harbor
04609

restaurant - (207) 288-9392
brewery - 288-9513

Located in downtown Bar Harbor, near the municipal parking lot.

 May - October: 3 pm - midnight daily

Bar Harbor Real Ale (1.048)
Coal Porter
Lompoc's Pale Ale

Roger's Tree Frog Stout
Ginger Wheat
Maine Blueberry Ale

Brewer: Roger Normand

Beer to go in 12-oz. bottles, six packs, and kegs. 300 barrels, distributed to area restaurants and shops. They have recently upgraded from a malt-extract brewery to full mash. Also on tap: Sam Adams, Geary's, Newcastle Brown, Bass, Yuengling's Lord Chesterfield, and Guinness. Bottled beers include Jenlin from France and Xingu from Brazil.

The menu has an international flavor and includes several Middle Eastern dishes. The two favorites are hummus and shawarma (a dish made of roast lamb, marinated in a curry sauce and served with fresh tomato and onion on pita bread). They also serve thin-crust pizza, New Zealand roast lamb, several vegetarian dishes, sandwiches, salads, and soups. Several wines are on the menu; full bar.

The Lompoc has both a neighborhood flavor and an international flair. It is a cozy one-room brewpub with 14 tables, and a mahogany bar. The brewhouse is next door and visible through a window at the end of the bar. There is no television (yeah!!). Doug Maffucci and Jon Hubbard opened the Lompoc three years ago, selling beer brewed out of state, with the exception of Geary's Pale Ale on draft. The bar was named after the Old Lompoc Cafe, featured in one of W.C. Field's classics, *The Bank Dick*. They began selling beer brewed locally and became interested in adding a brewery to the bar. They served their first beer on May 23, 1991. There is a brewery tour every afternoon at 4:30. They have a gift shop next door which carries 12-oz. bottles of their beer, T shirts, and homebrewing supplies.

♪ live music nightly

 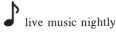 $$$ CA, VI

Sunday River Brewing
The Moose's Tale

 (207) 824-3541

1 Sunday River Road (P.O. Box 847)
Bethel
04217

Located at the intersection of U.S. Route 2 and Sunday River Road, near the Sunday River Ski Resort.

 Winter: 11:30 am - 1 am daily
Summer: Wed - Sun: 11:30 am - 1 am

Pyrite Golden	Black Bear Porter
Redstone Ale	Mollyecket (IPA)
Baron's Brown Ale	Cantdog
	Old Speck Stout

Brewer: Peter Leavitt

Seasonal:

Beer is all grain, served under pressure, filtered (except the stout); six beers on tap. Beer will soon be available to go in

Imperial Stout (St. Patrick's Day)
White Beer (due out this summer)

five liter refillable kegs. Ales made with Briess malts & a variety of American hops, including Cascade, Chinook, Cluster, Mount Hood, & Willamette varieties.

The menu features appetizers, soups, dinner specials and an extensive salad list, including a crabmeat salad and a grilled raspberry chicken salad. Start off with the appetizer list which includes among others, nachos, chicken fingers, or Head Poppers (stuffed jalapeños). Then choose from clam chowder, hamburgers, sirloin, deep-dish, Chicago-style pizza with red or white sauce, or design your own gourmet pizza. Dinner specials include fish and chips, fried seafood, fresh pasta, prime rib, shrimp and crab dishes, and several meat dishes. Full bar.

The pub area and separate restaurant, called The Moose's Tale, are located in a large building capable of accommodating nearly two hundred patrons. The establishment attracts both the winter skier crowd as well as vacationers to the area throughout the year. Opened December 18, 1992.

 extensive CD collection; live music three nights a week   2 (sports)

Events: They are planning a beer festival for homebrewers to be held in the fall.

 darts, horseshoes

  $$$ CA, VI

Maryland

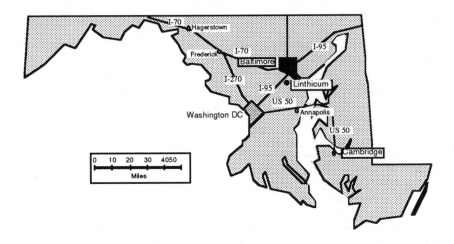

Baltimore Brewing

104 Ablemarle Street
Baltimore
21202

 (410) 837-5000

Next to the Flag House, one block from Little Italy and only a few blocks east of the Inner Harbor.

 Mon - Thurs: 11:30 am - 11:00 pm; Fri - Sat: 11:30 am - midnight; Closed Sunday

Dunkles (1.050)	Seasonal:
Helles (1.044)	Alt
Pils (1.050)	Maibock
Dark (1.051)	Wheat
Lager (1.046)	Wheat Bock
Pils (1.051)	Dobbel Bock
Märzen (1.051)	

Brewer: Theo De Groen
Beer is all grain; 950 barrels.

 The menu is American and German with a wide selection of items such as wursts, sauerbraten, spätzle, wiener-schnitzel, and soft pretzels. Six varieties of wine available; full bar.

The brewpub is located in a former food warehouse. It has been renovated with high ceilings and all interior walls have been removed, so that it resembles an upscale, German beer hall. The interior is brick and is open and airy. The brewery is directly behind the long, curving bar. Historic breweriana is displayed inside the brewpub. They served their first beer in 1989.

 $$$ AE, CA, CB, DC, VI

Oxford Brewing

611G Hammonds Ferry Road
Linthicum
21090

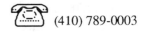 (410) 789-0003

Oxford Class (1.055, amber ale)
J. Pauls 1889 (1.055, amber ale)
McGarveys Aviator Ale (1.050, pale ale)
Seasonal:
   Oxford Santa Class (1.060, amber ale)
   Oxtoberfest (1.060, amber ale)
   Irish Class (1.060, amber ale)

<u>No beer sold on premises.</u>
Tours are held by reservation only with one month's notice. Best time to call is
Mon - Fri: 9 - 5. Formerly located in Glen Burnie and called British Brewing.

Sisson's
South Baltimore Brewing

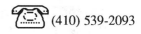 (410) 539-2093

36 East Cross Street
Baltimore
21230

Opposite the Cross Street Market & only 6 blocks from the Inner Harbor.

 Mon - Sat: 11:30 am - 2 am; Sun: 5 pm - 2 am

Stockade Amber (1.052, pale ale)
Marble Golden (1.044, golden ale)
Cross Street Stout (1.048)
So Bo HefeWeizen (1.046)

Seasonal:
Christmas Ale (1.068)
plus others

Brewer: Hugh Sisson
Beer is all grain, served under pressure, both unfiltered and filtered; 700 barrels.
64 oz. glass jugs to go. Many other draft and bottled beers available--
domestic, import, and micros.

Full service restaurant offering Cajun and Creole-style cuisine. They have been rated Baltimore's best for six years in a row. Reservations are highly suggested. Twenty-five varieties of wine; full bar.

An English-style, neighborhood restaurant/brewery situated in three adjacent row houses. Notice the copper tables. The brewery is visible through the wall of one of their dining rooms. The bar is quite small. The Cross St. Irregulars homebrew club meet here on a regular basis. They sold their beer first in 1990.

♪ background music - moderate; juke box

$$$ AE, CA, DC, DS, VI

The Wharf Rat Camden Yards
Oliver Breweries

206 West Pratt Street (410) 244-8900
Baltimore
21201

Located in the Camden Yards neighborhood, across from Festival Hall and one block east of Oriole Park.

 Winter: Mon - Sat: 11:30 am - 2:00 am; Sun: 11:30 am - midnight
Summer: Mon - Sat: 11:30 am - 2:00 am; Sun: 11:30 am - 2:00 am

Oliver's Best Bitter* (1.048)
Oliver's E.S.B.* (1.058)
Oliver's S.W.1 (1.048)
Oliver's Golden Best (1.040, pale ale)
Farrell Irish Strong (1.058)
Blackfriar Stout (1.050)

Seasonal:
Oliver's Pale Ale* (1.040)
Oliver's Summer Light (1.032)

Brewer: Howie Faircloth
Beer is all grain, both filtered/unfiltered, both cask-conditioned/served under pressure. Half gallons to go. Thirty beers on tap including 27 varieties such as Guinness and Murphy's Stout, Anchor Steam, Dock Street, Wild Goose, Sierra Nevada, Bass, Harp, Moosehead, Fosters, and Newcastle. (* indicates cask conditioned)

New English Cuisine inspires this restaurant's menu, as well as traditional entrees such as fish & chips and bangers & mash. Choose from numerous appetizers including Victoria & Albert (a warm crab and artichoke dip in a sour dough bread bowl, and Ruffians, traditional mini fish cakes made with delicate orange roughy. Soups include Ramsgate Seafood Chowder and English Beer and Onion Soup. For a main entree, pick from items ranging from Crab Cake to Fish and Chips to Mrs. Rooney's Chili to The English Channel (shrimp and scallops in a marinara sauce over angel hair pasta). Numerous salads and sandwiches also available. Thirty wines available; full bar.

This English-inspired yuppie pub, located in a historic 1850s building, is one of the last two cast-iron front buildings left in Baltimore. The first floor is the pub itself; upstairs are two Victorian dining rooms. The brewery opened January 27, 1993. They own another pub by the same name in Fells Point, where they are allowed to serve any beer but those which they brew, thanks to Maryland's modern and enlightened alc. bev. laws.

 live music (special events)
background music

 pool-billiards

    AE, CA, DI, DS, VI

Wild Goose Brewery

20 Washington Street
Cambridge
21613

 (410) 221-1121

Located off U.S. Rte. 50 in the old Phillips packing plant; two old smokestacks and a water tower indicate the site of the brewery.

Wild Goose Amber Beer (1.051)
Thomas Point Light Golden Ale (1.042)

Brewer: Mark Scease
Beer is filtered; 4,200 barrels.

Beer available for free sampling in tasting room, on tours only. No beer sold on premise.

Tours are conducted weekdays after 4 pm & on weekends; reservations required 3-4 days in advance. Best time to call for reservations: 8 - 4. Opened October 1989.

 **WILD GOOSE**

Massachusetts

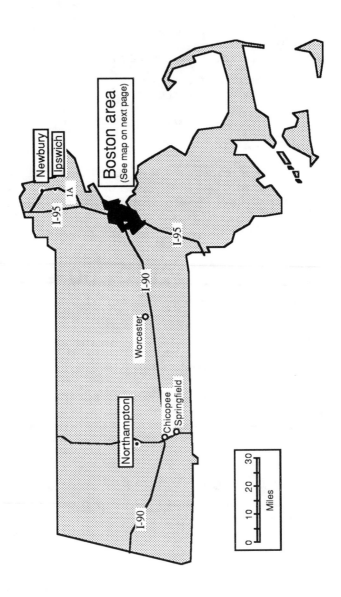

Newbury

Ipswich

Boston area
(See map on next page)

I-95

1A

I-95

I-90

Worcester

Northampton

Chicopee

Springfield

I-90

0   10   20   30

Miles

Boston Area Breweries

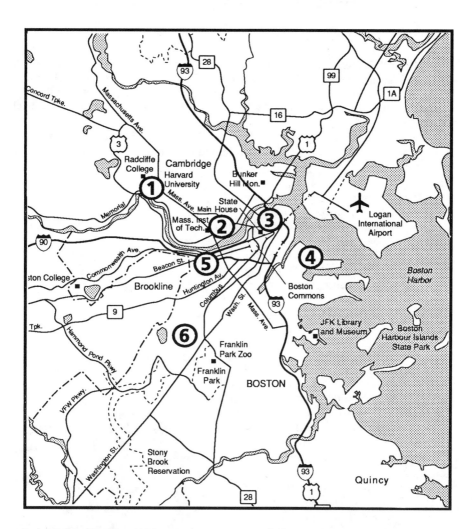

1. **John Harvard Brewhouse**
   33 Dunster Street, Cambridge

2. **Cambridge Brewing**
   1 Kendall Square, Cambridge

3. **Commonwealth Brewing**
   138 Portland Street, Boston

4. **Mass. Bay Brewing**
   306 Northern Avenue, Boston

5. **Boston Beer Works**
   61 Brooklin Ave., Boston

6. **Boston Beer**
   30 Germania Street, Boston

Boston Beer Co.

 (617) 522-9080

30 Germania Street
Boston
02130

Driving: Take I-93 to Exit 18 (Mass. Ave.) and bear left onto Melnea Cass Blvd. Turn left onto Tremont St. at the 8th stoplight (Tremont eventually becomes Columbus Ave.). Go to 11th stoplight & take right on Washington St. and then 4th right on Boylston St. Go 2 blocks & go left onto Bismark St. & look for the Samuel Adams signs.
Subway: Take the Orange Line outbound to Forest Hills. Exit at the Stoney Brook stop. Above ground, go left on Boylston St. and go to Bismark as described above.

Samuel Adams Boston Lager (1.052, lager)
Boston Stock Ale (1.056)
Boston Lightship (1.032, Pilsner)
Seasonal:
   Samuel Adams Octoberfest (1.056)
   Samuel Adams Winter Lager (1.064)
   Cranberry Lambic
   Samuel Adams Double Bock (1.084)
   Samuel Adams Wheat
   Samuel Adams Cream Stout

Brewer: Jim Koch

Beer available in the tasting room for sampling only.
Tours are held on Thurs. at 2 pm and on Sat. at 12 pm and 2 pm. No reservation needed. Call the brewery anytime for a recording giving complete times and directions.

The brewery is on the Register of Historic Places. The beer's namesake was a statesman, a patriot, and a BREWER. Samuel Adams Boston beers have won many awards at the Great American Festival, including four first places in the consumer preference poll and five gold medals in the professional panel judging.

Boston Beer Works
Slesar Brothers Brewing

 (617) 536-2337

61 Brookline Avenue
Boston
02215

Located across the street from the Red Sox box office at Fenway Park.

 11 am - 1 am daily

Acme Light (1.036)
Beer Works Raspberry (1.036)
Kenmore Kölsch (1.042)
Boston Red (1.050)
Buckeye Oatmeal Stout (1.055)
Hercules Strong Ale (1.100)

Many rotating seasonals

Brewer: Steve Slesar
They also make Major Root Beer and
Turnpike Lemonade. Three hard ciders
and three meads are served as well.

The cuisine is described as eclectic American. They specialize in fresh, grilled seafood, steaks, beer-basted burgers, and fresh pastas (fettucini, linguine, and 3-colored tortellini), served in a sauté pan at your table. Other popular entrees include stuffed quahogs and calamari. In addition they have appetizers, soups, salads, and sandwiches. Popular, freshly made desserts include mud pies and waffle boats. They have a Sunday brunch from 11 - 3, and specialize in omelettes and buckwheat waffles. They have a half dozen wines on the menu.

The brewpub is located in an old red and beige brick building between the stadium and the Mass. Turnpike. It was once a Goodyear tire factory and has Soho-style loft apartments on the upper floors. It has a large interior with a seating capacity of 225. Beer Works is 20th-century industrial in style, featuring lots of shiny metal, including a galvanized steel and aluminum, diamond-plate bar, and metalic industrial fans hanging from the 16-foot ceiling. This is contrasted with a black slate floor. They have an exposition char-grill with a shiny copper hood. The completely exposed brewhouse is next to the bar and the serving tanks are adjacent to the dining room. Be sure to check out the ample gift display area. The Boston Beer Nuts (homebrew club) meets here. Opened April 10, 1992.

 CD background music (mostly rock 'n roll)

 3

 validated parking, except during
Sox home games

 AE, CA, DC,
DS, VI

Cambridge Brewing

1 Kendall Square, Building 100
Cambridge
02139

 (617) 494-1994

On the corner of Broadway & Hampshire.

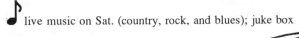

 Mon - Sat: 11:30 am - 1 am; Sun: noon - 1 am

 Regatta Golden (1.042, ale)
Cambridge (1.048, ale)
Charles River Porter (1.062)
Tall Tale Pale Ale (1.058)

Seasonal:
Wheaten Ale (1.036)
Winter Warmer (1.062, ale)
Bock (1.060)

Brewer: Philip Bannatyne
Beer is all grain, served under pressure, filtered; 2,100 barrels.
Beer to go in poly cube gallons.

 The food is quite eclectic, featuring many regional dishes--Southwestern and American. Menu includes vegetarian entrees. All go very well with the beer! Six varieties of wine available.

Cambridge Brewing is a neighborhood pub located in an old refurbished industrial mill with an exposed brick and light wood interior, bathed in sunlight from its many windows. The works of local artists are displayed on a monthly schedule. Opened May 1989.

 live music on Sat. (country, rock, and blues); juke box

  AE, DC, VI

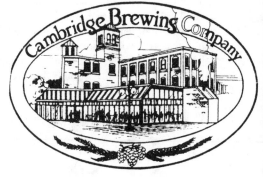

Commonwealth Brewing

138 Portland Street
Boston
02114

 (617) 523-8383

Located at the fork of Merrimac and Portland Streets, one block south of Boston
Garden and three blocks north of Faneuil Hall.

 Mon - Thurs: 11:30 am - midnight; Fri - Sat: 11:30 am - 1 am
Sun: 1 pm - 10 pm

Commonwealth Golden Ale (1.040)
Commonwealth Golden Export (1.042)
Boston's Best Burton Bitter (1.045, pale ale)
Commonwealth Amber Ale (1.048)
Commonwealth Classic Stout (1.050)
Blonde Ale (1.040, wheat)

Seasonal:
Celtic Ale
Ginger Ale (1.030)
Porter (1.055)
Special Old Ale
Winter Warmer (1.100)

Brewer: William Miller

Beer is all grain and cask conditioned. Beer to go in 12 oz. bottles.

 The cuisine is American with a selection of burgers, nachos, steaks and lobsters.

The brewpub walls are covered with English breweriana, including authentic Burton
Union casks over the bar. The downstairs is like an English pub and one can toss a
game of darts in full view of the brewing process. Their slogan: "let no man thirst for
lack of real ale." Beers are served from traditional English beer engines.
Commonwealth Brewing opened in 1986, making it the first brewpub in
Massachusetts since Prohibition.

♪ live music on Fridays and Saturdays (reggae); juke box - moderate

 darts

Ipswich Brewing

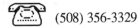 (508) 356-3329

25 Hayward Street
Ipswich
01938

Located in an industrial park in downtown Ipswich.

 Ipswich Ale (1.045, pale ale)

Brewer: Jim Beauvais

Tours are offered on Saturday at 1 and 3. Samples are given, but no beer is sold for consumption on the premises.

Partner Paul Sylva says their brew is all grain and unfiltered. Beer is made from two-row American pale malt, caramel malt, Willamette and Galena hops, Ipswich water, and their own yeast culture. Ipswich Ale is distributed in kegs, pony kegs, and half-gallon jugs to Kappy's in Peabody, Liquor Locker in Gloucester, Marcorelle's and Ipswich Bottle Shop, both in Ipswich. Beer also available in several restaurants in Boston, Ipswich, Gloucester, Rockport, Newburyport and Beverly.

Ipswich Brewing began distributing in October 1992 and is the first brewery to operate in Ipswich.

John Harvard Brewhouse

33 Dunster Street
Cambridge
02138

 (617) 868-3585

Located on Harvard Square.

 Mon - Wed: 11:30 am - 12:30 am; Thurs - Sat: 11:30 am - 1:30 am
Sun: 11:00 am - midnight

John Harvard Pale Ale	Seasonal:
Newtown Light Ale	Brown Ale
Irish Export Stout	Winter Ale
Crystal Pilsner Lager	Many more in the works.
Rauch Beer	

Brewer: Tim Morris
Beer is filtered and all grain. Some is cask-conditioned, some served under pressure.

 The restaurant has an extensive menu of classic American food. The speciality is house-made sausage. Many other items are also made from scratch including various pasta dishes. They have hard cider on draft and several wines.

Located in Harvard Square, this brewpub attracts the university crowd, tourists, and the neighborhood. A pictorial history of the life of John Harvard is depicted on the walls. The facility has a capacity of 300 people. Opened August 28, 1992.

 both live acoustic and jazz music is provided.

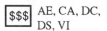 AE, CA, DC,
DS, VI

Mass. Bay Brewing

306 Northern Avenue
Boston
02210

 (617) 574-9551

Located in the Marine Industrial Park.

Harpoon Ale
Harpoon Golden Lager
Harpoon Dark
Bertucci's Light

Seasonal:
  Harpoon Octoberfest
  Harpoon Winter Warmer
  Harpoon Stout

Brewer: Tod Mott
Beer is all grain, served under pressure, filtered; 7,200 barrels.
Beer distributed in kegs and bottles.

Beer available for sampling only in tasting room.
Tours are held at 1 on Friday and Saturday. No reservations needed. Opened in 1987.

Northampton Brewery
Brewster Court Bar & Grill

 (413) 584-9903

11 Brewster Court
Northampton
01060

Located off Hampton Avenue, between the municipal parking lots and new parking garage in downtown Northampton.

 Mon - Sat: 11:30 am - 1 am; Sun: 1 pm - 1 am

Northampton Golden (1.048, Pilsner)
Northampton Amber (1.048, Vienna)

Seasonal:
  Northampton Steamer (1.050)
  Old Brown Dog (1.055, brown ale)
  Pale Ale (1.055)
  Hoover's Porter (1.050)

Seasonal (cont'd):
  Octoberfest (1.052
  Weizenheimer (1.044)
  Black Cat Stout (1.060)
  Pile Driver (1.048, dark lager)

Brewer: Rick Quackenbush
Beer is all grain, served under pressure, both filtered and unfiltered; 750 barrels.

 They offer a full menu with salads, appetizers, sandwiches, pizzas, entrees and daily specials. A favorite is chicken fajitas served on a "red hot" skillet with re-fried beans, guacamole, rice, tortillas and homemade salsa. 12-16 wines available; full bar.

Brewster Court Bar & Grill is located in a renovated, 19th-century carriage house-- brick with slate roof. The ample interior is a late 20th century mix & match style, which establishes a pleasant ambiance. Outdoor dining is available. Opened August 10, 1987.

 background music - eclectic

EVENTS: Halloween Charity Ball ,
Anniversary Charity Bash

$$$ AE, CA,
DS, VI

Ould Newbury Brewing

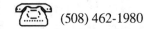 (508) 462-1980

227 High Road
Newbury
01951

The brewery is located in the basement of his home--call for directions.

Yankee Ale (1.045, amber ale)
Ould Newbury Porter (1.050)

Brewer: Joseph Rolfe
Beer is unfiltered.

Joseph Rolfe is a homebrewer, turned commercial. He began brewing in his basement and distributed his first kegs in September 1992. He has an account at the Thirsty Whale in Newburyport, which was buying all the beer he can produce at press time.

Rolfe has added a bottling operations to his two-barrel brewkettle. Bottles are 22-oz. in size.

Tours with tastings are offered--please to make a reservation. No beer sold for consumption on premise.

Michigan

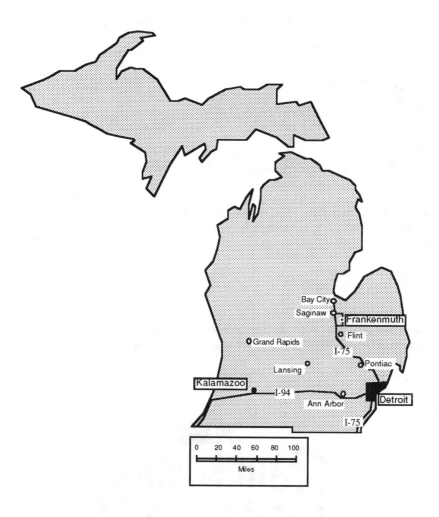

Bay City
Saginaw
Frankenmuth
Flint
Grand Rapids
I-75
Pontiac
Lansing
Kalamazoo
I-94
Ann Arbor
Detroit
I-75

0   20   40   60   80   100
Miles

Detroit & Mackinac Brewery

470 West Canfield
Detroit
48201

 (313) 831-BREW

Located in the midtown area, also known as the Cultural Center area, just south of Wayne State University and on the corner of 2nd.

West Canfield Ale (1.048)
Detroit & Mackinac India Pale Ale (1.052)
Detroit & Mackinac Red Ale (1.049)
Mackinac Black (1.050)

Brewer: Tom Burns
Beer is all grain, served under pressure, filtered; 500 barrels.

Owner Tom Burns gave up a law practice to become a brewer. In the early eighties he worked at Cartwright Brewing in Portland, Oregon, and later at Boulder Brewing in Boulder, Colorado. Ben Edwards, owner of a bar across the street called the Traffic Jam, built the brewery in 1988, but was been unable to brew beer because of a Michigan law which prohibits one person from being a brewer, wholesaler, and retailer of beer. Brewing began in March 1992. Burns began with kegged beer and hopes to expand to bottled beer in the future. Draft beers are available in seven Southeastern Michigan counties.

They conduct brewery tours the first Saturday of the month. Please call in advance. The brewery is licensed to sell beer directly to consumers for take out.

Frankenmuth Brewery

 (517) 652-6183

425 South Main Street
Frankenmuth
48734

Located a third of a mile north of Bavarian Inn & Zehnder's Restaurant.

Frankenmuth Extra Light (1.030)
Frankenmuth Old German Style Pilsner (1.046)
Frankenmuth Old German Style Dark (1.050)
Frankenmuth Natural Weisse (1.050)
Old Detroit Amber Ale (1.054)
Seasonal:
   Frankenmuth Old German Style Bock (1.067)
   Frankenmuth Cherry Weiss (1.046)

Brewer: Fred Scheer
Beers are all grain and filtered; 11,700 barrels.

Beer available for sampling only in tasting room during tours.
Tours are held daily from 11 - 5, May - October, and Wednesday - Sunday, November - April. No reservations needed. Beer is available to go by the six pack or case (i.e., no singles), and in five-liter cans. Opened for business in May 1988. They have added a new bottling line that includes a 22-ounce bottling capacity. They also added a five-liter canning operation.

Kalamazoo Brewing

 (616) 382-2338

315 East Kalamazoo Avenue
Kalamazoo
49007

Between Porter & Pitcher in downtown Kalamazoo.

Third Coast Beer
Bell's Amber Ale
Bell's Porter
Bell's Kalamazoo Stout
Bell's Beer
Seasonals:
  Deb's Red Ale
  Bell's Best Brown Ale
  Bell's Solsan Ale

Seasonals (cont'd):
  Third Coast Old Ale (1.093, barley
  wine)
  Bell's Expedition Stout (1.107, imperial
  stout)
  Bell's Cherry Stout (1.088)
  Bell's Double Cream Stout
  Bell's Eccentric Ale

Brewer: Larry Bell
Beer is all grain, some bottle conditioned, some not, unfiltered; 1,530 barrels.

Brewer Larry Bell got started as a homebrewer. While his passion in life was freshly brewed beer, he made ends meet as a disc jockey on a radio jazz program.

Tours available on Saturdays or by appointment. Beer to go available in 12 oz. bottles and kegs. Best time to call is between 9 - 5, Monday - Friday, and noon - 5 on Saturday. Bell began selling his beer September 1985.

Beer available for tasting.

  Hours: Mon - Fri: 9:00 am - 6:00 pm
          Sat - Sun: noon - 5:00 pm

Minnesota

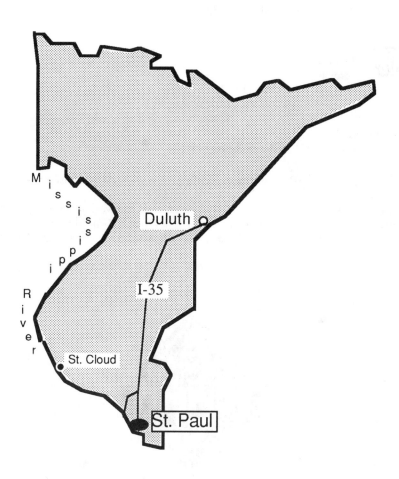

Duluth

I-35

Mississippi River

St. Cloud

St. Paul

Summit Brewing Company 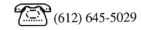 (612) 645-5029

2264 University Avenue
St. Paul
55114

Located five blocks east of Highway 280.

Summit Extra Pale Ale (1.048)
Great Northern Porter (1.054)
Seasonal:
    Summit Winter Ale (1.058)
    Summit Sparkling Ale (1.043)

Brewer: Mark Stutrud
Beer is all grain, served under pressure, filtered, 7,600 barrels.

<u>Beer available for free sampling in tasting room, on tours only; no beer sold on premises.</u>
Tours are held on Saturday at 1-- reservations required one week in advance; no tours over holiday weekends. Best time to call for reservations: 9 - 4, Monday - Thursday. Opened September 1986. Their equipment was purchased from a small Bavarian brewery, Hirshbrau, in Heimertingen.

New Hampshire

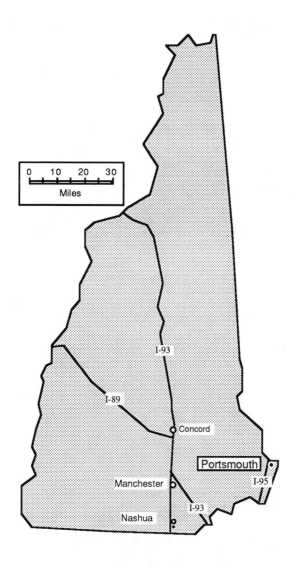

Frank Jones Brewing

225 Heritage Avenue
Portsmouth
03801

 (603) 433-2337

Located in the Portsmouth Industrial Park, south off U.S. Route 1 South (Lafayette Road).

Portsmouth Ale (1.052, IPA)
Granite State Golden Ale (1.043)
Seasonal:
  Special Reserve (1.058, extra special bitter).

Brewer: Sean Navish
Beer is all grain, served under pressure, filtered.
They are being distributed throughout New Hampshire in kegs and bottles.

The original Frank Jones Brewing Co. closed its doors in 1950. But in 1988 Don Jones and wife, LeaAnn Lombari-Jones, began distributing Frank Jones Portsmouth Ale brewed under contract. Jones is the great-, great-, great-, grand nephew of the man who made Jones Ale a household word in New England. The beer was brewed from an old Jones recipe at the Catamount Brewery in White River Junction, Vermont. Within two years they were able to raise the capital to start their own brewery in Portsmouth. The culmination of this effort was the official tapping of their first keg at the Rusty Hammer in Portsmouth in March 1992.

Brewer Sean Navish is currently brewing 180-barrel batches. They have a tasting room and conduct tours Saturday at 11 and 2 o'clock. They suggest that you make reservations two weeks in advance.

Portsmouth Brewing

56 Market Street
Portsmouth
03801

 (603) 431-1115

Located in the historic district, half a block off Market Square.

 11:30 am - 1 am daily

Golden Lager
Amber Lager
Pale Ale
Blond Ale
Old Brown Dog
Black Cat Stout

Seasonal:
Weisenhimer (summer)
Octoberfest (fall)
Cranberry Holiday Ale (winter)
May Bock
Hoover Porter
Blackcherry Stout
Steamer

Brewer: Peter Egelston
Clausterhauler (non-alcoholic) available.

 The restaurant offers an eclectic menu featuring everything from West Indian to country French cuisine. Many daily specials include fresh local seafood and gourmet pizzas. Chicken wings and nachos are popular appetizers. Entrees include several pastas, fresh seafood, steaks, and ethnic specialities. Also featured are grilled pizzas, signature burgers and sandwiches, and hot dogs. A raw bar with shrimp cocktail and various shellfish is available daily. Several wines served; full bar.

The building dates to the late 1800s. It features a restaurant and bar upstairs and a tavern downstairs with a raw bar and dance floor. Chief instigator of the new brewery was brewer and co-partner Peter Egelston, who started the Northampton Brewery in Northampton, Massachusetts, in 1987. Brewery tours are available; please call in advance. Opened June 1, 1991.

 live music five nights weekly: Sun. - acoustic/folk; Wed. - blues; Thurs. - alternative; Fri. & Sat. - rock 'n roll or rhythm & blues; background music with a CD system.

 darts and cribbage

$$$ AE, CA, DS, VI

New York

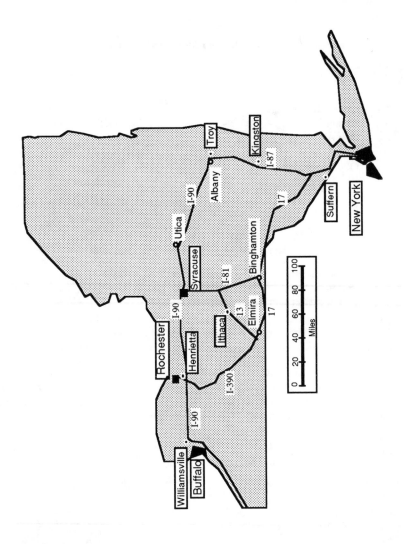

Abbott Square Brewpub
Buffalo Brewing

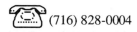 (716) 828-0004

1830 Abbott Road
Buffalo (Lackawanna)
14218

Located between Ridge Road & Rich Stadium. From the NY State Thruway, take exit 55 (Ridge Road). Turn left on Abbot Road. The brewery is one mile ahead on the left.

 11:30 am - 2 am daily

Buffalo Lager
Buffalo Pils
Limericks Ale
Buffalo Weisse
Buffalo Altbier

Seasonal:
  Buffalo Oktoberfest
  Buffalo Dopplebock

Brewer: Fred Lang

Beer is all grain, filtered, and made with a double decoction mash. It is distributed in bottles and kegs throughout New York and to 11 other states. Six packs & cases to go. Fifteen European drafts and 14 bottled beers (10 micro-brewed).

 Cuisine ranges from pub grub to barbecue, and steaks, with 20 sausages and meat pies to choose from (wings, of course).

Occupying a former roller rink, the pub has a beer hall atmosphere, with high ceilings, seating for 400, an 80-foot bar, a large balcony, and banquet facilities for up to 1,000. There is a large dance floor. The theme changed recently to country, with the main drinking/dining area now called the Alamo. The beautiful copper mash tun and brew kettle, imported from a brewery in Bavaria, can be seen from anywhere in the main dining room. In July 1990 they began bottling beer for the Buffalo area market. The brewery can be toured at 2:00 on Saturday, or at other times by appointment. The Sultans of Swig (homebrew club) meet here the third Wednesday of each month. Ask about the Mug Club.

 live music twice monthly (ethnic);
  background music - soft (oldies)

 darts   - 2 wide screens

Brown & Moran Brewing

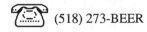 (518) 273-BEER

#417-419 River Street (P.O. Box 1629)
Troy
12180

Located on the Hudson River by the Troy Town Dock and Marina.

 Mon - Thurs: 11 am- midnight; Fri - Sat: 11 am - 2 am; Sun: noon - midnight

Golden Ale
Amber Ale
Dark Porter
Weizen Bier (hefe-weizen ale)

Seasonal:
  Belgian Cherry Ale
  St. Nick's Nectar

Brewer: Garry Brown

American or Canadian barley malt and British and American hops are used in this British modeled "tower" style brewery, that relies on gravity in transferring the brewery beer to the fermentation stage. Beer is available to carry-out in two liter glass, resealable bottles. Approximately ten other bottled beers available.

 Lunch and dinner selections include moderately priced American cuisine such as hamburgers, sandwiches, and appetizers. The bar also stocks a few other micro-brewed beers, wines, hard liquors, soft drinks, and homemade root beer.

The brewpub is located in the reconstructed 19th-century building which once housed the former Snyder's Printers. The mash/tun-brew kettles, surrounded by a glass-enclosed balcony, allow customers to see the brewing process firsthand. To climb atop his vat, Garry Brown ascends a steel spiral staircase salvaged from the illustrious Boradaile mansion. Legend says the mansion was once a speakeasy that gangster Jack "Legs" Diamond sometimes frequented. Painted murals on the walls of the dining area depict Troy's brewing past, including faces of former brewers. Although eighteen breweries were in Troy at one time, this is the only brewery now. The brewpub also sponsors a "Last Glass Club" and a homebrew competition.

 live and background music

 Outside deck faces the Hudson River

 antique shuffleboard

 $$$ VI, DC, AE

Buffalo Brewpub

6861 Main Street
Williamsville
14221

 (716) 632-0552

At the intersection of Main and Transit.

 Mon - Thurs: 11:30 am - midnight or 2 am
Fri - Sat: 11:30 am - 1 am or 3 am; Sun: noon - midnight

 Amber Ale (1.055)
Oatmeal Stout (1.060)
Pale Ale (1.050)
Buffalo Bitter (1.050)
Weiss (1.050)

Seasonal:
Kringle Beer (1.065, Ale)
Octoberfest (1.055)

Beer is made from malt extract and served under pressure. Twenty-four beers on draft, including their own, domestics, and imports-- some bottled beers.

 The food is pub style--mainly English and German--with regional favorites featured on the menu. Free popcorn and peanuts.

The pub is housed in an early 1900s, former coach stop with old shingles outside and a light pine interior. It has an old timey, pub with a stone fireplace and peanut shells on the floor. Kids are more than welcome. Ask bartenders Tom, Doug, or Tim about the Mug Club. Opened in October 1986.

 live music - acoustic & German (check for times and dates)
background music (soft)

 darts (dart teams play on a regular basis)   wide screen

EVENTS: Octoberfest is celebrated in June
(warm up), September, and October.

Chapter House Brewpub

 (607) 277-9782

400 Stewart Avenue
Ithaca
14850

Near Cornell University.

 Mon - Thurs: 4 pm - 1 am; Fri - Sat: 3 pm - 1 am; Sun: 5 pm - 1 am

 Clement's Pilsner (1.040)
Clement's Amber (1.040)
Clement's Dunkle (1.040)
Clement's Vienna Amber (1.040)
Cole Porter (1.065)
Nut Brown Ale (1.065)

Note: They stopped brewing in 1991, but have reapplied for a brewing license and hope to be brewing again soon.

Beer to go - bring your own container.

 The menu offers pizzas, nachos, and hot and cold sandwiches. Free popcorn as bar snacks. Wine is also served in addition to their own draft beers.

The pub occupies a turn-of-the-century building that has been a bar since 1939. It is a historic landmark and has a solid wood interior. The walls are covered with Cornell memorabilia. The brewpub caters to the college crowd and locals alike.

♪ live music every other Wednesday (acoustic guitar and folk)
background music - recorded (soft to loud depending on hour and day)

 Darts (real and electronic), videos -3, pool

EVENTS: Oktoberfest celebration.

Manhattan Brewing Co. Restaurant

40-42 Thompson Street
New York
10013

 (212) 925-1515

Corner of Broome and Grand Streets, between 6th Avenue and West Broadway, in the SoHo area of Manhattan.

 noon - midnight daily

 Names of beers to be announced.

Brewer: Garret Oliver

 They plan to offer fresh and hearty fare, including many vegetable dishes, seafood, sandwiches, pasta, and pizza. They will also serve several items prepared with beer such as malt pretzels and ale sausages.

The original owners converted an old Con Ed substation into an attractive brewery, pub, and restaurant in 1984. It closed in 1992 and was scheduled to reopen under new ownership in May 1993.

The brewery (3rd floor), tasting room (2nd floor) and restaurant (1st floor) are all located in this six story structure. The pub holds two large copper brewing kettles and offers a very congenial atmosphere. They have a space available for private parties.

 live entertainment planned (call for details)

  elevator

 pay parking garage across the street

 $$$ AE, CA, VI

Mountain Valley Brewpub

122 Orange Avenue
Suffern
10901

 (914) 357-0101
Fax your orders to 357-1088

 Sun - Thurs: 11:30 am - 2:00 am; Fri - Sat: 11:30 am - 4:00 am

 Porter
Copper (pale ale - amber)
Pale (pale ale-golden)
Copper Lyte (light pale ale)

Seasonal
Nut Brown Ale
Smoked Porter
Blonde Doppelbock

Brewer: Jay Mission
Beer is all grain, mostly filtered, and served under pressure.
Bring your own containers for beer to go.

 The extensive menu features Mountain Valley Barbecue (chicken, fish, and ribs) cooked in a slow-roast smoker, Texas style. Another popular item is Mountain Valley pasta with smoked fish. The menu also offers fresh chicken breast and fish prepared five different ways from creole to blackened to Francaise. They serve their own Rustica--an Italian recipe bread made from fresh dough, seasonings, and assorted vegetables. Many California wines and a full bar are also available.

The restaurant is housed in an old hotel located across the street from a train station. It has a rustic, mountain-like setting inside with four fireplaces, sculptured lifelike animals, and waterfalls. The brewpub itself allows for a full view with its numerous picture windows. Beer tasting and tours of the brewery are soon to be arranged. Opened October 26, 1992.

 Wed - Sat: live acoustic music (guitar); Southern country rock CD's and others and background music

 5 and a satellite

 AE, DC, VI

Rochester Brewpub

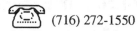 (716) 272-1550

800 Jefferson Road
Henrietta
14623

Located in the Marketplace Inn, a half mile west of I-390, near the airport and the Rochester Institute of Technology. From the NY State Thruway, take exit 46, follow I-390 north and turn left off of the exit ramp to Jefferson Road.

 6:30 am - 2 am daily

Amber Ale	Seasonal:
Oatmeal Stout	Octoberfest
Red Ale	Kringle
Nickel City Dark	Weiss
Buffalo Bitter	
Buffalo Pils	
Pale Ale	

Brewer: Peter Black
Ten beers on draft (incl. Guinness and Spaten) and 30 bottled beers
(many of them are micro-brewed).

 The restaurant offers pub food and features nightly dinner specials. Wine and full bar.

This Irish neighborhood brewpub is part of the Marketplace Inn Hotel and features a rustic interior with a very long, straight bar with a copper top. The floors are usually covered with peanut shells. Lots of breweriana. Opened March 1988.

 live music on Sunday nights - Irish. Background music at other times.

 darts, video games   wide screen

 $$$ AE, CA, DS, VI

Rohrbach Brewing

 (716) 244-5680

315 Gregory Street
Rochester
14620

Located in the South Wedge area, near Rochester's downtown, one block east of South Avenue.

 Mon - Thurs: 11:30 am - 11 pm; Fri - Sat: 11:30 am - midnight
Sun: 11:30 - 11 pm. Weekend hours are different in the summer--
Sat: 4 pm - midnight; Sun: 4 pm - 11 pm

 Old Nate's Pale Ale
Highland Amber (amber lager)
Gregory Street Lager

Seasonal:
Pilsner
Porter
Wheat

Brewer: John Urlaub
Also serves a full range of Genesee beers on draft, Coors and
Labatts on draft, and a limited number of bottled beers.

 The menu includes several kinds of appetizers ("beer buddies"), soups, salads, sandwiches, burgers, desserts, and a limited selection of entrees, including Polish potato dumplings, fish, New York strip steak, and pot pie. They have a good selection of wines and a full bar.

Located in a historic landmark known as the Old German House (built in 1908). Owner/brewer John Urlaub opened Rohrbach's May 1, 1992.

 background music  2

 darts

EVENTS: Oktoberfest (late September)

 $$$ AE, CA, VI

Where An
Olde Tradition
Becomes A New.

Syracuse Suds Factory

 (315) 471-2254

210-216 West Water Street
Syracuse
13202

Located in downtown Syracuse, across the street from Federal Plaza.

 Mon - Sat: 11 am - 2 am; Sun: noon - 2 am

 They have two regulars: a pale ale and an amber ale, plus one regularly changing beer. They are holding a contest to name the beers.

Brewer: Norman Soine
Beer is made from malt extract and served under pressure from kegs. Three other beers on tap, including Buffalo Lager; 62 bottled beers. Soine worked at F.X. Matt Brewing and Schlitz for several years and is an avid homebrewer (grows his own hops).

 Owner Al Smith describes the cuisine as American, featuring lots of finger food, including wings, sandwiches, burgers, nacho platter, veggie platter, and beer sticks; daily specials and soups and salads too. Fish fry on Friday. Most popular item is their Suds Bomber (Philly steak sandwich). Seven-eight wines; full bar.

This brewpub is located in an old four-story brick building which is listed on the National Register of Historic Buildings. The Erie Canal ran directly behind it. Barges once unloaded on the back steps. It was unoccupied for 15 years before becoming the Suds Factory. The main dining room and bar are on the the first level, with the kitchen and additional seating on the second floor. It has high ceilings with exposed beams, a wood parquet floor, and wood and brick walls. The main bar is oak, with a marble top. The brewhouse can be seen behind glass. Opened for business January 17, 1993; began serving their own beer April 17 of the same year.

 2 wide screens   pool, electronic darts

 free at night

 AE, CA, DC, VI

Woodstock Brewing

20 St. James Street
Kingston
12401

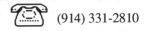 (914) 331-2810

Located near the edge of Kingston's Stockade section on the Hudson River. Take the New York State Thruway to exit 19; enter traffic circle and take 3rd right, Route 587; turn right as you get on Broadway on to St. James St.; the brewery is on the left, just beyond the corner with Prospect Street.

Hudson Lager (1.051 - 1.052, American lager)
St. James Ale (1.060 - 1.070, amber ale)

Brewer: John Nathan Collins
Plans call for Roundout Stout (1.065 - 1.070), Big Indian Porter (1.070 - 1.074), as well as some seasonal specialty beers, such as Ichabod Crane Ale (1.085, pumpkin ale) and Catskill Christmas Ale; 1,240 barrels.

Free brewery tours are available (reservations suggested) with sampling in the tap-room on Saturday, 11 am - 1 pm. You may buy six packs to go. The brick structure dates from 1830 when it housed the Hermance Foundry. The interior has been totally refurbished and houses a 6,000 sq. ft. traditional brewing operation. They brew with Catskill Mountain water, freshly ground malted barley from the U.S., and American hops. The beer is not pasteurized nor does it contain additives or chemicals of any type. It is cold filtered. When they begin to bottle later in 1993, all beer will be dated.

This is the first brewery to open in Kingston since the last one closed in 1942. Opened December 20, 1991.

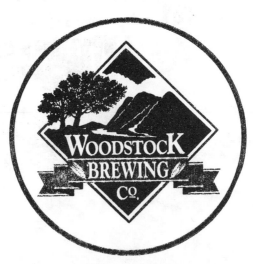

Zip City Brewing

3 West 18th Street
New York
10011

 (212) 366-6333

Located in the Flatiron District, on 18th Street, between Fifth and Sixth Avenues, and near Union Square Park.

 Bar: 11:30 am - 3 am daily (sometimes later Thurs - Sat.)
Kitchen: 11:30 am - 11 daily (late night menu Thurs - Sat)

Helles (1.057)
Pilsener (1.048)
Märzen (1.057)
Vienna (1.053)
Dunkel (1.053)

Seasonal:
Oktoberfest
Maibock (1.064)
Bock
Doppelbock

Brewer: Robert Berg

All beers are unfiltered and cask conditioned. Three house beers on tap at all times. They also serve several bottled microbrewed beers, and a few light and non-alcoholic beers. They are planning to have beer for take out (ask your waiter).

The menu is described as "upscale American pub fare." Featured appetizers include Calamari with Smoked Tomato Fennel Sauce and Littleneck Clams Steamed with Pilsner and Apple Cider. Light plates include Yellowfin Tuna Chili with Black Beans and Crème Fraîche and Honey Roast Turkey Reuben Sandwich. Entrees include Rabbit, Venison, and Wild Boar Sausages, and Chicken Pot Pie. Bar menu specialties include Zip City Nachos, served with or without wild boar sausage. Salads, grilled fish dishes, and a basic hamburger are also offered. Wine and full bar (extensive selection of single-malt Scotch).

The pub is located in an 1895 wrought-iron construction loft building that once housed the National Temperance Society. The interior brick wall and wrought-iron columns set the tone, and wood booths and banquettes give a feeling of comfort and intimacy. Zip City's beautiful two-vessel brewhouse, custom-manufactured in Austria, is situated inside the 90-foot long, U-shaped bar. A mezzanine overlooking the bar is often used for private parties and tasting events. The wort is piped to the basement, where it is fermented and stored for serving. The term "Zip City" comes from the novel *Babbitt* by Sinclair Lewis. Opened November 21, 1991.

$$$ AE, CA, DC, VI,
Carte Blance, JCB

North Carolina

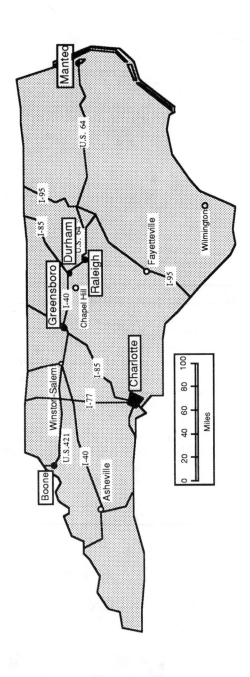

Dilworth Brewing

1301 East Boulevard
Charlotte
28203

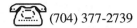 (704) 377-2739

Located at the corner of East Boulevard & Kennilworth.

 Mon - Thurs: 11 am - midnight; Fri - Sat: 11 am - 1 am; closed on Sunday

 Reeds Golden (1.044, pilsner)
Albemarle Ale (1.048, amber)
Dilworth Porter (1.052)

Seasonal:
Christmas Ale (1.056, dark ale)
Weizen (1.044)
Oktoberfest (1.056)

Brewer: John McDermott

Beer is all grain, served under pressure, filtered; 900 barrels.
Bottled Sharp available. Beer is distributed to other bars and restaurants.
22 oz. bottles to go.

They offer soups, salads, house specialties (fresh fish, marinated & grilled chicken breast, and rib eye), several kinds of burgers, deli specials, and desserts. Several wines available; full bar.

A neighborhood bar/restaurant which attracts an upscale crowd. The split level interior is roomy with a high ceiling and fans, and has a large beer mural on the upper level. A window opens onto a large brewing room behind the bar. The Carolina Brewmasters meet here the 1st Wednesday of every month at 6:00 pm.

♪ live music occasionally; background music (moderate)

  $$$ AE, CA, VI

French Quarter Cafe & Brewery

115 N. Duke Street
Durham
27701

 (919) 688-4586
FAX: (919) 688-4897

Near the Durham Bulls' ballpark, next to Liggett-Myers, and across the street from Brightleaf Square.

 Sun - Thurs: 4 pm - midnight; Fri - Sat: 4 pm - 2 am

 Golden Lager (1.048, helles)
Amber Lager (1.054, märzen)
Black Lager (1.058, dunkel)

Seasonal:
Wheat (1.048, California wheat)
Octoberfest (1.054, Vienna)
Maibock (1.072, helles bock)
Christmas (varies)

Brewer: Paul Hummer

Beer is all grain, unfiltered, and served under pressure. Beer to go in 1- liter bottles, 5- liter minikegs, and 30 and 50- liter kegs. Bottled beer available.

The restaurant features a New Orleans' type menu complete with various Cajun and Creole dishes. Popular items include crawfish boil and blackened prime rib. Twenty-five varieties of wine available; full bar.

Situated in a former tobacco processing building of the 1920s, this brewpub, with its exposed original brick walls has lots of open space and an exposed brewery. The interior is decorated with mardi-gras type decorations and original art featuring scenes of New Orleans. A separate club area upstairs from the restaurant sometimes features rock bands. Opened in November 1988 as the Weeping Radish, changed its name to the Old Heidelberg, and closed in 1992. Reopened October 1, 1992 as the French Quarter.

♪ Wed - Sat: live music upstairs (jazz, blues, rock bands)
Cajun background music downstairs.

 darts

EVENTS: Mardi Gras Festival (Feb.), Octoberfest (Oct.)

 3 wide screens

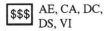 AE, CA, DC, DS, VI

Greenshields Pub & Brewery

214 E. Martin Street
Raleigh
27601

 (919) 829-0214

Opposite Moore Square Park.

 11:30 am - 1 am daily

Pilsner (1.048)	Seasonal:
Amber Bitter (1.052)	Wheat Beer (1.044)
Dark Lager (1.048+)	Nut Brown Ale
Porter (1.064)	Dark Wheat
Oatmeal Stout (1.064)	Christmas Bitter

Brewer: Gary Greenshields
Beer is all grain; 1,200 barrels. 20-liter kegs to go.
Bottles: Natural Light & Budweiser

 The menu places an emphasis on homemade English and American pub fare.
20 varieties of wine available; full bar.

The business is modelled after an upscale English pub and is located in a historical register building in the old city market. The interior has lots of oak paneling and a stamped tin ceiling. The atmosphere is casual and relaxed and appeals to a broad age spectrum. They have three floors of dining with fireplaces found in the bar and upper two dining rooms. The first floor has a library and piano. The back door opens onto a food court. Opened July 6, 1989.

 wide screen darts

  $$$ AE, CA, DS, VI

Loggerhead Brewpub & Restaurant

2006 W. Vandalia Road
Greensboro  (919) 292-7676
27407

At the corner of Pinecroft & Vandalia Road - 1 mile from the Four Seasons Mall.

 11 am - midnight daily (Sunday in summer: 1 pm - midnight)

 Loggerhead Pilsner
General Green Lager (amber lager)
Gate City Ale (pale ale)
Loggerhead Light
Cherry Pilsner

Brewer: Larry Stanley
Some house beers to take out. Bottles: Bud, Michelob, Lite, Heineken.
Beer distributed to other bars and restaurants.

 Wide variety of food--seafood, steaks, sandwiches, and salads. They offer 30 different appetizers. Try the baked, stuffed flounder.

The pub is located in a strip mall. The brewhouse is visible through glass as you go in. The pub has hardwood floors, seats 150, and features a 55' long L-shaped bar. PISS (Piedmont Institute of Suds Suppers) meets here on a regular basis. Named after the endangered loggerhead sea turtle, they have held several regular fund raising events to support the "Save the Turtle" Fund. Opened April 1990.

 live music Thurs -Sun (acoustical guitars, jazz on Sun);
background music (soft rock)

 (wide screen; satellite) four dart boards

Mill Bakery, Eatery & Brewery

122 West Woodlawn Road
Charlotte
28217

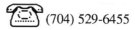 (704) 529-6455

Located on the south side of Charlotte; from I-77, take exit 6A.

 Mon - Thurs, Sun: 6:30 am - 11 pm (beer served beginning at 1 pm)
Fri - Sat: 6:30 am - 1 am

Harvest Gold	Harvest Light (Pilsner, contract)
Wheat Field Dry	Hornet Tail Ale (amber lager, contract)
Red October (amber)	Seasonal:
Weizen	Wooly's Winterfest
Stout	Spiced Ale

Brewer: Jason McKnight

This is a restaurant for those people seeking healthy, nutritious alternatives in their diet. A wide selection of homemade breads, sandwiches, pizza, soups and salads are offered, all with American Heart Association approval and recommendation. Each menu offering lists calories, fat, and sodium content. Emphasis on high-fiber foods. Desserts include "sinful" Danishes, cakes, and pies. Wine and mixed drinks available.

This is a yuppie, neighborhood restaurant that combines a bakery, eatery, and brewery. It is housed in a wooden building with metal roof and a large mill wheel out front. It has a light and airy feel, with cathedral ceilings, and is filled with plants and antiques and has country-style retail items for sale. It has a solid oak bar and backbar and light oak and pine walls.

live music: Wed.-Sat. (jazz, blues, pop, open mike on Wed.); (2)
background music: moderate, same as live

EVENTS: Full Moon Swamp Stomp Party - every month with live music, held outside, DJ, beer, crayfish, and T-shirts.

Spring Garden Brewing

 (919) 299-3649

714 Francis King Street (P.O. Box 8478)
Greensboro
27410

Located near the far western edge of the city limits. From I-40, take exit 213 toward Jamestown and Guilford College; it is just across the street from the College and behind the Wachovia Bank, off W. Friendly Avenue.

 Mon - Thurs: 11:30 am - 1:00 am
Fri - Sat: 11:30 am - 1:30 am; Sun: 11:30 am - 10:00 pm

 Humin' Bird Light   Blackbeard Bock
Oak Ridge Amber   Oktoberfest
                           Black Rose Lager

Brewer: Christian Boos
All beers are unfiltered and served at their proper temperature.
Two liter containers to go. Some domestic beers available.

The brewpub/restaurant offers a full-service menu featuring daily regional and ethnic specials which complement the freshly brewed beers. Some of the more popular items include smoked baby back ribs, a 13 oz. Angus ribeye steak, fresh fish, quesadilla crisps, and unique pastas. The restaurant takes pride in offering its guests a good value. Wine and mixed drinks available.

Spring Garden Brewing Company was established March 1991 as the flagship brew pub for the North Carolina-based Spring Garden Bar & Grills. The Brewery's all natural Bavarian style lager beers are brewed in the Munich-built brewhouse. Spring Garden adheres to the Bavarian Law of Purity. Accordingly, they use only the purest German Barley Malt, German and Czech hops and Bavarian Lager Yeast.

The restaurant's unusual decor appeals to the beer afficionado with its collections of beer antiques and memorabilia, the fountain made from an antique copper-tubed wort chiller and cathedral ceilings painted sky blue with clouds resembling jovial German folk drinking from beer steins. The three separate dining areas feature many plants, windows, and skylights. They are separated from the game room by a glass atrium. The Piedmont Institute of Suds Sippers (the local home-brew club) meets here.

♪ CD jukebox   🌿 large outdoor deck   📺

EVENTS: St. Patrick's Day, a summertime weekend Brew Ha Ha;
a German Oktoberfest and live entertainment Wednesday nights.

 shuffelboard, putt putt golf

  $$$ AE, CA, VI

Tumbleweed Grill & Brewery

122 Blowing Rock Road
Boone
28607

 (704) 264-7111

Located across form Appalachian State University.

 11:00 am - 10:00 pm daily

 Tumbleweed Amber
Gold Rush Ale

Seasonal:
  Smoked Porter
  Stout
  Rauch

Beer is made from malt extract, unfiltered, and cask - conditioned. A pepper beer is in the works. Beer to go. Other brands are sold on tap or in bottles.

This ethnic style restaurant offers approximately fifty unique Mexican menu items as well as regional Southwestern specialties. Popular items include a penny pasta with veal, a mesquite-grilled grouper with pineapple-rum relish, grilled sea scallops over Monterey Jack cheese quesadillas, medallion of pork tenderloins, and Cajun crab cakes. For dessert, try the chocolate enchilladas or the caramel flan.

The interior decor of this brewpub, with its open kitchen, coincides with its menu theme. Indian and Southwestern paintings adorn the wall; a variety of clay bowls, antiques, flora, and peppers hang from the ceiling surround the bar. An enclosed porch overlooks the tennis courts and baseball field of the university. Owners along with consultant, Kenny Bowman, are planning to reorganize the local homebrew club here for the many local homebrewers. Opened June 1989; brewery added in March 1992.

♪ CD, background music (jazz to modern rock; some classical)

 3

 $$$ AE, CA, DC, DS, VI

Weeping Radish Restaurant & Brewery

Highway 64 E. (P.O. Box 147)
Manteo
27954

 (919) 437-1157

Adjacent to The Christmas Shop.

 Mon - Sun: 11:30 am until . . .

Helles Bier (1.050, golden lager)
Fest Bier (1.052, amber lager)
Black Radish Bier (1.052, dark lager)

Brewer: Andy Duck
Beer is all grain, served both under pressure and cask-conditioned, unfiltered; 850 barrels. 1 liter refillable bottles, 5 liter mini kegs to go, party kegs available.

 The restaurant offers an array of German dishes such as veal, sauerbraten, and sausages as well as traditional American fare. Black Forest and Sacha Tortes are specialties of the house. Lighter fare is available for take out or to eat in the biergarden. Don't miss the fresh soft salted pretzels served with spicy hot mustard. Seven varieties of wine available.

This is an authentic Bavarian restaurant, pub, and biergarten located on historic Roanoke Island, the location chosen by Sir Walter Raleigh for his ill-fated Lost Colony, on the Outer Banks of North Carolina. Observe the brewery behind glass while you enjoy the fruits of their labor. The Reinheitsgebot is strictly adhered to here. The term "Weeping Radish" refers to a German radish served with beer in Bavarian restaurants. When sliced and salted, the radish sweats moisture, or "weeps." You may want to join the brewery tours held daily during the season. They began selling their own beer in July 1986.

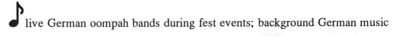

♪ live German oompah bands during fest events; background German music

 darts, video games in pub

EVENTS: Springfest - Easter weekend
Octoberfest - Labor Day weekend

 - in the pub

 CA, VI

Ohio

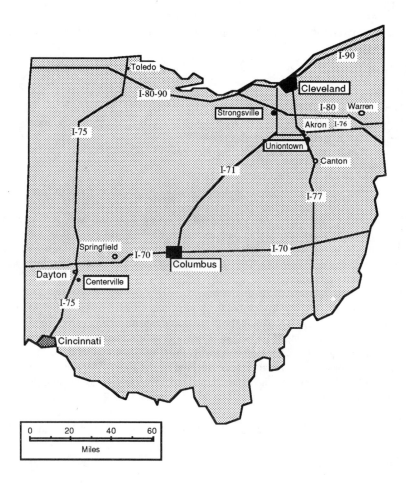

Barley's Brewpub

  (614) 228-2537

467 N. High Street
Columbus
43215

Located across the street from Columbus' new convention center and next door to the North Market.

  11 am - 1 am daily

Pilsner (1.040)	Seasonals:
Pale Ale (1.048)	to be announced
Irish Rogue (1.040, red ale)	
Ivan Porter (1.060, named after the brewer's son)	

Brewer: Scott Francis
Beer is all grain, filtered, and served under pressure; all English, 2-row malt.

 They offer a full menu, emphasizing pub type fare. Favorites include Beef & Ale Soup, onion rings prepared in pale ale batter, Sauerkraut Balls (made with sauerkraut, potatoes, cheese, and sausage), beer-cheese spread, 3-alarm chili, and wings with Gates of Hell sauce. They have several salads and sandwiches, turkey burgers, ribs, and daily specials.

Barley's is located in an old brick building, next door to the historic North Market, a farmers' market. It has a traditional alehouse style, with brick walls, wood floors, high ceilings, and a stamped tin ceiling. It has a beautiful, antique, carved cherry and mahogany and glass back bar from Germany. From the dining area, the brewhouse is visible in the basement through a large opening in the floor. There are large murals on the walls. The dining room-bar accommodate 150. They are renovating the basement in order to provide more room. Opened November 1992.

♪ background music (Celtic, classical, and traditional music from the British Isles)

 2 (1 wide-screen)

&

$$$ AE, CA, VI

The Burkhardt Brewing

 (216) 896-9200

3700 Massillon Road
Uniontown
44685

Take I-77 onto route 241 Massillon Road; located in "the shops of Green".

 Open Mon - Sat; closed Sunday

North Star (American light ale)
White Cliff Ale (british bitter)
Eclipse (Scotch ale)

Seasonal:
Bock (March)
Holiday Honey Ale
Irish Red
Mug Ale (dark ale)
Oktoberfest

Brewer: Tom Burkhardt, Jr.
Their beer is made using malt extract. Beer to go in kegs.

The cuisine is international, featuring many German, British, and Irish dishes. American entrees are also offered including steaks and burgers.

The exterior has modern lines and features a central arch and green awnings. The brewhouse is located in a building adjacent to the pub. The interior features brass and oak and has a casual pub atmosphere. Thomas Burkhardt Sr., president of Burkhardt's Brew Pub, says his son, Thomas Jr., is head brewer, making him a fifth generation Burkhardt brewer. The Burkhardt family has been brewing beer in the Akron area since 1877. In 1874 Wilhelm Burkhardt came to America to practice the trade he had perfected in his German homeland. After serving as an apprentice and brewmaster, he acquired the Wolf Ledges Brewery in Akron. Upon his death in 1882, his wife and children carried on the business. During prohibition the brewery switched to ice manufacturing. The last brewery, Burkhardt Brewing Co. was sold to Burger Brewing. It reopened as a microbrewery May 31, 1991.

♪ contemporary music; local talent

The Chickery

453 Miamisburg-Centerville Road
Centerville
45459

 (513) 439-9100
FAX: (513) 439-9290

Located in the Normandy Square Shopping Center, two miles east of the Dayton Mall on State road 725.

 Mon - Fri: 11:00 am - midnight; Sat - Sun: 8:00 am - midnight

 725 Brand Beer (Pilsner)
Chickery Red (red ale)
Wët (wheat beer)

Brewer: David Foster
They sell gallon and half-gallon jugs of beer to go, as well as homemade Chickery Root Beer. Beer available for wholesale and contract brewing.
Many brands of domestic bottled beer are available.

 A family-style restaurant featuring rotisserie-roasted chicken, pork, and turkey; BBQ ribs; burgers; soups; salads; appetizers; pasta; and desserts. They also serve breakfast Saturday and Sunday and have their own bakery. Minors can try the Chickery Root Beer, and there is a children's menu too. They specialize in take out.

Located in an open and airy building in a red-brick shopping center. The restaurant seats 200. Opened November 4, 1991.

 fifties & sixties background music   2 big-screens

Columbus Brewing
Hagen's Ale & Tee
Gibby's

476 S. Front Street
Columbus
43215

Columbus	(614) 224-3626
Hagen's	(614) 621-2600
Gibby's	(614) 464-4297

Located in the old brewery district, across from the old Hoster Brewery.

Hagen's: Mon - Sat: 11:00 am - 2:30 am; Sun: noon - 1:00 am

Gibby's: Mon - Wed: 11 am - 1 am; Thurs - Sat: 11 am - 2 am
closed Sunday

Gold (1.036, Pilsner)
Pale Ale (1.048)
Nut Brown Ale (1.050)
Black Forest Porter (1.052)
1492 Lager (1.048)

Seasonal:
Special Reserve (Scottish ale)
Octoberfest
Stout
Christmas Warmer

Brewer: Scott Francis/ **Assist.:** Vince Falcone
Beer is made from a combination of malt extract and grain, served under pressure, filtered; 700 barrels. Bottled beer to go. They distribute to several Columbus area bars and restaurants. Hagen's has 15-20 bottled beers in addition to the "house" brews.

Hagen's, a golf theme restaurant known for huge portions and low prices, offers a wide variety of American food, including pizza, burgers, Philly steak sandwiches, grilled sword fish, and huge slabs of ribs. They serve the Columbus Brewing Pale Ale, Nut Brown Ale, and 1492 Lager.

Columbus Brewing is a microbrewery with two bars, Hagen's and Gibby's, each connected to it. All three are separately owned by members of the same family. Tours are by reservation only. No beer is served on tours, but the beer is readily available on either side. The brewery is also visible from Hagen's, but the beer is not piped in directly. Opened August 1989.

♪ live music available in both Hagen's and Gibby's - weekends

Great Lakes Brewing

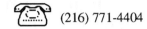 (216) 771-4404

2516 Market Street
Cleveland
44113

Across from the West Side Market on West 25th Street & Lorain Avenue.

 Mon - Thurs: 11:30 am - midnight; Fri. - Sat: 11:30 am - 1 am
closed Sunday

Moon Dog Ale (1.050)
Burning River Ale (1.056)
Heisman (1.056, Dortmunder)
The Elliot Ness (1.056, amber)
Commodore Perry I.P.A. (1.064)
Edmund Fitzgerald Porter (1.060)
Seasonal:
   Weizen (summer)
   Dunkel Weizen
   Weizen Bock
   Cleveland Brown Ale

Seasonal (cont'd):
   Christmas Ale
   Winter Warmer
   Ohio City Ale
   Honey Ale
   Emmett's Stout
   Holy Moses Ale
   Helles Bock
   Nosferatu Red Ale (Halloween)
   Conway's Irish Ale
   Oktoberfest
   Rockefeller Bock (dark)

Brewer: Thaine Johnson

Beer is all grain, served under pressure, both filtered and unfiltered. Beer to go in 12-oz. six packs and half-gallon jugs from the bar. They distribute their beer to other bars and restaurants.

The kitchen prepares a variety of lunch and dinner dishes, each a complement to the house beers -- many kinds of salads, ribs, crab cake, and homemade pastries and desserts. They hold a clam bake in the autumn. Wine available; full bar.

Great Lakes is Cleveland's only brewery and the state's first brewpub since Prohibition. The building, dating from 1860, was an old feed store and later a saloon. It includes the Beer Cellar, a lower-level dining area of brick and stone, where you can see the kegging operation; the Tap Room, with a century old mahogany bar, brick floor, high ceiling, and lots of breweriana; the Market Room, with Victorian decor and view of the historic West Side Market; the Great Lakes Room, which is filled with nautical memorabilia; the Rockefeller Room (reported to be John D. Rockefeller's first office in Cleveland), for small groups (seats 15); and the patio, which offers a view of Market Street. This was Elliot Ness' favorite watering hole-- ask the bartender to show you the bullet hole. The Society of Northeast Ohio Brewers (SNOB) meets here the first Monday of each month at 7:30 pm.

 patio

EVENTS: Oktoberfest, Halloween

 First floor only

$$$ AE, CA, DC, VI

Hoster Brewing

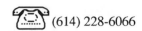 (614) 228-6066

550 S. High Street
Columbus
43065

On the corner of High & Hoster Streets, in the old brewery district.

 Mon - Sat: 11 am - 2 am; Sun : 4 pm - 11 pm

Eagle Light (1.032, starkbier)
XX Pale (1.048, Pilsner)
Gold Top (1.048, lager)
Amber Lager (1.052, Munich dark)

Seasonal:
Independence English Ale (pale ale)
Oktoberfest
Maibock
Black Top Doppelbock
Eagle Dark S.O.B. (Some Of Blacktop)

Brewer: Allen Young
Selected bottled beers. Five liter cans to go. Their beer is distributed to several Columbus bars and restaurants.

 The menu is filled with hearty American style favorites and includes appetizers, salads, soups, sandwiches, and entrees. Try the beer cheese soup and the home-made bologna and bratwursts.

This 100-year-old streetcar shop has been converted into a turn-of-the-century saloon, filled with oak, brass and breweriana. It has the longest bar in Columbus. The outside is brick with stained glass windows. Brewery tours are available; please call in advance.

♪ background music - contemporary hits (moderate); juke box

EVENTS: Oktoberfest in the German village (early September)

Melbourne's Brewing

 (216) 238-4677

12492 Prospect Road
Strongsville
44136

 Mon - Sat: 11 am - midnight; Sun: 1 pm - 10 pm

Bondi Beach Blonde (1.050, helles)   Seasonal:
Wombat Wheat Beer (1.046)   Perth Pale Ale (1.046)
Down Under Beer (1.048, brown ale)   Octoberfest (1.059)
                                                           Christmas Bock (1.065)
                                                           Irish Red Ale (1.048)

Brewer: Mark Ward

Beer is all grain and filtered. They distribute to other bars and restaurants in the area.
Beer to go in 64 oz. glass jugs.

 They offer both American and Australian cuisine with a variety of appetizers,
burgers, sandwiches, seafood, pasta, pizza, steak, meat pies, and bangers. They
prepare from only the freshest ingredients; all desserts are made from scratch
daily. Don't forget to ask about the daily specials: pasta of the day, chef's special,
and catch of the day--special items for the kiddies too. Full bar.

This is a neighborhood brewpub with an Australian flavor. It is filled with wood and
brass and is decorated with large numbers of beer posters. The copper brewing vessels
are visible from the restaurant. Opened in 1989.

 background music (soft/ moderate)

$$$ AE, CA, DC, VI

Pennsylvania

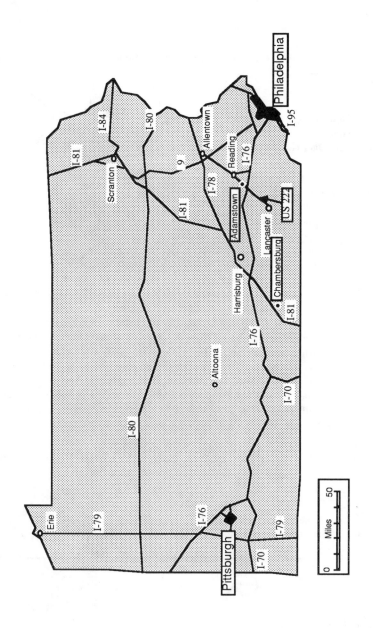

Allegheny Brewery & Pub
Pennsylvania Brewing

 (412) 237-9402

800 Vinial Street
Pittsburgh
15212

At the corner of Troy Hill Road and Vinial Street, on the north side.

Mon - Sat: 11 am - midnight; closed Sunday

Penn Pilsner (amber)
Kaiser Pils
Penn Dark (Dunkel)
Penn Light Lager (Helles)

Seasonal:
Oktoberfest
Celebrator Bock
Maerzen Fest
Alt
Weizen
Weizen Bock

Brewer: Alexander Deml
Beer is all grain (pure 2-row barley malt),
served under pressure, filtered; 7,000 barrels.
20 liter kegs, and pony kegs are available to go.

Cuisine is authentic German and features dishes such as sauerbraten, schweine-braten, bratwurst, and weiner schnitzel. Great variety of selection.

The building is a 19th-century brewery (Eberhardt & Ober) in the German section of Pittsburgh and is listed on the National Register of Historic Buildings. The attractive interior is an authentic German beer hall with large heavy maple tables and benches, high ceilings, and has brewery and industrial memorabilia on display. A Ratskeller party room is in the lower level. The brewery and pub are owned and operated by the Pennsylvania Brewing Co., brewers of Penn Pilsner, making it the first "tied house" in Pennsylvania since Prohibition. Copper brewing kettles are in full view from the restaurant. They bill their brew as "the beer that beats the imports." The brewery opened in 1987; the pub was added in 1989 and expanded in 1992.

♪ strolling accordion player Tues and Wed; Blues band on Thurs; DixieLand Jazz or German bands on Fri and Sat; German background music
ANNUAL EVENTS: Oktoberfest- giant outdoor
fest Fri. - Sun. of the last 2 weekends in
September. It features live, non-stop music, a
special brew, and outdoor grills.

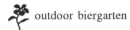

 outdoor biergarten

    $$$ AE, CA, DS,VI

Arrowhead Brewing

1667 Orchard Drive
Chambersburg
17201

 (717) 264-0101

From I-81, take exit 5, turn right on Wayne Ave., then left at light onto Orchard; it's the last drive on the right.

Red Feather Pale Ale (1.047)

Brewer: Fran Mead

Red Feather is made from British pale malt, crystal malt, chocolate malt, and small amounts of torrified wheat (for crispness and head retention) along with Cascade and Northern Brewer pellets and dry hopped with Cascade and Willamette leaf hops. Alcohol content is 4.75% by volume and the beer is unpasteurized.

They began selling beer in December 1991. It is now distributed in 12-oz. bottles and kegs in Pennsylvania, western Maryland, and northern Virginia.

Tours are offered during the week and can be arranged for the weekend if you will call a day or two in advance. Samples of Red Feather are given at the end of the tour.

President/brewer Fran Mead began as a homebrewer and later apprenticed with D.L. Geary in Portland, Maine, before contracting for a 25-barrel Peter Austin brewhouse. Alan Pugsley, who works with Austin, assisted Mead in starting up the brewery and formulating the beer.

Dock Street Brewing Brewery & Restaurant

Two Logan Square
Philadelphia
19103

 (215) 496-0413

At 18th and Cherry Streets, next to the Four Seasons Hotel, in downtown Philadelphia.

 Mon - Thurs: 11:30 am - midnight; Fri - Sat: noon - 2 am; Sun: noon - 11 pm

Pale Ale (cask conditioned)	Seasonal (cont'd):
Weiss Beer	Dunkle
Pilsner	Dortmunder
Bitter	Scotch Ale
Brown Ale	Bock
Seasonal:	Barleywine
Helles	& others

Brewer: Nicholas D. Funnell

Beer is all grain; most are served under pressure; 1,800 barrels. There are always six beers on tap, from a selection of more than 30. Beer to go in five liter kegs. They also brew under contract Dock Street Amber Beer and Dock Street Bohemian Pilsner, which are distributed in 18 states.

 The full-service, award-winning restaurant features a brasserie menu of char-grilled meats and fish, game pies, and hearty sandwiches. Breads and desserts are baked on premises.

The brewpub is situated in the ground floor of a new 40-story office building. They occupy 7,500 sq. ft. and have 14-foot ceilings and a 1930s decor, with cherry wood paneling and a cherry bar with a granite bar top. A lounge area for drinking is available along the street side windows. The brewhouse is visible behind the bar. Check out the canvas murals over the bar. Tours are available--reservations suggested. State law forbids them from serving other beers, wine, or liquor! Happy hour is held Monday - Thursday from 5 - 7 pm. Opened in October 1990. Collector T-shirts, mugs and glasses are available for sale.

♪ live music Fri - Sat (jazz and blues)
  background music

 darts and 2 pool tables
  (free of charge)   3

EVENTS: Oktoberfest, Annual Homebrewer Competition, The Book and the Cook, St. Patrick's Day, Monthly Beer Style Classes

   AE, CA, DC, DS, VI

Samuel Adams Brewhouse
Philadelphia Brewing

 (215) 563-ADAM

1516 Sansom Street, 2nd Floor
Philadelphia
19102

Near 15th Street and two blocks from City Hall; upstairs from the Sansom Street
Oyster House.

 Mon - Thurs: 11 am - midnight; Fri - Sat: 11 am - 1 am; closed Sunday

 Ben Franklin's Gold (golden ale)   **Brewer:** Jim Pericles
Poor Richard's Amber (amber ale)   Beer is filtered. Beer to go: 22-oz.
George Washington's Porter   bottles, hand-filled daily.

 The dining room seats 80 and features fresh, hearty pub fare with lunch and dinner menus and bar snacks. Everything is made from scratch and they use their
beer in many of the recipes. Some of the foods are typically English, others are
good American standbys. Check out the daily specials. Have the designated driver try
the homemade root beer or the cream soda. Beer served in 12-oz. glasses and in 20-oz.
imperial pints.

It is located in a turn-of-the-century, two-story shop front. It is an American version
of an English pub and features a solid mahogany bar, hand-carved in Lancastershire,
England. Be sure to see the collection of Royal Doulton china mugs on display. They
can only serve what they brew on the premises - no wine, no liquor, and no other
beers! The brewpub is a partnership between Jim Koch, of the Boston Beer Co. (mak-
ers of Sam Adams) and David & Judy Mink, owners of the Sansom Street Oyster
House. The annual competition of the HOPS (Homebrewers of Philadelphia) is held
here. Opened Thanksgiving of 1989.

♪ live music on Wednesday (folk), Thursday (open mike), and Saturday nights
(guitar player/singer); background music (bartender's choice).

EVENTS: 4th of July - a week long party

 darts

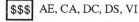 $$$ AE, CA, DC, DS, VI

Stoudt Brewery
Black Angus Brewery House

Box 880, Route 272 (P.O. Box 809)
Adamstown
19501

 (215) 484-4387

From the Pennsylvania Turnpike, take Exit 21 and follow State Rd. 272 north.

 Mon - Sat: 5 pm - 11 pm; Sun: noon - 9 pm

 Golden Lager (1.049)
Pilsener (1.049)
Adamstown Amber (1.049, lager)

Brewers: William Moore and Rick DeBar
Beer to go in 750 ml. bottles; 3,000 barrels.

Seasonal:
Raspberry Wheat (1.049)
Bock (1.060)
Wheat (1.049)
Sour Mash Ale (1.049, alt)
Beer Fest Bock

 The restaurant offers fine dining and features steaks and seafood. They offer German entrees and have a raw seafood bar. Eighty varieties of wine; full bar.

The blue, red, and white building is Victorian in style and features an antique mall and beer garden. Tours are offered at 3 on Saturday, and 1 on Sunday. It is best to call ahead. Enjoy your time in Pennsylvania Dutch country while you visit! Opened May 1987.

 live German music from mid July until Labor Day: Friday: 7 pm - 11 pm; Saturday: 2 pm - midnight; Sunday: 3 pm - 7 pm

EVENTS: Bavarian Summer Festival (see days and times under live music), Bock Bier Fest (in late March), and Christkindlsmarkt (5 weekends before Christmas).

$$$ AE, CA, DC, VI

Tennessee

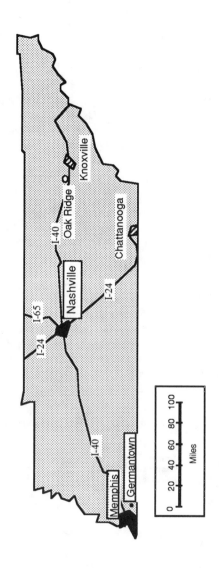

Bluff City Grill & Brewery

235 Union Street
Memphis
38103

 (901) 526-BEER

Located at the corner of 4th and Union, in downtown Memphis.

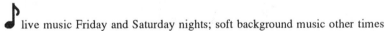

 Sun - Wed: 11 am - 1 am; Thurs - Sat: 11 am - 3 am

ESB	Seasonal:
Porter	Bonaparte Ale (Scotch ale)
Amber	many more seasonals planned
Gold	

Brewer: Bryan Jones
Beer is all grain, served under pressure; some brands are filtered, others not.

 A great variety of items are featured on the menu, including appetizers (try the beer bread), soups, salads, sandwiches, burgers, entrees, and desserts. Rotisserie barbecued meat is their specialty. Try the blue plate special. Several wines on the menu; full bar.

The brewpub occupies the old Trailways bus terminal in downtown Memphis. The interior has an eclectic style and features lots of cherry wood and plush carpeting. From the dining room one can see the brewhouse in full display behind glass. The spacious interior seats 260, and there are separate banquet facilities for 60. Owner Mark Metzger says he has opened two other brewpubs: Portsmouth Brewing in Portsmouth, New Hampshire, and the Northampton Brewery in Northampton, Massachusetts. When it opened April 1, 1993, it was the first brewery to operate in Memphis since the Schlitz Brewery closed in 1982.

♪ live music Friday and Saturday nights; soft background music other times

  valet parking

 AE, CA, DC, DS, VI

Bohannon Brewing

 (615) 242-8223

134 2nd Avenue North
Nashville
37201

Located on the historic "Market Street" in downtown Nashville.

Market Street Pilsner Draft
Market Street Golden Ale
Market Street Wheat Beer
Seasonal:
  Market Street Bock Beer (spring)
  Market Street Oktoberfest Beer (fall)

Beer is filtered.

No beer sold on premises. However, by later summer 1993 Bohannon should be a brewpubs.

The brewery is located on the site Nashville's first brewery, Crossman & Drucker (est. 1859). Beer is available in tasting room (the original tasting room from 1888 Greenbrier Whisky Distributor) for sampling only during tours. The tasting room overlooks the Cumberland River and is decorated with inlaid oak paneling, stained glass windows, and leaded glass. Scheduled tours are held Monday through Friday at 2 pm. Reservations may be made for tours at other times with one week's notice asked for large groups. Best time to call is Monday - Friday, 9:00 am - 4:30 pm. Opened May 1989.

Boscos Pizza, Kitchen, & Brewery

7615 W. Farmington # 30
Germantown
38138

 (901) 756-7310

Located in the Saddle Creek Shopping Center.

 Mon - Thurs: 11 am - midnight; Fri - Sat: 11 am - 1 am
Sun: noon - midnight

 Tennessee Cream Ale (1.042, blonde ale)   Seasonal:
Neshoba Amber Ale (1.046)   Boscos Holiday Ale
Germantown's Own (1.050, alt)   (1.056, ale-bock)

Brewer: Chuck Skypeck
Bud Light is available on draft.

The menu features fresh gourmet pizzas from a wood-fired Italian oven. Fresh ingredients ranging from duck to lamb to seafood are cooked on the grill and rotisserie. Also featured on the menu are handmade pasta, and a variety of soups, salads, and desserts made with regional ingredients. Twenty-five wines on the menu; full bar.

There is a fountain directly outside this brewpub, which is accessible through large glass doors. Inside are a modern look-in demonstration kitchen and brewery. Old World Mediterranean decor adorns the dining room. Opened December 15, 1992.

 background music   beer garden to open spring 1993

$$$ AE, DC, DS, VI

Vermont

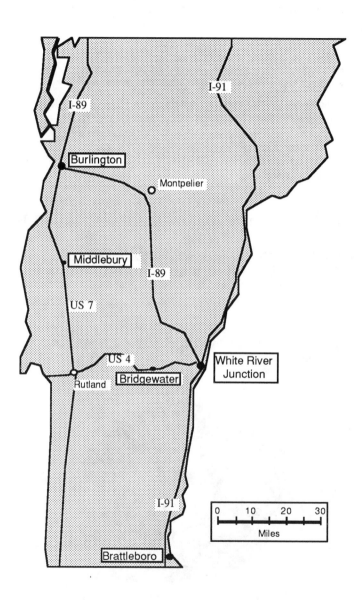

Catamount Brewing

 (802) 296-2248

58 South Main Street
White River Junction
05001

Located in downtown White River Junction.

Catamount Gold (1.040, blond ale)
Catamount Amber (1.048, pale ale)
Catamount Porter (1.052)
Seasonal:
  Christmas Ale (1.056)
  Octoberfest (1.042)
  Bock (1.050)

Brewer: Stephen Mason
Beer is all grain, served in pressurized kegs and bottles, filtered; 12,000 barrels.

<u>Beer is available in tasting room for sampling only during tours.</u>
Tours are held daily July 1 - October 31 and on weekends throughout the year. No reservations required but they suggest a call when planning a visit in the off season (November - May). Best time to call: Monday - Saturday, 9 - 5 and Sunday 1 - 5. Beer may be purchased for off-premise consumption after tours in the brewery store; available in 12 oz. bottles in 6 packs and cases. They are the contract brewer for Post Road Real Ale of Massachusetts and Pike Place IPA. Began brewing in 1986; sales commenced in February 1987.

McNeill's Brewery

 (802) 254-2553

90 Elliot Street
Brattleboro
05301

Located in downtown Brattleboro, at the junction of Elliot and Church.

 Sun - Fri: 4 pm - 2 am; Sat: 4 pm - 1 am

Duck's Breath Bitter (1.035)   McNeill's Special Bitter
Dead Horse IPA (1.054)   Nut Brown
Slop Bucket Brown (brown ale)   Bohemian Pils
Best Blond   Pay Day Beer (Vienna)
Exterminator Doppelbock   Oatmeal Stout
Firehouse Pale   Bucksnort Barley Wine

Brewer: Ray McNeill.
All beers are cask conditioned and served through hand pumps. There is a wide
variety of other draft beers including: Catamount Gold, Catamount Amber,
Catamount Porter, Rolling Rock, and Woodpecker Cider.
Thirty bottled beers, including several Belgians.

 Their specialty is homemade chili. They also have nachos, guacamole and
chips, and several kinds of sandwiches. Three wines on the menu; full bar.

This is a family pub which even keeps toys on hand for the kiddies. It is housed in
one of the oldest wood-frame buildings in Brattleboro, which has served as fire station, police station, jail, and finally a pub (Dewey's Ale House) since 1985. The
brewery was added in May 1991. The interior has high ceilings and lots of oak and
mahogany. Local artists pictures and sculptures are frequently on display. The bar has
an interesting ceramic cat from which the Catamount beers are served.

 background music (moderate)

EVENTS: Morris dancers on Memorial Day weekend

darts, board games,
and toys for the wee ones

 CA, VI

Mountain Brewers

 (802) 672-5011

Box 140, Route 4, The Marketplace
Bridgewater
05034

On U.S. Route 4, a few minutes west of Woodstock, Vt.

Long Trail Ale (pale ale)
Northern Light Lager (continental light, 120 calories per 12 ozs.)
Long Trail Ale (altbier)
Long Trail Light (light ale, 115 calories per 12 ozs.)
Long Trail India Pale Ale
Long Trail Stout (classic, Irish style)

Brewer: Dave Hartmann
Beer is all grain, served under pressure, filtered; 8,000 barrels.
Original gravities range from 1.048 - 1.050.

<u>No beer sold for consumption on premises.</u>
The brewery is located in the basement of The Marketplace At Bridgewater Mill, a former woolen mill - - now a Vermont crafts center and factory outlet. Free tours and tastings daily from noon to 5 p.m. No reservations required. Six packs, cases, and singles to go. Shirts, glassware, etc. on sale. First brewed on November 7, 1989. Picnic area on the Ottauquechee River. The brewery was expanded considerably in 1992.

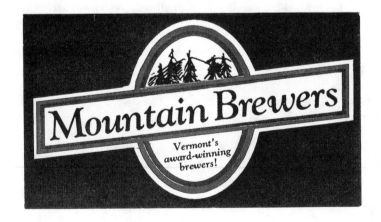

Otter Creek Brewing

74 Exchange Street, # 1
Middlebury
05753

(802) 388-0727
(800) 473-0727

North of downtown, in the industrial area.

Copper (1.052, alt)
Summer Wheat Ale (1.046)
Seasonal:
    Hickory Switch Smoked Amber Ale
    Stovepipe Porter
    Mud Bock Spring Ale

Brewer: Lawrence Miller
Beer is all grain, served under pressure, filtered; 600 barrels.

Open house Friday 4 - 6; tours Friday at 4:30 and 5:30, and by reservation. In addition, they have tours in the summer Saturday at 3:00 and 4:00. Beer available in 15.5 gallon kegs, five-gallon kegs, half-gallon bottles, and 12-oz. bottles. T-shirts, sweat shirts, etc. also available.
In 1992 they substantially expanded their brewing capacity and in 1993 added a new bottling line.

The Vermont Pub & Brewery of Burlington

144 College Street
Burlington
05401

 (802) 865-0500

At the corner of St. Paul & College Street, across from the City Hall Park.

 Sun - Thurs: 11:30 am - 12:30 am; Fri: 11:30 am - 2 am
Sat: 11:30 am - 1 am

 Burly Irish Ale (1.044, mild ale)
Vermont Smoked Porter (1.048)
Dogbite Bitter (1.048, best bitter/SPA)
Seasonal:
   Rock Dunder Brown Ale (1.042)
   Billybuck Maibock (1.060)
   Grand Slam Baseball Beer
      (1.046, Canadian ale)
   Pesky Sarpent Original Vermont
      Lager (1.049, Pilsner)
   Hellish Bock (1.072)
   No. 5 Ale (1.036)

Seasonal (cont'd)
   Wee Heavy (1.093)
   Hornes's 80/-Scottish Export Ale
      (1.050)
   Black Bear Dunkelager (1.052)
   Bombay Grab India Ale (1.050)
   Vermont Maple Ale (1.045)
   Betelguise Weiss (1.045)
   Kellerbier (1.053)
   O'Fest (1.056)
   Vermont Spruce Ale (1.051)
   Frambrosia (1.042)

Brewer: Greg Noonan
Beer is all grain, served under pressure, both filtered and unfiltered; 847 barrels.
Guinness Stout and a Vermont guest beer on draft; bottled beer
represents world beer styles. Vermont Hard Cider on draft.

 British Isles & American pub food - wide variety of specials ranging from nouveau to various ethnic styles. All-beef burgers, roast beef, chili, etc. are from organically raised black Angus. Six wines available; full bar. For the designated driver and the kiddies: homemade seltzer, root beer, and ginger ale.

This brewpub sports an 80-foot long greenhouse; mahogany, brick and tile with lots of glass; and a monolithic brick and cobbled terrace. The emphasis is on fresh, flavorful beer in a relaxed atmosphere. The Green Mountain Mashers meet here two to three times a year. Opened October 1988.

♪ live music Thursday (pub sessions), Friday and Saturday (R&B/blues/bluegrass)

 darts, chess, backgammon

  $$$ AE, CA, DC, DS, VI,

Windham Brewery
Latchis Grille

 (802) 254-4747

6 Flat Street
Brattleboro
05301

Located in downtown Brattleboro, not far from McNeill's Brewery, on the corner of Flat and Main streets, in the basement of the Latchis Hotel.

 Mon - Sat: 11 am - midnight; Sun: 10 am - midnight

Whetstone Golden Lager
   (made with honey and wheat)
Moonbeam Pale Ale
Ruby Brown Ale
Red Clover Lager

Seasonal:
   Frankenspice Xmas Ale
   Oktoberfest

brewer: John Korpita
All house beers are cask-conditioned, unfiltered, and all grain.
Beer to go in 2.2 gal. beer globes. Guinness on draft. There are six
bottled beers, including Xingu and Ballentine IPA.

The menu features items prepared with fresh, local ingredients. There are many grilled items, including catfish, Thai chicken, and shrimp. The bratwurst and kraut, the fettucini, and beer-batter fried calamari are very popular items. There is a light-dining menu, featuring such items as salads, soups, and sandwiches. Try the burrito bar with authentic Mexican offerings.

The brewpub is located in the Latchis Building, which was built in 1938 in the late art deco style. It is listed in the National Registry of Historic Places. The building also contains the famous Latchis Hotel and Latchis Theater. The brewpub has a stand-up bar and a large dining area with picture windows overlooking the Whetstone Brook. There is also a private dining room. In all, it seats 130 people. Displayed on one wall is a large painting of Brattleboro in the old days as well as postcards of old Brattleboro. It has an English "pubby" feel. Brewery tours are available--please call in advance. The local homebrew club, Beer Nuts & Valley Fermenters, meets here for regional tasting events. Opened July 17, 1991.

♪ live music on Tues. nights (traditional Irish music)

Virginia

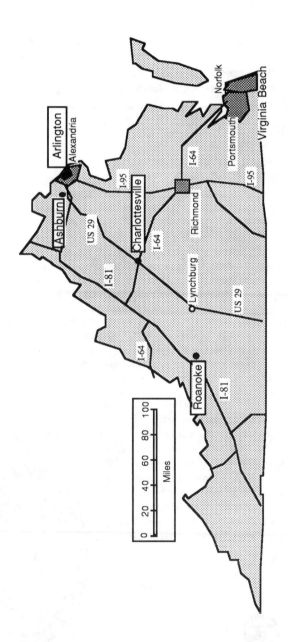

Bardo Rodeo

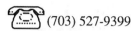 (703) 527-9399

2000 Wilson Boulevard
Arlington
22201

Located near the Court House Metro stop (the staff at Bardo encourage patrons to take the Metro).

 5 pm - 2 am daily

 Names of beers to be announced; styles of the first brews will be:

California common
California red
Stout
Porter
Wheat

Brewer: John Mallett
Beer is all grain; some filtered, some not; some served under pressure, some not. They have a total of 36 taps, including their own; many craft-brewed beers on tap; about 12 bottled beers, including West Coast beers and Belgian ales.

 They offer a limited menu listing six international appetizers and six entree featuring several items made with chicken. We suggest the Honey Where's the Keys to the Ducati? (vegatable lasagna with fresh herb ricotta and red sauce). All but one of the items can be made vegetarian. Wine served as well.

Bardo is located in the old Olmsted Oldsmobile dealership. You can't miss it, the entire building has been painted bright blue. The old showroom has been converted into a beer hall and has an enormous plate glass front with a Plymouth Fury crashing through it (the CD jukebox is IN the Fury). The brewhouse is exposed in the middle of the main room, with two open fermenters. There are two other rooms, including the Bardo Room which has a 240 foot mural wrapping around it, depicting scenes from Bardo. The seating capacity for the complex is 600+.

This is Bill Stewart's second attempt at opening a brewpub. His first, Amdo Rodeo, is still open and has a fantastic selection of draft beers, but, alas, never brewed. In case you were wondering where the name came from, the "Amdo" was taken from the province in western Tibet where the Dalai Lama was born. Stewart visited Tibet in 1985 and ever since has been an enthusiastic supporter of the International Campaign for a Free Tibet. The name Bardo comes from the Tibetan Book of the Dead, where Bardo is a place where the dead spend 49 days before proceeding on their journey in the underworld. When you see Stewart's two places, you will understand where the "Rodeo" came from. Opened in March 1993 and began brewing in May.

 no smoking, period

Blue Ridge Brewing

 (804) 977-0017

709 West Main
Charlottesville
22901

Across from the Amtrak station.

 Mon - Fri: 11:30 am - 2 pm; 5 pm - 2 am
Sat: 11:30 am - 2 am; Sun: 10:30 am - 2 am

 Hawksbill Lager (Pilsner)   Seasonal:
Piney River Lager (amber lager)   White Oak Wiezen
Afton Ale (red ale)
Humpback Stout

Brewer: A. Burks Summers
Beer is all grain, filtered, and served under pressure.
Kegs and bottles to take out. Also: Bud, Bud Light, & Amstel in bottles.

 This is a full-service, fine-dining restaurant that offers steaks, seafood, pastas, traditional Southern fare, burgers, pizzas, and desserts. Check out the daily specials on the chalkboard. About 30 wines; full bar.

They are located in an old building with a stamped tin ceiling. This is a neighborhood/sports bar, with an upscale character.

♪ live music on Sunday (rock/ blues)
background music (rock/ jazz/ classical, moderate - loud)

   handicapped access to all areas but
the bar

$$$ CA, MA, VI

Lone Star Cantina & Brewery
108 Campbell Avenue SE
Roanoke
24011

 (703) 344-0200

Located in the historic city market in downtown Roanoke.

 Mon - Wed: 11:30 am - 10 pm; Thurs - Sat: 11:30 am - 1 am
Sun: 11:30 am - 3 pm

 Cerveza de la Estrella de Oro
    (1.032, golden ale)
Cerveza Paloma
    (1.028, golden light ale)
Cerveza de la Estrella Negra
    (1.045, dark ale)

Seasonal:
    Cerveza de la Esmeralda
        (1.038, blue Khaffir)
    Cerveza Navidad
        (1.052, dopplebock)

Brewer: Patrick Carroll
Beers are all grain, filtered, served under pressure. The Cerveza de la Esmeralda is made
with sorghum seed. Several bottled Mexican and American beers are available.

 Lone Star features authentic Tex-Mex cuisine, but also offers a Gringo Burger for
those who can't make the switch. The menu includes appetizers, chilis and
soups, salads, and about 15 entrees, including Fajitas, Tostadas, Mesquite
Grilled Chicken, Camarones Enchipotlados, and Pescado Enperejilado. Several vegetarian dishes are offered. About a dozen wines and full bar.

Lone Star occupies an old retail building dating from 1909. It operated as the Army
Navy Surplus Store from 1922 until the mid-fifties. It is now a Texas-style cantina
with colors and textures of the Southwest. The brewery is located behind glass in the
bar area of the restaurant. The brewpub first opened in 1991 as Blue Muse Brewing,
closed in 1992, and reopened October 22 of the same year as the Lone Star. They
hoped to be brewing again by May 1993.

♪   live music on occasion; usually background music (country/western/rock)

   &

 pay

$$$ DS, MA, VI

Old Dominion Brewing

44633 Guilford Drive
Ashburn
22011

 (703) 689-1225

Located in the Corporate Centre at Beaumeade, a few miles from Dulles Airport. To reach the brewery from Washington, D.C., take the Dulles Access Road (Rte. 267) (be sure to take the toll road, with local access) to exit 1 (Rte. 28). Go north on Route 28 for about three miles to Rte. 625 (Waxpool road). Go left on Rte. 625 for 1.2 miles to the Corporate Centre at Beaumeade. Turn right at the flags onto Panorama Parkway. Turn left at the first street (Beaumeade Circle) and follow this street until you come to the red brick buildings with a blue stripe. Turn left after the red-brick buildings onto Guilford Drive. Old Dominion is the third building on the left.

Dominion Ale	Virginia Native Brite
Dominion Lager (1.049)	Hard Times Select
Dominion Stout	Blue Point
Portner's lager	O'Bannon Dark Beer
Victory Amber Lager	St. Georges Lager

Brewer: John Mallett
Beer is all grain, filtered, served under pressure; 6,000 barrels.

Beer is provided for tasting only in their hospitality suite.
Tours are held on Saturdays at noon and 3 pm. No beer sold on the premises. Opened for business in May 1990. Their slogan: "Don't drink more. Drink better. Drink Dominion Beers."

Old Dominion was founded in 1989 by Jerry Bailey, a former population expert with Agency for International Development. He had brewed at home for ten years "because he couldn't stand to drink tasteless American industrial beers." With the help of friends and Washington area beer lovers he began distributing in May 1990. Old Dominion beers are carried at more than 250 restaurants and retail stores in Washington, northern Virginia, and southern Maryland.

West Virginia

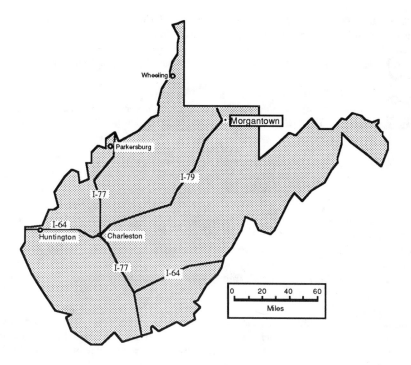

One Onion Brewery & Bistro

1291 University Avenue
Morgantown
26505-5450

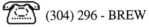 (304) 296 - BREW

Located in downtown Morgantown, on the corner of University and Walnut, near the University of West Virginia campus and the Riverfront Park.

 Mon - Thurs: 11 am - 2 am; Fri - Sat: 11 am - 3 am; closed Sunday

AJ Gold (light ale)
Fennen Celtic Ale (amber ale)
Cameron Scottish Stout
Gabriel's Wheat

Seasonal:
   several are planned

Brewer: Jim Martin
Beers are all grain, filtered, and served under pressure.
Imported beers are also available.

 The bistro offers a variety of gourmet dishes with the majority of entrees being centered around the fresh, homemade pasta. Entrees change daily depending on the availability of fresh ingredients. Visits are made weekly to the Baltimore docks to purchase catch-of-the-day items, such as catfish and tuna. Try the Onion Brew Stew, a thick gumbo, or pick from a variety of homemade breads. Several wines are available and they offer a full bar.

The brewery itself, with its six stainless steel vats, is visible from the streets as well as from inside the pub. The name, The One Onion, comes from an old Russian parable about a woman who died. Her patron saint needed to know some good deed she did in her life to get her into heaven, and she recalled a time when she gave an onion to a beggar woman who asked her for food. Out from the sky floated a huge onion, which the woman grabbed hold of as it started to rise heavenward. Suddenly, it unraveled layer by layer and the woman fell into the abyss of hell. The moral of the story is that one onion is not enough to get you into heaven. Owners Andrew Gongolla, Jim Martin, and David McClure are hopeful the One Onion will prove to be the good deed necessary to help revitalize the older part of the city in which it is located. Opened October 16, 1992.

♪ live jazz and blues on occasion

Wisconsin

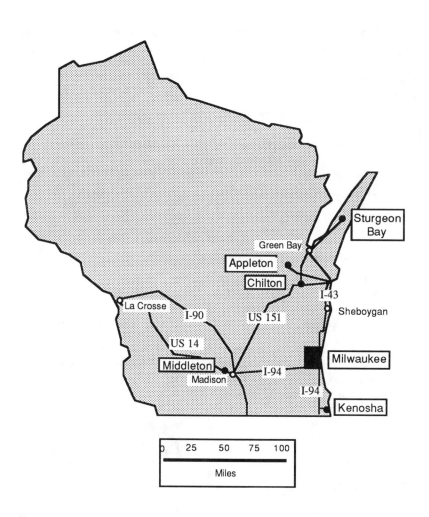

Sturgeon Bay

Green Bay

Appleton

Chilton

I-43

La Crosse

I-90

US 151

Sheboygan

US 14

Milwaukee

Middleton

Madison

I-94

I-94

Kenosha

| 0 | 25 | 50 | 75 | 100 |

Miles

Appleton Brewing - Adler Brau
Dos Bandidos Restaurant
Johnny O's Pizzeria

 (414) 731-3322

1004 South Olde Oneida Street
Appleton
54915

Located in the Between-the-Locks Mall at the southeast end of the Oneida Skyline Bridge, which crosses the Fox River.

 Dos Bandidos: Mon - Sat: 11 am - 10 pm; Sun: 4 pm - 10 pm
Johnny O's: Sun - Thurs: 4 pm - 2 am; Fri - Sat: 4 pm - 2:30 am

Adler Brau Light (1.038)
Adler Brau Lager (1.045)
Adler Brau Pilsener (1.050)
Adler Brau Amber All Malt (1.048)
Porter (1.054)
January special:Ginzing Dr. Brau

Seasonal:
  Bock (1.050)
  Weiss Brau (1.054)
  Holliday (1.040, dark lager)
  Fallfest (1.056, Oktoberfest)
  Pumpkin Spice (1.050)
  Oatmeal Stout (1.054)

Brewer: John Jungers

Beer is all grain, served under pressure, both filtered and unfiltered (dark); 430 barrels. Beer to go in 25 oz. bottles. Johnny O's also has nine other bottled beers.

Dos Bandidos is a Mexican restaurant offering an extensive south of the border menu, mixed drinks, wine, and American dishes too. Beer tastings are offered, followed by a gourmet Mexican lunch or dinner. Johnny O's offers several kinds of pizza, appetizers, and sandwiches. Several wines available; full bar.

Once the old Muench Brewery built in 1858, the brick building was remodeled into the Between-the-Locks Shopping Mall in 1978. The building also houses specialty shops, offices, a dance studio, and a hair-styling sylon. The brewery pipes the beer directly to the two restaurants. Visitors are welcome to tour the brewery. Breweriana located throughout the building. The S.O.B.'s Oshkosh Wi Club meets here. Began selling own beer September 1989.

 background music (top 40, soft/moderate)

 Dos Bandidos - 4; Johnny O's - 7
   (2 wide screens)

 Johnny O's - darts, video games, pool, pinball

$$$ AE, CA, DC, DS, VI

Brewmasters Pub Restaurant & Brewery

4017 - 80th Street
Kenosha
53142   (414) 694-9050

Located in a masonry barn in Friarwood Country Village, on Kenosha's south side.

 Mon -Fri: 11 am - midnight (stays open later on weekends)

 Harborside Light (1.032, lager)   Seasonal:
Kenosha Gold (1.046, lager)   Liberty Lager (1.070)
Amber Vienna Style (1.058)   Maibock (1.066)
Royal Dark (1.058)   Mocha Stout (1.063)
                                  Nort's Cream Ale (1.052)
Brewers: Jim Jensen, Jim Johnson,   Oktoberfest (1.055)
            Dave Norton   Old St. Nick (1.090, dopplebock)
Beer is all grain, served under pressure,   Plymouthe Bock (1.066)
unfiltered; 400 barrels. Beer to go in quart
Mason mugs and 5-gal. containers.

 The cuisine is mainly American with a variety of burgers, sandwiches, seafoods, and steaks. They also offer stir fries, Cajun specialties, and pastas. Portions are generous. Twelve wines available; full bar.

The brewpub is housed in a turn-of-the-century stable for show horses. It has a brick exterior with wooden interior and offers an old English atmosphere. The brewhouse is visible from the bar. Tours are available--reservations are suggested two days in advance. The Bidel Society of Kenosha meets here the first Thursday of every month. Began selling their own beer in February 1987.

 Live music on special occasions & weekends; background music (light jazz, etc.)

EVENTS: Octoberfest - last weekend of Sept. & first weekend of Oct.; Halloween party; pig roasts in Biergarten (weather permitting; call for details).

$$$ CA, VI

Capital Brewery

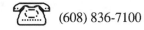 (608) 836-7100

7734 Terrace Avenue
Middleton
53562

From Highway 12 (The Beltline) take the Greenway Boulevard Exit. The Brewery is two blocks from the exit.

 Fri: 3:30 - 8 pm; Sat: noon - 8 pm during the summer.

Gartenbrau Lager
Gartenbrau Special (1.047, lager)
Gartenbrau Dark (1.053, lager)
Gartenbrau Weizen (1.048)
Wisconsin Amber (1.0510

Brewer: Kirby Nelson
Beer is all grain, filtered; 8,700 barrels.

Seasonal:
Gartenbrau Bock
Gartenbrau Maibock
Gartenbrau Oktoberfest (1.054)
Gartenbrau Wild Rice
Winterfest
Bock

 They serve appetizers in the Bier Garten during the summer.

Summer tours are held Monday - Thursday at 1 pm, Friday at 1 pm and 3:30 pm, and Saturday at 1, 3, and 4 pm. Off-season tours are held at 1 pm. Call ahead to make arrangements for large groups or private tours. Tour charge is $1.00 for persons 21 years and older. The tour includes beer samples. They have recently added tanks to increase capacity to over 12,000 barrels.

The Gift Haus is open Monday - Friday from 9 am - 4:30 pm all year. It offers German glassware, a selection of collectors' mugs and glassware from other breweries, and Capital Brewery and Wisconsin souvenirs of all kinds. Opened for business in June 1986.

 volleyball, horseshoes ♿

Cherryland Brewing

341 North Third Avenue
Sturgeon Bay
54235

 (414) 743-1945

The brewpub borders on both Third & First Avenues.

 10 am - 4 am daily

 Golden Rail (1.050, lager)
Silver Rail (1.046, lager)
Weizen (1.044, ale)
Irish Light (1.046, ale)
Cherry Ale (1.048)
Apple Bock (1.056)

Brewer: Mark Feld
Beer is made from malt extract, filtered. 800 barrels. Beer to go in
six packs, cases, and 12- oz. bottles. Available for distribution.

 The menu features pub fare with a variety of Italian items. Try the beer battered
fried perch. Ask about daily specials.

This is a neighborhood brewpub situated in a turn-of-the-century train station with a
railroad theme on the inside. Opened in 1988.

 Background music - soft to moderate

 CA, DS, VI

Lakefront Brewery

 (414) 372-8800

818A East Chambers Street
Milwaukee
53212

Chambers Street is one block north of Locust Street & west of the Milwaukee River.

East Side Dark (1.075, dopplebock)
Riverwest Stein Beer (1.068, amber lager)
Klisch Lager (1.060, Pilsner)
Cream City Pale Ale (1.060)
Seasonal:
  Big Jim's Pumpkin Beer (1.055)
  Klisch Cherry Beer (1.060)
  Pumpkin Ale (lager)

Brewers: Mark May & Gary Versteegh
Beer is all grain, served under pressure, unfiltered; 840 barrels.

No beer sold for consumption on premise.

Tours are available on Saturdays at 1:30 and 2:30 pm--reservations suggested. Many draft outlets are located in Riverwest neighborhood - several within walking distance of the brewery. Opened December 2, 1987. Began limited bottling in 1990.

Lakefront Brewery Inc.

Rowland's Calumet Brewing
The Roll Inn

25 North Madison Street (414) 849-2534
Chilton
53014

Located on Highway. 57, one block north of the only stop light in town.

 Tues - Thurs: 2 pm - 2 am; Fri - Sat: noon - 2:30 am; Sun: noon - 2 am
closed Monday

 Calumet Beer (pilsner)
Warpath Beer (wheat)
Ambush Beer (amber)
Calumet Dark

Seasonal:
  Calumet Bock
  Calumet Wheat & Bock

Brewer: Robert Rowland
Beer is all grain, served under pressure, filtered; 100 barrels.
Beer to go in half barrels, quarter barrels, and five gallon kegs.

 Currently the cuisine is sandwiches *a la microwave* and pizzas. Try Rowland's
Old Fashion Root Beer.

This neighborhood brewpub occupies the town's original firehouse, built before
1880. It has 14-foot ceilings and a back bar built in the 1920s. Lots of tile and wood
in the interior. The bar opened in 1983; the brewing operation was added in the fall
of 1990.

Background music and juke box

 darts, pool on a 100 year old table, pinball, electronic poker

Sprecher Brewing

 (414) 272-2337

730 West Oregon Street
Milwaukee
53204

Located in the shadow of the Old Phillip Best (Pabst) Brewery.

Special Amber (1.052, lager)
Black Bavarian (1.060, doppelbock)
Hefe Weiss (1.044)
Milwaukee Weiss (1.044)
Milwaukee Pils (1.042)
Dunkel Weizen (1.049)

Seasonal:
Mai Bock (1.060)
Oktoberfest (1.056, lager)
Winter Brew (1.058, dark
lager)
Irish Stout (1.060)

Brewer: Randal Sprecher
Beer is all grain, served under pressure, filtered (except Hefe Weiss); 8,200 barrels.

<u>Beer available in tasting room only during tours.</u>
Tours are conducted on Saturday at 1, 2, and 3 pm--reservations recommended. Beer for
sale for off-premise consumption only, in 16- oz. bottles and kegs, pony kegs, and
one liter German flip top bottles. A gourmet root beer soda is also available in 16- oz.
bottles and kegs. Opened in 1986.

Water Street Brewery

 (414) 272-1195

1101 North Water Street
Milwaukee
53202

Located one block north of the Performing Arts Center.

 Sun - Thurs: 11 am - 2 am; Fri - Sat: 11 am - 2:30 am

Water Street Amber (1.034, ale)
Sporten European Lager (1.054, Pilsner)
Water Street Weiss (1.060)
Old World Oktoberfest (1.056)

Seasonal:
Kilbourn Special Bock (1.062)
Callans Irish Red (1.042)
Irish Oatmeal Stout (1.042)
Nut Brown Ale

Brewer: John Dallman

Beer is made from malt extract, served under pressure, both filtered/unfiltered;
670 barrels. Two other beers on draft (Miller, Miller Lite), 34 bottled beers
(11 Wisconsin brews and 19 imports - Bip, Pilsner Urquell, Hacker-Pschorr,
Swan, and Samuel Smith Lager).

 The restaurant offers a varied selection of salads, appetizers, sandwiches, and
nightly dinner specials - try the Old World Selection (bratwurst and knackwurst)
and the smoked sausage platter. Entrees are designed to enhance house beers.
Don't miss the Brewmaster's Deli for lunch. Several wines available; full bar.

Housed in a restored, 100-year-old building with 1890s red brick walls and ornate, tin
trim. The interior has exposed brick, arches, and offers panoramic views of the city.
Check out the antique beer bottle collection and brewery lithographs. The brewhouse
is visible. Souvenir T-shirts and glasses for sale. Opened 1987.

♪ Background music (soft)

 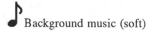 $$$ AE, CA, VI

Canada

Many Americans are unaware of the beer renaissance going on in our neighbor to the north. In this respect, Canada definitely does not play second fiddle to the United States. As a matter fact, during the current revival, the first brewery to make real ale in North America was the Horseshoe Bay Brewery in Vancouver, British Columbia. It was also the FIRST brewpub in North America, beating out Bert Grant in Yakima, Washington, by a few weeks.

The Canadian revival, as in the United States, began on the West Coast, and later spread eastward. John Mitchell, part owner of the Troller Pub, in Vancouver, had become bored with Canadian beers and was intrigued with the brewpubs springing up in the United Kingdom. Upon returning from a trip to England where he investigated the brewpubs, Mitchell received permission to open the Horseshoe Bay Brewery and sell its ales at the Troller Pub, albeit, the brewery and pub were required to be no less than 100 meters from each other. The venture was a success from the pouring of the first pint in the summer of 1982, and the Troller had to turn away thirsty customers when the beer sold out.

The year 1983 saw the opening of two more breweries in British Columbia: Mountain Ales in Surrey (a craft brewery making British style ales) and the Prairie Inn in Saanichton, a suburb of Victoria. The Prairie Inn brewpub is still open today and continues to make its beer from malt extract.

Within a year of starting Horseshoe Bay, Mitchell had left to start another brewery, Spinnakers Brewpub, across the channel in Victoria. Spinnakers opened in the summer of 1984, as did Granville Island Brewing (a craft brewery making lagers) in Vancouver.

By 1984 the excitement had spread across Canada, and 1984, 1985, and 1986 saw an outbreak of craft breweries and brewpubs all across Canada. The pace has abated since those heady years, but the climate still seems to be reasonably good for new breweries. Several of the breweries, such as Upper Canada, Brick, Big Rock, and Sleeman, have prospered and grown to the size of regional breweries.

Canada has also seen a higher mortality rate among the new breweries than in the United States, especially during the current recession and among malt-extract breweries. Canada has a far higher percentage of malt-extract breweries than in the U.S. While a malt-extract brewery is capable of producing perfectly good beers (and I've had some, for example at Pacific Coast Brewing, in Oakland, California), they generally don't seem to do so. Perhaps the problem is one of not taking the brewing process seriously enough.

Also, a third kind of "brewpub" has sprung up in Canada. These are breweries that don't mill the malt, mash the grist, nor boil the wort--they just ferment and age the beer, the wort being trucked in from another brewery. Technically, they meet the definition of a brewery, so I suppose I will include them in the next edition of *On Tap*.

As in the United States, brewpubs have become quite fashionable and one doesn't have to visit some hole in the wall to get a selection of good beer. These upscale establishments, such as the Rotterdam and Amsterdam in Toronto, are drawing in more and more converts to the cause. The time has come when good restaurants are providing a beer list, in addition to their wine list.

Homebrewing is even more popular in Canada than in the U.S., partly due to the high "sin taxes." Many "you-brew-it" establishments have opened where all of the equipment and ingredients are provided by the shop. An increasing number of Canadians have turned to this method in order to get good beer at a reasonable price. The Lion Brewery in Waterloo, Ontario, operates its own "you-brew-it" shop right next to the brewpub.

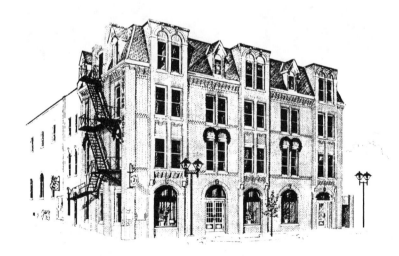

The Lion Brewery, Museum, & Malt House
in Waterloo, Ontario

Brewpub - Craft Brewery
Count by Canadian Province

April 1993

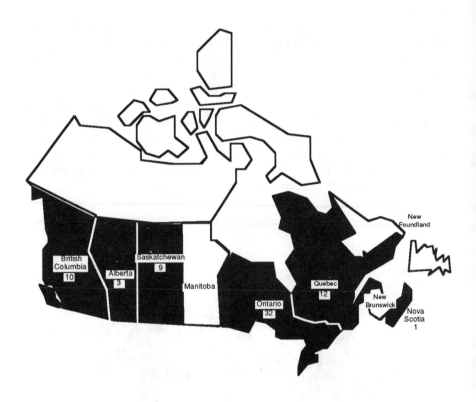

Alberta

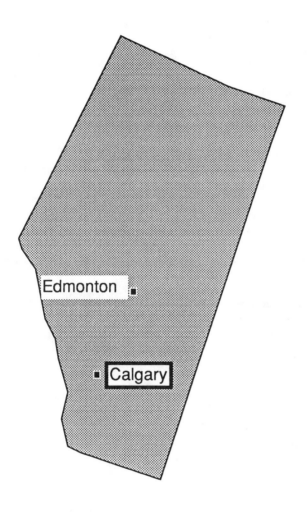

Edmonton ■

■ Calgary

Big Rock Brewery

 (403) 236-7523

6503 35th Street, S.E.
Calgary
T2C 1N2

Big Rock Traditional Ale
Big Rock Bitter
Big Rock Cock O' the Rock Porter
Big Rock Classical
Pale Ale
Royal Coachman Dry Ale
McNally's Extra Ale
XO Lager

Brewer: Bernd Pieper
The beers are all grain and filtered. They also brew a few contract brands and export
some of their beers to the United States.

Former corporate lawyer and rancher Ed McNally started working on his brewery in
1984 and had it open and brewing within a couple of years. He started with ales and
later added several lagers. Brewing output has increased steadily over the years. Big
Rock beers are available in kegs and bottles in western Canada and many parts of the
United States.

Tours of the brewery are available by appointment and they sell souvenirs and their
own beer for take out.

$$$ CA, VI, AE

Brewsters Brew Pub & Brasserie

834 11th Avenue, S.W.
Calgary
T2R 0E5

 (403) 263-2739

Located downtown at the corner of 11th Avenue and 8th Street SW.

 Mon - Wed: 11 am - 1:30 am; Thurs - Sat: 11 am - 2 am; closed Sunday

Hammerhead Red (1.046, ale)
Palliser Pale (1.046, ale)
Bow Valley Brown (1.046, ale)
Big Horn Bitter (1.046, ale)
Shaughnessy Stout (1.058, ale)
Blue Monk Barley Wine (1.074, ale)

Seasonal:
Brewster IPA (1.046, ale)
Ginger Ale (1.045)
Original (1.045, lager)

Seasonal (cont'd)
Flying Frog (1.045, lager)
Ernest Bay Premium (1.045, Pilsner)
Wild West Wheat (1.045, lager)
Rocky Mt. Dark (1.045, lager)
Continental Light (1.035, lager)
Cranberry (1.045, ale)
Brewsters Spring Bock (1.055)

Brewers: Clifford Auckland and Mike Tymchuk
The beers are all grain, filtered, and served under pressure.
Beer to go in one-liter bottles and 19-liter kegs; six guest bottled beers.

 The pub style cuisine includes hamburgers, fish 'n chips, sandwiches, nachos, soups, and salads, chicken wings, ribs, pork dumplings, steaks and low calorie options. Wine served and full bar available. Look for lunch, happy hour and evening food specials. They feature a house beer of the week.

The interior is modern Canadian with plants, lots of oak and brass. It seats 350 and the brewery is glassed-in on two sides. It features a special 40-seat, private room with a view of the brewery. This was Alberta's first full mash brewpub when it opened in May 1991.

 background music (moderate)   6   darts

EVENTS: Octoberfest (celebrated all month)

  free

$$$ CA, VI, AE

Brewsters Brew Pub and Brasserie

755 Lake Bonavista Drive
Calgary
T2J 0N3

 (403) 225-2739
Fax order #: 265-2620

Located in the Lake Bonavista Mall, overlooking the lake.

 Mon - Thurs: 11 am - 1 am; Fri - Sat: 11 am - 2 am; Sun: 11 am - 8 pm

Hammerhead Red Ale (1.046)
Palliser Pale Ale (1.046)
Qu'Appelle Valley Brown Ale (1.046)
Big Horn Bitter (1.046)
Shaughnessy Stout (1.058)
Brewsters Barley Wine (1.074)
Seasonal:
  Brewster IPA (1.046)
  Ginger Ale (1.045)
  Original Lager (1.045)

Seasonal (cont'd)
  Flying Frog Lager (1.045)
  Ernest Bay Premium
    (1.045, Pilsner)
  Wild West Wheat (1.045)
  Rocky Mt. Dark (1.045, lager)
  Continental Light Lager (1.035)
  Cranberry Ale (1.045, ale)
  Brewsters Spring Bock (1.055)

Brewer: Michael Tymchuk.
The beers are all grain, filtered, and served under pressure.
Beer to go in one-liter bottles and 19 liter kegs

 The pub style cuisine includes burgers, fish 'n chips, sandwiches, nachos, soups and salads, chicken wings, ribs, pork dumplings, steaks and low calorie options. Wine served and full bar available. Check out lunch, happy hour and dinner specials. They feature an in-house beer of the week.

The interior is modern Canadian with plants, oak, ceramics and brass. This neighborhood pub seats150 and the brewery is glassed on two sides. Full bar and wine. Opened July 1992. Children welcome.

♪ background music (moderate)   4   🎯 darts   🌼

EVENTS: Octoberfest (celebrated all month)

 free

 $$$ AE, CA, VI

British Columbia

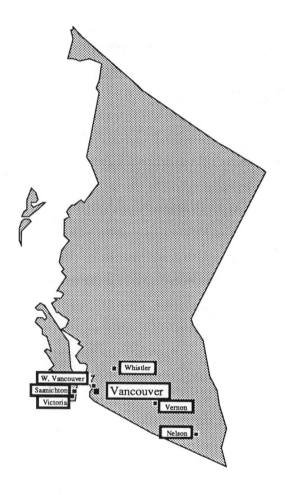

Granville Island Brewing

 (604) 688-9927

1441 Cartwright Street
Vancouver
V6H 3R7

Located on Granville Island, near the entrance to the island.

Granville Island Lager (Bavarian Pilsner)
Granville Island Light (lager)
Granville Island Bock (dark Bavarian bock)
Lord Granville Pale Ale

Brewer: Mark Simpson
Their beer is all grain and they follow the German Reinheitsgebot; 12,775
barrels.

Granville Island is located in the old Lecky Paper Warehouse on the trendy Granville
Island. They offer tours at 1:00 and 3:00, seven days a week. Samples of their beers
are given out during the tours. Reservations are not necessary, but large groups
should call in advance.

They are licensed to sell their beer for take out. In addition, they sell several
wines from the Pacific Northwest, as well as T-shirts and souvenirs of the brewery.
They distribute their beers throughout British Columbia in kegs and bottles.
Granville Island beers were first sold in June 1984.

Horseshoe Bay Brewing

6695 Nelson Avenue
West Vancouver (Horseshoe Bay)
V7W 2B2

 (604) 921-6116

Bay Ale (1.041, amber)
Raspberry Triple (1.065, Belgian)
IPA (1.055, traditional)
Nut Brown (1.043, dark mild)

Seasonal:
    Christmas (1.065, traditional)

Brewer: Philip Watney
Their beer is all grain and they brew in 1,200 liter batches.

This was originally founded as the Troller Pub-Horseshoe Bay Brewing Co. by brewing pioneer John Mitchell. Opening in June of 1982, it was the first brewpub to open in North America and also the first brewpub to offer cask-conditioned beer in North America. The brewery closed in 1987 and Mitchell went on to open Spinnakers Brewpub in Victoria.

Horseshoe Bay Brewing reopened in 1989 as a craft brewery. They do not have a taproom but they do offer beer during tours. Tours are by appointment only, with three weeks advance notice requested. Best time to call is between 10 am and 3 pm. Their beer is both bottled and kegged. They sell beer to go in six-packs. They have outgrown their facility at the marina and plan to move soon.

Nelson Brewing

 (604) 352-3582

512 Latimer Street
Nelson
V1L 4T9

Located across the street from the Nelson Fire Hall.

Old Brewery Ale (1.048, English pale ale)
Silverking Lager (1.048, Pilsner)

Brewer: Dieter Feist
The beer is all grain; 2,200 barrels.

Tours are possible--please make advanced reservations. They do not have a license to provide samples on the tours, nor to sell beer for take out. However, they do have Nelson T-shirts for sale.

The batch size is 550 gallons. The Silverking is made with German malt and Czech hops. They distribute their beer both in kegs and in one-liter bottles. Of historical interest, the first Nelson Brewery opened at this location in 1893. The new owners purchased the Nelson trademark and opened in April 1991.

Okanagan Spring Brewery

2801 27th A Avenue
Vernon
V1T 1T5

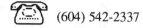 (604) 542-2337

Spring Premium Lager
Old English Porter
Old Munich (dark wheat)
St. Patrick Stout

Brewer: Stefan Tobler
Their beer is all grain, all natural, and filtered. They distribute both in kegs and bottles.

To open this brewery, German immigrant and owner Jakob Tobler had to refurbish a warehouse, which was once an apple packing house. Brewer Raimund Kalinowski, a graduate of the brewing school at the University of Berlin, designed the brewhouse. The beers meet the Reinheitsgebot standard and have been exported to Germany. Opened December 1985.

Tours are available--please call for an appointment. They have a retail store where you can buy their beer to go, as well as brewery souvenirs.

Prairie Inn Neighborhood Pub & Cottage Brewery

7806 East Saanich Road
Saanichton
V0S 1M0

 (604) 652-1575

From Victoria, take Route 17 toward the ferries; when you get to the McDonald's, turn left on Mount Newton Cross Road; when you come to the four way stop; the Prairie Inn is on the corner.

 11 am - 1 am daily

English Gold
Black Bitters
Aussie Rules

Brewer: Brian Mayszes
Their beers are made from malt extract.

 They have a full menu with appetizers, sandwiches, burgers, and many entrees.

This is one of Canada's earliest brewpubs, even though the the brewhouse is not actually in the same building. The brewpub is in a yellow, wood frame house with a wrap around porch. Inside, it has an English pub feel to it. Opened in 1983.

 pool

Shaftebury Brewing

 (604) 255-4550

1973 Pandora Street
Vancouver
V5L 5B2

Located in East Vancouver, five minutes from downtown.

Shaftebury Cream Ale (1.042)
Shaftebury E.S.B. (1.050)
Shaftebury Traditional Ale (1.043, bitter)

Seasonal:
    Shaftebury Wheat Ale (1.045)
    Shaftebury London Porter (1.056)
    Christmas Ale (1.075, barley wine)

Brewer: Mike Stewart
Their beer is all grain, batch size is 33 hectolitres.

Tours are available; please call one day ahead. Tasting area exists for sampling but there is no beer to go.

They sell their kegged beer to many accounts: try these British-styled ales in any of the five Fogg 'N Sudds locations, as well as in over 270 other establishments. Opened on August 21, 1987.

Spinnakers Brewpub

308 Catherine Street
Victoria
V9A 3S8

 (604) 386-BREW

Located on the south shore of Victoria's Inner Harbor.

 7 am - 11 pm daily

Spinnakers Ale (1.046)	Dunkle Weizenbrau (1.054)
Doc. Hadfield's Pale Ale (1.046)	Jameson's Scottish Ale (1.040)
Weizenbrau (1.044)	Dunkle Heffeweizen (1.058)
RotesWeizen (1.048)	Oatmeal Stout (1.060)
Heffeweizen (1.048)	Empress Stout (1.053)
India Pale Ale (1.050)	Genoa Dark Lager (1.048)
Imperial Stout (1.052)	Genoa Lager (1.048)
Christmas Ale (1.080)	Copper Bock (1.074)
Mitchell's ESB (1.050)	Jameson's Spiced Ale (1.040)
Mt. Tolmie (1.046, dark)	Old Knucklehead Stout (1.052)

Brewer: Jake Thomas
Their beer is all grain, unfiltered, and cask conditioned.
Beer to go in 22-oz. bottles and 4-liter polypro. 4-6 drafts & 6-8 bottled beers.

 The cuisine is Northwest and traditional. Specialty of the house is halibut 'n chips in brewer's yeast batter.

They are situated in a renovated old waterfront building dating from the 1920s. The restaurant is on the main floor with taproom/pub upstairs. They have warm interior furnishings with terra cotta tile floors and extensive wainscotting throughout. They have a south facing patio with seating for forty, as well as balcony seating for twenty. They claim to be the first "in-house" brewpub in Canada. Victoria's CAMRA chapter meets here five to six times a year. The brewpub was first opened by John Mitchell in June 1984.

 live music 5 - times per week (piano, jazz, folk); background music (soft)

 darts

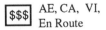

$$$ AE, CA, VI,
En Route

Swan's Brewpub

Buckerfield Brewery
506 Pandora Avenue
Victoria
V8W 1N6

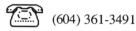 (604) 361-3491

Located in Olde Town Victoria on the corner of Pandora & Store Street opposite Johnson St. Bridge.

 Mon - Sat: 11:30 am - 2 am; Sunday: 11:30 am - midnight

Arctic Ale (1.044, pale ale)
Buckerfield's Bitter (1.048)
Empress Stout (1.058)
Appleton Brown (1.050, ale)
Pandora Pale Ale (1.042)
Bavarian Lager (1.050)

Seasonal:
Christmas Cracker Ale (1.072, barley wine)
Northern Lite (1.036)
Beacon Hill Lager (1.054, strong lager)

Brewers: Frank Appleton and Chris Johnson
Beer is all grain, unfiltered, some cask-conditioned, some served under pressure. Beer to go in 650 brown glass bottles; one draft and twelve bottled beers.

Classical pub cuisine includes hot or BBQ wings, pub burgers, chicken strips, steak sandwiches, calamari, fish 'n chips, and a "Ragin Cajun Halibut Burger." These offerings are rounded out with soups, salads, vegie-plate, nachos, and garlic or cheese toast.

The building was built as Buckerfield's seed warehouse in 1913 and completely remodeled into an English, neighborhood pub in 1989. The exterior is brick with wrought-iron balconies with hanging floral baskets (in summer). The interior includes a polished-oak bar with gleaming brass English hand pumps. Original art is displayed on an antique brick wall with original wood posts and beams. Space is divided into pub, restaurant, and banquet room. CAMRA -Victoria meets here quarterly. Opened in 1989.

♪ live music Mon, Tues, & Wed (acoustic, folk); background music (soft)

$$$ AE, CA, DS, VI

Vancouver Island Brewing

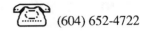 (604) 652-4722

#24- 6809 Kirkpatrick Crescent
R.R. #3
Victoria
V8X 3X1

Located just off Keating Cross Road.

Premium Lager (1.046, Pilsner)
Pipers Pale Ale (1.044)
Herman's Dark Lager (1.050)

Seasonal:
Hermannator Xmas Boch
Easter "Hoppin' Ale
Oktoberfest

Brewer: Ross Elliot
Beer is all grain; batch size is 40 hectoliters.

Tap room is available on premises and beer is on sale for take out in 12-oz. bottles. Tours are available by appointment with one month's reservation required. Best time to call is between 8:30 am and 4:30 pm. Beer to go in six or 12-packs. Beer is marketed in bottles and kegs. Opened in the winter of 1984.

Whistler Brewing

1209 Alpha Lake Road
Whistler
V0N 1B1

 (604) 932-6185

Located a few miles south of Whistler, in an industrial park.

Whistler Premium Lager
Black Tusk Ale
Albino Rhino

Brewer: Thilo Buchholz
Their beer is all grain and filtered. They also make some contract beers for area restaurants. Their beer is distributed in bottles and kegs.

Tours are available, please call for an appointment. The brewery was opened in 1990 by Rob Mingay and Gerry Hieter. Since then, it has changed hands and is now owned by Don Konantz.

Nova Scotia

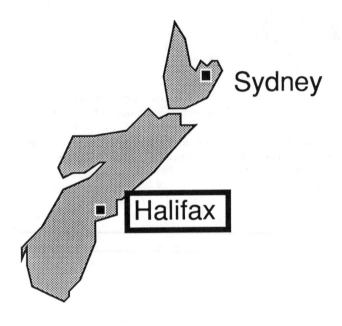

Sydney

Halifax

Granite Brewery

1222 Barrington Street (P.O. Box 114)
Halifax
B3J 1Y4

 (902) 422-4954

 11:30 am - 12:30 am daily

 Best Bitter (1.046, bitter)
Peculiar (1.056, old ale)
Keefe's Irish Stout (1.040)

Brewer: Kevin Keefe
Beer is all grain, unfiltered, some cask-conditioned, others served under
pressure. One guest draft and various bottled beers

 They offer a varied cuisine with a wide range of styles and tastes. Wine and full
bar.

The brewpub is housed in a restored 1830's stone house, "The Henry House." It is a
landmark building that was home to William Alexander Henry, father of the
Confederation, and framer of the Canadian Constitution. Opened in April 1985.

 background music (moderate)   3

 darts

 free

 $$$ AE, CA, DC,
VI, En Route

Ontario

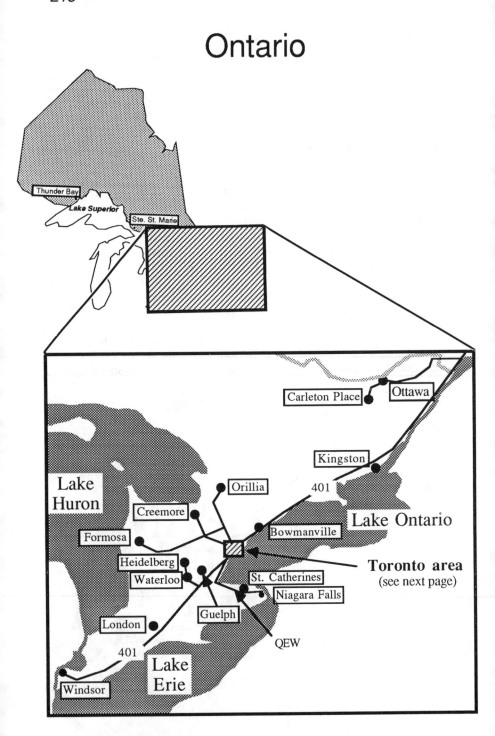

Toronto Area Breweries

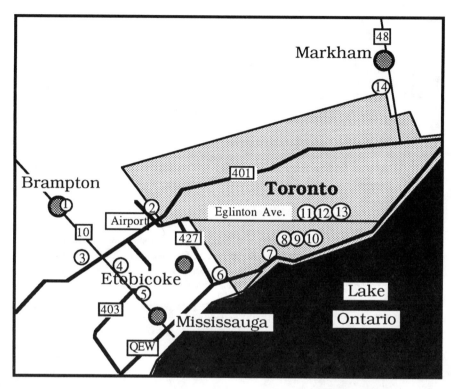

1. **Tracks Brewpub**
   60 Queen Street E., Brampton

2. **Marconi's Restaurant & Br.**
   262 Carlingview, Etobicoke

3. **CC's Brew Pub**
   6981 Mill Cr. Dr. # 1, Mississauga

4. **Tapsters Smokehouse Grill**
   100 Brittania Road E., Mississauga

5. **Brax 'n' Brew**
   4230 Sherwoodtowne Blvd.
   Mississauga

6. **Great Lakes Brewing**
   30 Q. Elizabeth Blvd., Etobicoke

7. **Upper Canada Brewing**
   2 Atlantic Avenue, Toronto

8. **Rotterdam Brewing**
   600 King Street West, Toronto

9. **Amsterdam Brasserie & Br.**
   133 John Street, Toronto

10. **Denison's Br./Growler**
    75 Victoria Street, Toronto

11. **Spruce Goose Brewing**
    130 Eglinton Ave., E., Toronto

12. **Vinefera**
    150 Eglinton Avenue E., Toronto

13. **Granite Brewery**
    245 Eglinton Avenue, E., Toronto

14. **Barb's Union Station Pub**
    4396 Steeles Avenue, East
    Markham

Algonquin Brewing

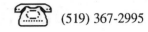 (519) 367-2995

Number One Old Brewery Lane
Formosa
N0G 1W0

Algonquin Special Reserve Ale
Algonquin Country Lager
Algonquin Light
Formosa Draught
Formosa Light
Royal Amber Lager
Bruce County Lager
Marconi European Lager (brewed under license)
Banks Beer of the Caribbean (brewed under license)

The beer is filtered and served under pressure.

Algonquin opened in 1989 as Northern Algonquin and has shortened its name since then. It occupies the old Formosa Spring Brewery, founded in 1870. It was acquired by Benson & Hedges in 1970 closed within a year. Beers were first brewed under contract. Since the plant opened production has increased steadily.

No beer sales for consumption on premise. Tours can be arranged--please call in advance. Their retail store is open 9 - 5 daily.

Amsterdam Brasserie & Brewpub

133 John Street
Toronto
M5V 2E4

 (416) 595-8201

Located at the corner of John and Adelaide in downtown Toronto, near the Toronto Dome and the theater district. The Queen Street West streetcar line is nearby.

 11:30 am - 1 am daily

Lager (1.046)	Seasonal (cont'd):
Nut Brown Ale (1.048)	Christmas Bock
Bitter	Spring Bock
Seasonal:	Blonde Ale
Stout	Weisse
Rauch	Amber Wiessen
Oktoberfest	

Brewer: Harley Smith

Beer is all grain, made from single-step, infusion mash; filtered; served under CO_2-nitrogen pressure. Lagers are krausened. Black & Tan (Nut Brown & Stout) pints are $2.95 until 8 pm. Large selection of bottled beers.

 Appetizers include home-smoked Atlantic salmon, bruchetta (with tomatoes & virgin olive oil). Soups, salads and a variety of entrees, including deep-fried calamari, catch & pasta of the day, lamb curry, and grilled German sausage on a poppy seed bun are available. Desserts include Old World, Black Forest Cake, and Amsterdam Apple Pizza. Nightly $10 special. Wine and full bar available.

Located in a renovated, brick warehouse, it is airy with high ceilings; red, white, and blue theme. Spiral steps take you to the galleried drinking-game room upstairs. It has a 40'+ bar, and three dining areas on left. A small bar and the brewery are in the basement. The beer is served from serving tanks on the main level and from kegs upstairs.The Little Amsterdam is next door-- it offers keg beer, has tiled and brick walls, and two gas fireplaces. When the Amsterdam opened in 1986, it was the first brewpub in Toronto. Blue Jays fans flock here (in season). Seats 430. Tours of the brewery can be arranged.

 background music (medium-loud)   4   pool

 two patios   EVENTS: Halloween, New Years Eve

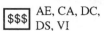 AE, CA, DC, DS, VI

Barb's Union Station Pub & Eatery

4396 Steeles Avenue, East (P.O. Box 61)
Markham (416) 940-3130
L3R 9W1 940-3131

Located in the Market Village Plaza, at the corner of Steeles and Kennedy. Markham is a suburb of Toronto.

 11 am - 1 am daily

 Lager
Ale

Brewer: John Lippert
Beer made from malt extract, filtered, served under pressure.
Nine guest beers on tap, including Smythewick's. Twenty - thirty imported bottled beers, plus a few domestics.

 They have a varied menu, including soups, salads, appetizers, desserts, and finger foods such as nachos, pizza, wings, sandwiches, burgers (kiddies's menu too). Entrees include pasta, filet of sole, rainbow trout, Bombay chicken, souvlaki,and rib eye steak. The brewpub is under new ownership and they are plan to expand the menu. Check out the daily specials. Happy hour--free hors d'oeuvres brought to your table. Monday night is pitcher night (buy a pitcher and get a discount on food). Wine and full bar.

This brewpub has been made to resemble an old-fashioned train station, complete with old- fashioned train station ornaments, such as street lights and benches and, for effect, a model train, which runs completely around the inside of the pub. The brewhouse is behind glass next to the front door. The inside has two levels--the 40-foot, L-shaped bar and pool table on the upper level, and most of the booths and dance floor on the lower. In contrast to the railway antiques, the interior is modern industrial, with exposed ductwork and brick walls, sporting neon beer signs. Now under new ownership, they sponsor a slow pitch softball team and a hockey team. The crowd is mostly 25 and above, with some families coming in.

 DJ Thurs - Sat night; moderate background music other times

 8 and a dish; Tavern TV also patio seats 100
EVENTS: St. Patrick's Day (green beer, etc.)

 darts, pool, and video

$$$ AE, CA, VI

Blue Anchor Restaurant & Brewpub

47 West Street, SE
Orillia
L3V 5G5

 (705) 325-7735

In downtown Orillia.

   Mon - Sat: 11 am - 1 am; Sunday: noon - 1 am

   Bitter Amber Ale
Lager

Brewer: Rick Neil
Beer made from malt extract.
Various other beers on draft.

   The menu features typical pub grub such as meat pies, burgers, sandwiches, fish 'n chips, etc. Daily specials available.

Located in a renovated 19th century building, the pub has a circular bar in the middle, varnished pine trim, and has a light and airy feel, with many windows. The brewery is visible behind glass both from the outside and inside. The pub was copied after a 15th century pub in Cornwall, England. Opened in 1988.

 live music on Sunday - jazz and blues jam (4:30 pm until), background; karaoke on Sat. (8:30 pm)

 4   darts, pool (3 & 8 ball tournaments)

$$$ AE, CA, VI

Brax 'n' Brew

 (416) 897-0900

4230 Sherwoodtowne Boulevard
Mississauga
L4Z 2G6

From the QEW, take Route 10 west and turn right at Rathborn West, and then right on Sherwoodtowne.

 Mon - Fri: 11 am - 1 am; Sat: 2 pm - 1 am; Sun: 4 pm - 1 am

 Knight's Ale (1.050, dark American ale)
Harvester (1.045, lager [winter]; 1.035 [summer])
Seasonal:
   Winter Warmer (1.070, made with cinnamon, ginger, & almonds)
   IPA (1.059)
   Märzen (1.060, fall)

Brewer: Alan Knight
Beer is all grain, filtered, served under pressure.
Seven other draft beers; several bottled beers available.

 The menu has a large assortment of soups and salads, including Popeye's Spinach Salad, and a seafood chowder. They also offer an array of appetizers, sandwiches, kabobs, pub pies, pasta, and a selection of entrees. Quick business lunches are available during the week. Special desserts include Blackout Tort and Very Berry Cheesecake. Wine and full bar.

This used to be the Luxembourg Brewpub and is now named for owner Brax Diab. It is housed in a yellow brick building. The interior is split level, with the restaurant in the front and the bar in the rear. The brewhouse is visible in the rear of the building. The walls are adorned with Canadian breweriana. Brewery tours are available. Ask about the Mug Club.

♪ live music Thurs-Sat (folk, rock, blues); background music other times

 2   patio   darts

$$$ AE, CA, DC, DS, VI

Brick Brewing

181 King Street, South
Waterloo
N2J 1P7

 (519) 576-9100

Located south of the center of town near the old Labatt's Brewery.

Brick Premium Lager
Brick Red Baron (lager)
Anniversary/Spring Bock (Christmas & spring bock)
Amber Dry
Henninger Kaiser Pils (brewed under license)

The beer is not pasteurized , but is cold, sterile filtered to extend shelf life.

Tours are available Tuesday - Thursday by appointment; one month's notice is required.

Brick is situated in a renovated warehouse built in 1827, and has a traditional European brewhouse. They offer a hospitality room. Beer to go is available in bottles and kegs from their retail store in back. The store also offers a variety of souvenirs such as hats and shirts. They opened December 1984, and became a public corporation in December 1986. Shares are traded on the Toronto Stock Exchange. Beer is available in Beer Stores throughout Ontario.

CC's Brew Pub

6981 Mill Creek Drive, Unit 1
Mississauga
L5N 6B8

 (416) 542-0136

Located at the corner of Mill Creek and Derry, in a white office building.

 11 am - 1 am daily

 CC's Own Lager

Brewer: Murray Voaks
Beer made from malt extract, filtered, and served under pressure. Large selection of bottled beer available.

 CC's started out as a wing house and has expanded their menu from there. They have a large variety of chicken wings and other appetizers, salads, and sandwiches. Entrees include roast beef, fajitas, veal parmigiana, and pizza. They offer a children's menu. Every Sunday is Italian night; Monday is wing night; Tuesday, burger and fries; Wednesday, fish 'n chips. Wines and full bar.

CC's is housed in the first floor of a modern, bright- white office building. Inside, it is a dimly lit, spacious sports bar seating 325. Families are welcome during the day and evening; it is mostly singles at night. They have cigarette happy hour from 5 - 7:30 (in case you didn't know, cigs and alcohol are very expensive in Canada). Thursday night is casino night with special beer prices. Opened April 1991.

♪ live music Monday evening (style varies); Tuesday - country music; Wed - Sat - DJ & dancing; Sunday - karaoke night

EVENTS: Halloween, St. Patrick's Day, Beach Party,

 12, large screen, and 2 dishes   4 pool tables, darts, videos, NTN

$$$ AE, CA, DS, VI

CEEPS
Barney's

 (519) 432-1425

671 Richmond Street
London
N6A 3G7

Located near the University of Western Ontario.

 11 am - 1 am daily

 CEEPS Lager (1.048)
Seasonal:
 Wheat

Brewer: Charles MacLean
300 hectoliters
Seven-eight guest beers on draft, 40+ bottled beers.

 Burgers, club sandwiches, and daily specials. Wine and full bar at CEEPS.

This is actually two pubs, located across the hall from each other, and served by the same brewery. Barney's is a businessmen's bar. CEEPS is your basic student tavern, with brewhouse in the front corner, together they seat 300. Opened April 1991.

 background music - Barney's   6 at CEEPS; 2 at Barney's

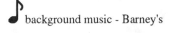 two patios   CEEPS - pool

Charley's Tavern

4715 Tecumseh Road, East
Windsor
N8T 1B6

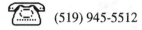 (519) 945-5512

At the corner of Tecumseh and Pillette Roads, ten minutes from the tunnel on the east end.

 Mon - Sat: 11 am - 1 am; Sunday: noon - 1 am

 TimeOut Lager
TimeOut Ale

Brewer: Mike Dumochelle

 Food selections are limited to bar snacks and catering by Pizza King. They bill themselves as "the best lunch bucket in Canada."

This is a typical Ontario sports tavern located one mile from Chrysler's mini van plant. They have a dance floor. Clientele ranges from 19 to 90 years old with a mix of white and blue collar types. Souvenirs are available for sale.

 live - top forty on Tues. & Wed., country western (Sat.); karaoke on Sun. & Mon.; background (top 40)

 patio (seats 150)   12 (2 dishes and a 100" screen)

 pool, pinball for 75

Conners Brewing

227 Bunting Road
St. Catharines
L2M 3Y2

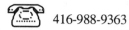 416-988-9363

Conners Best Bitter (ale)
Conners Ale
Conners Special Draft (ale)
Conners Imperial Stout (ale)

Brewer: Liam McKenna.
Beer is all grain; batch size is 20 hectoliters.

Tours are available by appointment only. They require that you call one week in advance; best time to call is from 9 am - 4 pm, Monday - Friday. A tasting room is available. Beer to go in mixed six-packs, 12-packs, and kegs (10L, 20L, 30L, and 58.6 L). Opened in January 1991.

Creemore Springs Brewery

139 Mill Street (P.O. Box 369)
Creemore
L0M 1G0

 (705) 466-2531

Located in Creemoreouth of Collingwood.

Creemore Springs Premium Lager (1.047)

Brewer: Kurtis Zeng
Beer made with two and six-row Canadian and imported malts, and
Czechoslovakian Pilsner hops. They use spring water and employ no ad-
juncts, additives, or chemicals.

Creemore is a handsome brewery located in a restored 1890s building which was once
the May Hardware Store. They have no sales team. Bars must approach them and must
pass muster to be allowed to sell Creemore Lager. Their beer is sold in bottles and
kegs.

They have a retail store with bottles and souvenirs. Tours are available by appointment.

Denison's Brewing (Chophouse & Fish Grille)
Growlers Bar
Conchy Joe's Oyster Bar

75 Victoria Street
Toronto
M5C 2B1

(416) 360-5877 Denison's
(416) 360-5836 Growlers

Located at the corner of Victoria and Lombard in downtown Toronto.

 Mon - Sat: 11:30 - 1 am; closed Sunday

Growler's Lager (1.047, filtered Pils)
Growler's Lager (unfiltered)
Royal Dunkel (1.053, Munich dunkel)

Seasonal:
  Bock (1.067, Jan-Mar)
  Weizen (1.050, Apr-Sept)
  Spezial (1.053, Oct)
  Märzen (1.054, Oct-Jan)

Brewer: Michael Hancock
Beer is all grain and served under pressure.
Seventeen bottled beers. The Royal Dunkel and Weizen are unfiltered.
Hancock worked at Molson for twelve years before coming to Denison's.

Denison's offers full service, lunch and pre-theater dining, featuring an extensive list of beef, pork, fowl, and fish. Conchy Joe's has a raw bar featuring oysters and clams, as well as steamed shellfish, appetizers, chowders, fish entrees, pasta, sandwiches, burgers, and desserts. Growler's includes many of the Conchy Joe's cooked items, plus salads and pizza. About 20 wines and full bar are available at all three restaurants. Two independently run kitchens.

The complex of three glitzy restaurants and a brewery are located in a historic red and yellow brick building. The brewing operation is in the center of the building with the restaurants wrapped around the brewhouse on three levels. The brewhouse is visible through glass from all three of the restaurants. Growlers (in the basement) has a serpentine copper-topped bar and wrap-around booths. Tours of the brewery are available by appointment. Opened November 1989.

♪ Denison's & Conchy Joe's -- soft background
Growler's -- moderate (videos too)

  pay 3

 Conchy Joe's & Denison's

$$$ AE, CA, DC, VI

Granite Brewery

 (416) 322-0723

245 Eglinton Avenue, East
Toronto
M4P 3B7

Located on the corner of Eglington Avenue and Mt. Pleasant.

 11:30 am - 1 am daily

Best Bitter (1.046, English bitter)   Peculiar (1.056, strong ale)
Best Bitter Dry Hopped (1.046)   Keefe's Irish Stout (1.042)

Brewer: Ron Keefe
Beers are all grain and unfiltered; dispensed from serving tanks; served under pressure, with the exception of the Best Bitter Dry Hopped; Try the Black and Tan (Bitter mixed with Stout) or the Amber and Tan (Bitter mixed with Peculiar). Three guest drafts and 25 bottled beers. Don't leave Toronto without trying the Best Bitter Dry Hopped.

 The cuisine offers a mix from down-home cooking to exotic European. Appetizers include artichoke dip, garlic herb mussels, and bruschetta. For entrees, try the traditional fish 'n chips, burgers, shrimp and sausage jambalaya, Spanish paella, raspberry curry chicken, or a variety of stir-fries. Soups, salads, stews, chili, sandwiches and desserts round out the menu and, of course, don't forget to check the board for daily specials. Menus available in braille! Several wines and full bar .

They occupy the ground level of the Storey Building. It overlooks a private garden and covered outdoor patio. The interior offers four distinct spaces: the library, with seating for 30; the bar, with space for 30; the snug, a quiet space for 28; and the brew room with seating for 110. The brew room has a fireplace, plush carpeting, and a long, wooden racing shell hanging from the ceiling. The latter two rooms have a view of the brewery. They have another brewery in Halifax. T-shirts and other merchandise are on sale. Opened October 1991.

EVENTS: St. Patrick's Day, Anniversary Party darts, board games

 2

  free

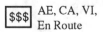 AE, CA, VI,
En Route

Great Lakes Brewing

 (416) 255-4510

30 Queen Elizabeth Boulevard
Etobicoke
M8Z 1L8

From the QEW, take exit 142, go north on Islington Avenue, right on The Queen's Way, then right on Plastics Avenue, and finally left on Queen Elizabeth. It's on the left side of the street.

 Great Lakes Lager (1.044)

Brewer: Bruce Cornish
Beer made with two row Canadian malt, Goldings, Hallertauer, and Northern Brewer hops.

Tours available but reservations are suggested. They have a retail outlet selling keg beer and souvenirs. They have six beer tanks outside. This brewery originally opened in Brampton, closed, and then reopened in Etobicoke.

Hart Breweries

 (613) 253-4278

175 Industrial Avenue
Carleton Place
K7C 3V7

 Hart Amber Ale (1.052)

Beer is all grain and made from Canadian two-row, chocolate, and Karastan malts, corn syrup, and roasted wheat, and Cascade, Hallertauer, Tettnanger, and Willamette hops.

Tours are offered--please call for reservations. They brew Dragon's Breath for Kingston Brewing. They are using open fermentation vessels. Much of the brewhouse is from the old Ottawa Valley Brewing Company. Beer is distributed in bottles and kegs. Opened in the fall of 1991.

Heidelberg Restaurant & Brewery

2 King Street (P.O. Box 116)
Heidelberg
 (519) 699-4413
N0B 1Y0

Right in the center of town, at the corner of regional roads 15 and 16.

 Mon - Thurs: 11 am - midnight; Fri - Sat: 11 am - 1 am; Sun: noon - 8 pm

 O.B. Draft (4.5% alc., lager; stands for "Our Beer")

Brewer: Howie MacMillan
Beer made from malt extract and dispensed from serving tanks. A few other drafts and bottled beers available.

 Dinner entrees include smoked pork hock, ribs & pigtail combo, weiner schnitzel, chicken, roast beef, country sausage, and trout. Variety of sandwiches, side orders, such as battered onion rings and chicken wings. Different dinner special each night. Half-size dinners available for children. Full bar.

Built in 1838, in the heart of Amish and Mennonite country, the Old Heidelberg was the first licensed brewpub in central Ontario. It is the social gathering place for the town and has a rustic feel to it.The brewhouse is on the left, behind glass, as you enter the dining room. The the bar is in the rear, and there is a separate game room on the side. Fake wood beams and neon beer signs make up the decor. Caps and T- shirts for sale. Banquet facilities. They began brewing August 1986.

 honkey tonk piano every day; sing along Fri & Sat 7 - 11   2

EVENTS: St. Patrick's Day

 Rooms available in new 16-room Heidelberg Motel next door.

 shuffleboard, pool, miniature golf, and video

  CA, VI

Jolly Friar Brewpub & Dining Lounge

320 Bay Street
Sault Ste. Marie
P6A 1X1

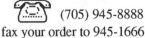 (705) 945-8888
fax your order to 945-1666

In downtown, across from the Memorial Gardens (the main arena).

 Mon - Sat: 11:30 am - 2 am; closed Sunday

Friar's Ale
Friar's Oktoberfest
Dales Bitter
Strong Bitter
Brown Ale
Stout
Bock

Draught Bitter
Pilsner Light

Seasonal:
  Wheat Beer
  Christmas Ale (cranberry)
  Sparrowhawk Porter

Brewers: Dale Mammar and John Sicoli
Beer is made from malt extract (with some grain
added), filtered, and served under pressure.

 The cuisine is English and Canadian. Popular items include beer battered fish 'n chips,home smoked meats, steak 'n kidney pie, and Scottish eggs.

This is an English-Canadian pub with a old timie, neighborhood pub atmosphere. The interior decor is what they describe as a "pub/roadhouse style." They offer a beer and wine making demonstration every Monday. Wine and full bar available.

 live music - weekends (country, English, soft rock); background (soft to moderate)

 2

EVENTS: Saginaw Friendship Games Dart Tournament, St. Patty's Day Buffet, New Year's Party, Super Bowl Party

 darts

$$$ AE, CA, VI

Kingston Brewing
The Pilot House of Kingston

 (613) 541-1218

34 Clarence Street
Kingston
K7L 4V1

Located one block from City Hall, the tourist information center, and the downtown Marina.

 11 am - 1 am daily

Regal Lager (1.045)
Dragon's Breath Ale (1.050, cask conditioned)
Downtown Brown (1.048)
Dragon's Breath Pale Ale (1.049)

Seasonal:
 Strong Autumn Ale
 Bock (spring)

Brewster: Marta Turner

They offer both cask-conditioned beers and beers served under pressure. Guinness on draft: large selection of bottled imported beers. Dragon's Tooth Pale Ale available in 12- oz. bottles (brewed under contract at Hart Breweries.)

They offer a wide selection of appetizers, sandwiches using bread baked daily on the premises, salads, burgers, chicken, smoked meats, and fish and chops--dryland New Zealand lamb chops that is! Check out the daily specials with Thursday for curry specials and Friday for Mexican. They serve wines made on the premises. Full bar available.

They are housed in a historical, limestone building dating to 1860. This neighborhood, English pub is multi-leveled with the brewery visible behind the bar and the wine room on display downstairs. Decorations include a large collection of beer towels, beer trays, and posters from other brewpubs. Opened April 1986.

EVENTS: Chili Fest Founder - 1st Saturday in October.

♪ background - moderate

  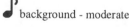   darts

 pay

$$$ AE, CA, DC, VI, En Route

KINGSTON BREWING COMPANY

Lighthouse Brewpub
Flying Dutchman Hotel
The Motel

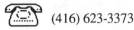 (416) 623-3373

143 Duke Street
Bowmanville
L1C 2W4

Located at Liberty Street South, at Highway 401, Interchange 432.

 Mon: 11 am - 5 pm; Tues - Wed: 11 am 8 pm; Thurs: 11 am - midnight
Fri: 11 am - 12:45 am; Sat: noon - 12:45 am; Sun: noon - 4 pm

 Beer brewed on an irregular basis and made from malt extract.

Brewer: Christopher Mendez

 Offer a variety of appetizers, sandwiches, entrees, and deseerts. Try the prime
rib. Daily specials are offered. Wine and full bar.

This family- style brewpub, featuring wooden booths and tables was founded in 1990.
It has a separate gameroom.

 background, DJ after 9 pm on Thurs   pool and videos

 58 rooms

  AE, CA, DC,
VI, En Route

Lion Brewery, Museum, & Malt House
Huether Hotel

 (519) 886-3350

59 King Street, North
Waterloo
N2J 2X2

Located on the north side of the downtown, on the corner of King and Princess.

 Mon - Sat: 11 am - 1 am; Sun: 5 pm - 1 am

Lion Lager (1.046)	Adlys Ale (1.052)
Lion Lite Lager	English Ale (1.056)
Huether Premium Lager (1.046)	Lion Dry

Brewer: Kelly Adlys
Beer is all grain; the two ales mixed make a nice black and tan.

They have a great selections of appetizers, including gourmet, breaded chicken wings; chicken fingers and fries; potato skins; deep fried wontons; and nachos. Full dinners include roast beef, rolled ribs, roast chicken, schnietzel, and grilled ham steak. In addition, the menu features salads, hot sandwiches, seafood, a large selection of sandwiches, pizza, and a deli bar. Several wines; full bar.

This brewpub is located in a four-story building which housed a brewery and inn, dating from 1842. The Victorian facade was added in 1880. The restored building now has rented rooms for University of Waterloo students, a movie theater, dining room and museum, a high-ceilinged, stone rathskeller, a large billiard hall, and a karaoke bar. All of the walls throughout the two bottom floors are adorned with pictures and breweriana from the old hotel-brewery and old Waterloo (called Berlin until the First World War). The dining room and vaulted rathskeller have beautifully restored stone floors, and stone and brick walls. Customers include families, students, and off-duty police. They sponsor a local junior hockey team. This brewpub is a total beer-breweriana-dining experience; so, put it on your "must list" when visiting Ontario. Stop in and see the U-Brew it place (The Lion Beer Factory) next door, owned by the same family. Facilities throughout can accommodate 900. Despite the name, they do not have rooms for guests. Don't miss the barrel-making display. Souvenirs for sale. Opened in 1987.

♪ live music Sunday night; Karaoke Thurs - Sat night and Sunday 5 pm - 1 am, exotic dancing (check for days and times)

 several, & a large screen, & 2 satellite dishes

 pool, snooker, darts, shuffleboard, videos

$$$ CA, VI

Marconi's Restaurant & Brewery
Journey's End Suites

262 Carlingview
Etobicoke
M9W 5G1

 (416) 675-6854

Located near the Toronto Airport, at the corner of Dixon and Carlingview, off the main lobby of the Journey's End Suites.

 11:30 am - 1 am daily

 Marconi's Dry Lite
Marconi's European Lager
Superiore (contract, brewed by Algonquin)

Seasonal:
Octoberfest
Christmas Beer

Brewers: Alda & Gord Slater
Beer is all grain, filtered, and served under pressure.

Marconi's features an array of appetizers, pizza, Mexican dishes, sandwiches, burgers, fajitas, meat and fish entrees. Their specialty is a New York steak, pasta, and shrimp combo. They have many pasta entrees and also have a large variety of desserts. Free hors d'oeuvres during happy hour. Lunch buffet and salad bar. Special Sunday brunch. Free soft drinks for the designated driver. They make and serve their own wines. Wine and full bar.

Marconi's currently has a Mexican theme with cactus, fish nets, and mariachi hats adorning the walls, but plan to switch to country and western in the future. The restaurant has a light and airy look with a pastel and white color theme and many picture windows. Brewery tours are offered. Opened in 1990. The original Marconi's Restaurant is in Sudbury (central Ontario).

♪ live music on occasion; background music other times (soft-moderate); karaoke Friday & Saturday night

 Journey's End Suites: tel. (416) 674-8442   3 and a big screen

 pool (hexagonal), foosball,
videos, darts

 patio

  $$$ AE, VI, en Route

Master's Brasserie & Brewpub
Skyline Hotel

330 Queen Street
Ottawa
K1A 5A5

 (613) 594-3688

 Mon - Sat: 11 am - 1 am; Sun: noon - 10 pm

 Master's Ale (5% alc.)
Master's Lager (5% alc.)

Beer made from malt extract. One domestic draft and several bottled domestics and imports.

 The menu offers quiche, wings, stromboli and homemade bread. Entrees include Cornish pasty, bratwurst, prime rib, seafood, lasagna, and chili. Check out the seafood bar, soups, salads, and English rarebit. Desserts include chocolate cheesecake and strawberry-rhubarb pie. House wines and full bar.

This trendy brewpub is located in the hotel's old bakery. It features art deco style. Clientele includes area residents and the civil servants working in the area. Aging tanks are visible from the bar and dining area.

  pay

 AE, CA, DC, DS,
VI, En Route

Niagara Falls Brewing

 416-374-1166

6863 Lundy's Lane
Niagara Falls
L2G 1V7

Near the corner of Dorchester Road, near the QED.

Niagara Trapper Premium Lager (1.051)
Gritstone Premium Ale (1.057, dark ale)
Olde Jack (1.062, bitter strong ale)
Trapper Light (1.045)
Brock's Extra Stout (1.057)

Seasonal:
  Eisbock (1.060, specialty strong beer -- 8 %)
  Maple Wheat (1.076 -- 8.5 %)

Brewers: Wally Moroz and John Lavery.
Beer is all grain, 60- barrel batch size; annual capacity: 11,000 hectoliters.

Reservations are generally not needed as tours are given every day, seven days a week. Call between 9 am and 5 pm for tour times. However, group tours of 10 - 50 people require reservations. Beer is available for sampling only in the tasting room. Beer to go in the retail store in 341 ml. bottles, six and 12-packs, 26-oz. bottles, quart bottles, and kegs. Check out the T-shirts and other types of breweriana in the retail store.

Brewing Company

Port Arthur Brasserie & Brewery

901 Red River Road
Thunder Bay
P7B 1K3

 (807) 767-4415

Exit off Expressway (# 1117) to Red River Road.

 Mon. - Sat.: 11 am - 1 am; Sunday: 11 am - 11 pm

Arthur's Lager
Seasonal:
   Octoberfest
   Halloween Witches Brew

Seasonal (cont'd):
   Christmas Beer
   St. Patrick's Ale

Brewer: John Tilbury
Selected domestics and imports available.

 A wide selection of food much like the roadhouses of old is offered. Soups, salads, steaks, pasta dishes, Mexican dishes, seafood and stir fries.

Tanks are glassed in behind the bar and are visible from everywhere in the pub. This neighborhood bar is decorated with reds and greens and has many original neon lights. The bar is in the middle with dining areas on both sides. They sponsor a four-man volleyball team that plays on their beach volleyball court. Seats 150. Opened in 1988.

 background, DJ at night   patio (with heaters) for 120   20

EVENTS: St. Patrick's Day, Halloween, Christmas Beach Party, Friday Night Party

 NTN, volleyball (sand court)

    AE, CA, DC, DS, VI, En Route

Rotterdam Brewing

 (416) 868-6882

600 King Street West
Toronto
M5V 1M6

Located at the corner of Portland and King.

 11:30 am - 1:30 am daily

Rotterdam Lager (1.045)
Rotterdam Scotch Ale (1.055)
Rotterdam Pilsner (1.054)
Rotterdam All Night Lager
Seasonal:
  IPA
  Octoberfest
  Nut Brown Ale
  White Cap Ale
  Tartan Ale
  Framboise
  Doppelpils

Seasonal (cont'd):
  Weizenbock
  Irish Stout
  Father John's Ale
  Dogbolter
  Dunkel Lager
  Amber Weizen
  Milk Stout
  Cherrywood Lager
  Weizbier
  Edelbock

Brewer: Joel Manning
Beers are all grain, filtered, and cask conditioned.
House pints special 'til 8 pm. Forty drafts, including Smythwicks, Guinness, Conners, Murphy's, Younger's Tartan, and Stones Best. More than 200 bottled beers.

 For lunch they have starters such as soups, salads, homemade bread, fried calamari, guacamole, nachos, and spicy chicken wings. There is a lengthy list of entrees, including sirloin steak, grilled German sausage, pastas, fish, smoked turkey, many sandwiches, and a falafel platter. They also have Rotter-Damn good burger and fries, and daily specials. Dessert entrees include Old World Black Forest Cake, apple pizza, fresh cranberry cheesecake. The dinner menu is equally inviting. Wine and full bar. They have their own bakery. Several items are prepared in beer.

Rotterdam is housed in a century-old, red-brick building. Inside it has beautiful old-fashioned street lamps, stone walls, marble topped tables, a long bar, and windows onto the street. The copper jacketed brewing vessels, on the second level gallery, are visible through the glass ceiling. There is a basement with a nice old flagstone floor.

 background rock (medium-loud)　 2　 tree-lined patio

 pool　

 $$$ AE, CA, DC, DS, VI, En Route

Sleeman Brewing & Malting

551 Clair Road West
Guelph
N1H 6H9

 (519) 822-1834

Located on the south side of Guelph.

Sleeman Cream Ale
Sleeman Silver Creek Lager
Sleeman Premium Light

The beer is brewed from water coming from deep wells. No additives or preservatives are used and they use Canadian two- and six-row malt and some yellow corn grits. They fire brew in copper kettles.

Beer is sold at the brewery along with a variety of collectibles. Their beer is also sold in Beer Stores throughout Ontario. They do not open on Sundays. They also contract brew Stroh's and Stroh's Light. Sleeman Brewing originally opened in 1834, but was sold in 1933 marking the end of Sleeman beer until they reopened in 1988 with the backing of Stroh's. Motto: "Sleeman . . . the choice is clear."

Spruce Goose Brewing

 (416) 485-4121

130 Eglinton Avenue, East
Toronto
M4P 2X9

Located in downtown Toronto, on the north side of Eglington Avenue, west of the Vinefera (brewpub).

 Mon - Fri: 11 am - 1 am; Sat: 5 pm - 1 am; closed Sunday

 Canuck Lager (1.050)
Amber Ale (1.050)
Seasonal:
    4% Lager
    Dry Beer

Brewer: Charles MacLean
The beer is all grain, filtered, and served under pressure; 250 hectoliters.
Ten-twelve guest beers on tap; 20-30 bottled beers.

 Their appetizers, include Great Wall Spring Rolls, Sprucechetta (Goose-style Italian bread topped with herbs and mixed cheeses), and wings. They offer a variety of salads, pizza, burgers, and sandwiches, including the Howard Hughes Original (baguette stuffed with onion sprouts, ham, and cream cheese) and the Jane Russell (croissant served open faced with Monterey Jack, ham, sweet pepper, tomato, and onion sprouts). Entrees include Szechwan chicken, shrimp, and vegetarian lasagna. The late night menu includes shrimp and chicken, nachos, wings, and pizza. Check out the daily specials. Wine and full bar.

The front entrance opens onto a large two-story gallery where a large model of the Spruce Goose hangs from the ceiling, over the dance floor. There are two bars on the main floor and one on the lower level. The back bar on the main level is decorated with a full-size canoe, a stuffed goose, and an old airplane propeller. The brewery is toward the back on the top floor. The Spruce Goose airplane theme permeates this 9,000 sq. feet establishment, with photos of Howard, Jane, and friends along with drawings of the airplane. The very large dance floor on the lower level becomes a discotheque at night; business people predominate during the day. This trendy brewpub opened October 1991.

♪ DJ, loud rock music at night 3 pool and video games

 seats 200

 pay during the day;
free at night

Tapsters Smokehouse Grill & Brewery
Metro Hotel
100 Brittania Road East
Mississauga
L4Z 2G1

 (416) 890-8909

From the QEW, take route 10 north, cross over route 403, continuing until you reach an old red-brick church and cemetery on the right (Britannia Church)--the next street is Brittania Road East--turn right.

 11 am - 1:30 am daily

 Dark Lager (1.044, Dusseldorfer dark ale)
Blond Ale (1.040)

Seasonal:
  SpringBock (1.060)

Seasonal (cont'd)
  Wheat Beer (1.035
  Best Bitter (1.050)
  Scotch Ale (1.050)

Beer is all grain, filtered, and served under pressure.
Five drafts and 40 bottled beers (many imports)

Appetizers include soups, shrimp, escargot, smoked salmon, and quesadillas. There are many salads, pastas, and sandwiches. Beef and pork, grilled kabobs, sizzling fajitas, chicken, and seafood are offered as entrees. Kiddie menu offered with free drink refills. Several wines and full bar available.

Tapsters is housed in a modern building with plate glass windows and is attached to a hotel called the Metro Hotel (ask the manager about Tapsters special patron rates). It is casual and open with unique displays of hundreds of imported beer bottles and cans. It caters to the business crowd. They opened in the summer of 1987. Brewery tours are available. Their motto: "In heaven there is no beer, that's why we 'brew' it here."

live music on occasion (light rock & roll)
background music (moderate)

 wide screen

 video, pool, shuffleboard
NTN Interactive Trivia

EVENTS: Patio Party, Customer Appreciation Party

 Metro Hotel: tel. (416) 890-5700
(free buffet breakfast)

 free

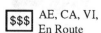 AE, CA, VI,
En Route

Tracks Brewpub

 (416) 453-3063

60 Queen Street East
Brampton
L6V 1A9

From the QEW, take Route 10 north until you reach downtown Brampton. Turn right on Queen Street. Tracks is located one block ahead on the left, in the rear of a building known as The Mill.

 11:30 am - 1:30 am daily

 Old Mill (1.045, amber lager)

Brewer: Alan Knight
Their beer is all grain, filtered, and served under pressure.
Four draft beers and 33 bottled beers (imports and domestics).

 They serve what they refer to as classic Canadian pub food--burgers, sandwiches, stir fries, salads, wings etc. Popular entrees are chili, steak and kidney pie, lasagna and fettucini Alfredo. Monday night is Wing Night. Specials offered every day at lunch and dinner. Wine and full bar.

The building was constructed in the late 1800s as the Brampton Knitting Mills. The exterior is red brick with large windows and features a large, secluded beer garden. The building shakes when trains rumble by, hence the name "Tracks." The interior features red brick and light wood with old wood beams on the ceiling. The exposed beams show off the old pulleys hanging from the ceilings. It offers four distinct areas with a different atmosphere in each. A lounge in rear has wicker tables. Lounge in middle has fireplace, Persian carpet, high-backed chairs, and antique copper doors. The small brewery is in the middle of the bar area. Opened August 1987.

 live music Thurs. - Sat. (pub rock, blues, folk); background music (moderate)

 8   NTN Interactive Trivia Games

 pay parking across
the street

$$$ AE, CA, VI

Upper Canada Brewing

 (416) 534-9281

2 Atlantic Avenue
Toronto
M6K 1X8

Located in central Toronto. From the QEW, exit at Jameson, north to King Street West, go right (east), cross Dufferin, then right (south) on Atlantic to end of street.

Pale Ale
Colonial Stout (1.046)
Dark Ale (1.048)
Lager (1.046)
Light Lager (1.037)
Publican's Special Bitter Ale (1.046)

Rebellion (1.056, malt liquor)
Point Nine
Seasonal:
Wheat
True Bock

Tour times are normally at 4 pm, but special arrangements can be made by calling in advance. Tasting room offers samples of all their beers. They are open seven days a week. Their own retail store has beer for off-premise consumption along with a wide selection of souvenirs such as shirts, caps, glassware and other breweriana. Bottled and draft are available for take out.

Upper Canada was founded in 1985 by Frank Heaps. It is located in an early 1900s brick warehouse. All beers are brewed in conformity with the Bavarian Purity Law of 1516. Water is pure spring water from the Calecdon Hills, 30 miles northwest of Toronto. It is trucked to them daily. They triple cold filter their beers and bottle only in brown glass.

UPPER CANADA
Pale Ale
Brewed to the Highest Standards in the
World to Satisfy the Most Discriminating
Beer Connoisseurs

4.8% alc./vol.

Vinefera Bar & Grill

 (416) 487-9281

150 Eglinton Avenue East
Toronto
M4P 1E8

Located in downtown Toronto on the north side of Eglington, close to the Spruce
Goose and Denison's.

 11:30 am - 1 am daily

 Bavarian Lager

Brewer: Alan Knight
Beer is all grain, filtered and served under pressure.
Four guest drafts.

 A full menu includes soups, salads, appetizers, sandwiches, burgers, pasta, and
pizza. In addition they have a large selection of entrees, including chicken te-
riyaki, sole Florentine, grilled medallions of beef. Check out the daily lunch and
dinner specials. Happy hour: Mon. - Fri. from 3 - 6 pm. Wine and full bar.

The owners are Der Chia Lin from Taiwan, a Ph.D. in Biomechanics and his wife Shou
Lin. The bar is in front and the dining area is in rear. They have cushioned booths.
Old car headlamps decorate the corners of the bar. A small dance floor is on the far
side of the bar. The brewery is in the back, behind glass. Opened March 1992 and began serving their beer January 1993.

 background music; DJ sometimes   7 sets and a dish

 pool

Wellington County Brewery

950 Woodlawn Road West
Guelph
N1K 1B8

 (519) 837-2337

Located on the northeast side of Guelph, on the outskirts of town.

Arkell Best Bitter (1.038)
County Ale (1.052)
Iron Duke (1.065)
Premium Lager
Special Pale Ale (1.045)

Brewer: Michael Stirrup

Wellington County opened in 1985 and is one of the oldest microbreweries in Ontario. They make traditional English brews that are not pasteurized. These ales reflect the British roots of the area. The Special Pale Ale and Premium Lager are available in one-liter bottles. The Arkell Best Bitter, County Ale, and Iron Duke are cask conditioned beers available on draft.

Please make an appointment if you would like to tour the brewery. The retail store is open Monday - Friday, from 9 am - noon and from 1 pm - 5pm.

These real ales are offered in a number of establishments in Ontario. WBR suggests sampling the ales in the Woolwich Arms on Yarmouth Street in Guelph. Having the "privilege" to serve their ales is a process of being "interviewed" and selected. They don't have the need to market their brews in the traditional sense; they market themselves.

Quebec

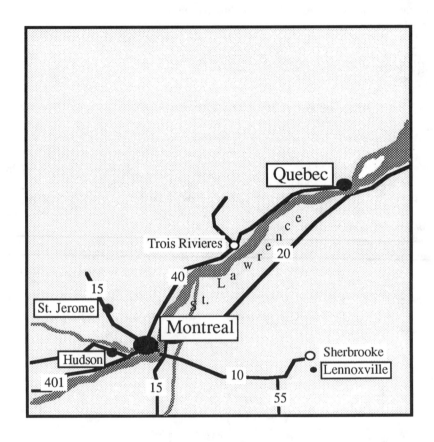

Brasal-Brasserie Allemande

 (514) 365-5050

8477 Cordner
Lasalle (Montreal)
H8N 2X2

Hopps Brau (lager)
Brasal Special (strong lager)
Brasal Light (light lager)
Seasonal:
  Brasal Bock

Brewer: Harold Sowade
Beers are cold aged and filtered. Batch size is 32 hectoliters.

Tours are available weekly and beer is made available for sampling. There is no beer to go. Reservations are required and they request that you call three weeks in advance; call between 8 am - 7 pm, Monday - Friday. Beer is bottled and kegged and is available in over 3,000 outlets. They brew according to the traditional Bavarian Purity Law of 1516.

Brasserie McAuslan

4850 Rue Street, Ambroise, Bureau 100
Montreal
H4C 3N8

☎ (514) 939-3060

Located on the corner of St. Ambroise Street and St. Remi Street in the St. Henri District of Montreal.

St. Ambroise Pale Ale (1.047)
St. Ambroise Oatmeal Stout (1.065)
Griffon Brown Ale (1.045)
Griffon Extra Pale (1.045, Canadian premium ale)

Brewster: Ellen Boonsall

They are housed in a 10,000 sq. ft. industrial building near the historic Lachine Canal and Atwater Outdoor Market. Beer is available for sampling only during tours, held on Wednesday night. Call at least one day in advance for reservations. Best time to call is 8 am - 6 pm, Monday - Friday. Beer is available in 12-oz. bottles and in five-liter kegs. Batch size is 50 hectoliter. Quebec's first microbrewery opened for business in February 1989. Beer is sold widely in city grocery stores.

Brasseurs du Nord

 (514) 438-9060

18 Boulevard J. F. Kennedy # 3
St. Jerome
J7Y 4B4

Located in an industrial park.

Boreale Rousse (1.048, red ale)
Boreale Blonde (1.044, blond ale)
Boreale Noire (1.060, stout)

Brewster: Laura Urtnowski.
Beer is all grain; 14,000 hectoliters.

Tours are offered about once a month with some sampling. Reservations are required at least one week in advance (best time to call is late morning). Beer is available in both bottles and kegs. Batch size is 30 hectoliters. They recommend Boulevard, St. Laurent in downtown St. Jerome as the best place to taste.

LES BRASSEURS DU
NORD INC.

G.M.T. Brassuers

📞 (514) 274-4941

5710 Garnier Street
Montreal
H2G 2Z7

Near Rosemont Boulevard in the Rosemont area.

 Belle Guele (1.049, lager)

Brewer: Andre Lafreniere
Beer is all grain.

Beer is available for sampling on tours. Reservations are required with one month's notice expected. Best time to call is 9 am - 5 pm, Monday - Friday. They market in both bottles and kegs; batch size is 20 hectoliters. Opened in April 1988.

La Cervoise

4457 Boulevard, St. Laurent
Montreal
H2W 1Z8

 (514) 843-6586

Near the corner of Mont and Royal.

 3 pm - 3 am daily

 La Futee (1.045 - 48, lager)
La Main (1.045 - 48, amber ale)
Seasonal:
   Hydromel (1.052, ale mead)
   Oktoberfest (1.050 - 54)

Brewer: Sean Tordon
Two local micros on draft (Boreale & Belle Guelle); bottled beers (a selection from Belgium, England, France, Denmark, Germany, Norway, and Mexico).

 Appetizers include chips, popcorn, and pretzels to accompany the French style hot dogs.

The brewpub is part of a main downtown strip. The front is like a garage door and opens wide during warmer weather. It offers a front row seat for the best people watching in town! The interior is informal in style. The clientele ranges from businesspeople to artsy students.

 background music - soft to moderate

 darts, pool

$$$ AE, CA, VI

Cheval Blanc

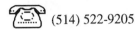 (514) 522-9205

809 Ontario Street
Montreal
H2L 1P1

Located on the northeast corner of St. Hubert and behind the Voyaageur Bus Station, near St. Denis Street. The Berre - Uquam metro stop is nearby.

   Mon - Sat: 3 pm - 2 am; Closed Sunday

Amber Ale	Seasonal:
Pale Ale	The Titanic (Christmas beer)
Golden Wheat Ale	Cap Tourmente (wheat)
Brown Ale	Loch Ness (Scottish Ale)
	Maple Syrup Beer

Brewer: Jerome Denys

Beer is all grain, recipes are changed four times annually to fit the season. Selected brews are refermented in 750- ml. bottles (cherry and raspberry for example)

 They offer appetizers and a limited menu including Hungarian sausage and tacos. Go for the beer!

This is an upscale tavern that was remodelled from the family's old tavern that they have operated since 1937. Seats 80. When it was opened by Jerome Denys in 1987 it was the province's first brewpub.

 live music on Sunday (rock), background

Crocodile Club

 (514) 733-2125

5414 Gatineau
Montreal
H3G 1Z5

Located at the corner of Gatineau and Lacombe, near the Cote-des-Neiges metro stop.

 Mon - Sat: 11:30 am - 3 am; Sunday: 5 pm - 1 am

 L'Alligator (ale)
La Cayman (brown ale)
La Crocodile (ale)
Le Gavial (lager)
Croc Pale Ale (contract brewed)

Brewer: Guy Meilleur

 Limited menu includes appetizers and finger foods--wings, burgers and fries.
Evening serving hours are from 4 - 9 pm.

They have a California style with a Canadian accent. The exterior is covered in pressed chrome. It features a bar on the first floor, pool playing area upstairs, and a disco downstairs. They are located near the University of Montreal and have a large student clientele.

 background music, disco in basement 7 patio

 pool, pinball

$$$ AE, CA, DC,
DS, VI

Crocodile Club St. Laurent

4238 St. Laurent
Montreal
H2W 1Z3

 (514) 848-0044

Located near the St. Laurent metro stop. St. Laurent is the main dividing line between East and West.

 Mon - Fri: 11:30 am - 3 am; Sat: 5 pm - 3 am; closed Sunday

 La Crocodile (blond ale)

Brewer: Guy Meilleur
Bottled beers include 12 imports and 25 domestics.

 The cuisine is fine French dining and features a variety of meat and fish entrees: lamb, veal, steak, salmon, and swordfish. Dinner specials are offered each night such as "Surf and Turf," Leg of Lamb with Wine and Shrimp with Wine. There are all you can eat and drink specials.

Four levels offer from bottom to top: a disco, bar, restaurant, and brewery. A sky dome at the bar gives a view of the brewhouse from anywhere. Lots of light, chrome, and stainless steel define the look. It features a fountain and has a capacity for 800 with seating for 140 in the restaurant.

 background, disco   terrace    giant screen

 video, electronic darts

$$$ AE, CA, DC, DS, VI, En Route

Golden Lion Brewing

6 College Street (P.O. Box 474)
Lennoxville
J1M 1Z6

 (819) 565-1015

On the corner of Queen and College Streets, at the traffic lights.

 Mon - Sat: 10 am - 3 am, closed Sunday

 Township's Pale Ale (1.040, Canadian pale ale)
Lion's Pride (1.042, British brown ale)
Bishop's Best Bitter (1.042, bitter)
Black Fly Stout (1.045)
Seasonal:
   Cream Ale (1.038)
   Biere d'Amour (1.042, "love tonic")
   Santa's Suds (1.042, Christmas Pilsner)

Brewer: Stan Groves.
Beers are all grain, filtered, and served under pressure.
Thirty bottled beers also available.

 The brewpub offers Mexican and Cajun pub fare with chicken wings, potato skins, burgers, and burritos. They also offer wine and a full bar.

This English style, neighborhood pub opened for business in 1973 and added the brewery later.

 live music: Tues (acoustic) & Thurs (rock/blues) - winter

background music (moderate)

 free

 $$$ VI

L'Inox

37 Rue Street Andre
Quebec City
G1K 8T3

 (418) 692-2877

 noon - 3 am daily

 Trouble Fete (white beer)
Trois de Pique (bock)
Bitter (English Ale)
Transit (European pale ale)

Seasonal:
Stout
Viking Beer (honey and fruit ale)

Brewer: Pierre Turgeon

 They have no kitchen but offer three different European hot dog sausage plates.

An urban style brewpub with old stone, brick and metal. It is decorated with an art exhibition that changes each month. The bar is in the middle with tables to each side. This is a place to talk and be with friends. Began serving their own beer in 1987.

 live music - Thurs. night (folk, folk rock, background)   seats 90

 pool, darts, videos

 $$$ AE, CA, VI

Massawippi Brewing

33 Winder (P.O. Box 34)
Lennoxville
J1M 1Z6

 (819) 564-2444

Massawippi Bitter
Massawippi Dark Dutch (amber ale)
Massawippi Special Brau
Massawippi Quai Lager
Pale Ale
Seasonal:
   Massawippi Stout

Brewer: Scott Thompson

They brew according to the Bavarian Purity Law of 1516. No direct sales are permitted from the brewery in Quebec. Beers are available in Montreal and eastern Quebec. The name Massawippi comes from the river that flows near the brewery. Founded in June of 1986, it is Quebec's first microbrewery. They originated as the Pilsen Brewpub in North Hatley. The Pilsen was later sold and they moved to Lennoxville. The beer is still featured in the Pilsen which offers fine hospitality, beer, and bed and breakfast.

Mon Village Brewery

514-458-5331

2760 Cote Street Charles Road (P.O. Box 794)
Hudson
J0P 1H0

Located off exit 22 of Highway 417, the Trans-Canada Highway.

  11:30 am - 2 am daily (kitchen closes at 10 pm)

 Dark Gold
Gold

 Fine dining includes soups, appetizers, and entrees such as corned beef and cabbage, BBQ ribs, steak, chicken and scampi. Try the pig's knuckles served with potatoes and sauerkraut. Desserts include cheesecake and pecan pie served with specialty coffees. Full bar and wine available. Kitchen closes from 3 - 5 pm and after 10 pm. Sunday buffet offered.

A country inn in a charming old wooden farmhouse built in 1829, featuring a bar, drinking loft, and several lounges and dining rooms. It features lots of wood, stained glass, fireplaces and historic farm tools. The old bakery was converted into the brewhouse.

 background music   terrace

$$$ AE, CA, DC, DS, VI, En Route

Saskatchewan

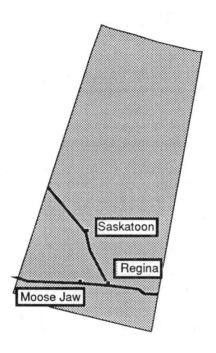

Barley Mill Brewpub

 (306) 949-1500

6807 Rochdale Boulevard, N.W.
Regina
S4X 2Z2

Located in the Rochdale neighborhood, in northwest Regina.

  Mon. - Sat.: 11 am - 2 am; Sunday: noon - 11 pm

  Prairie Lager
Barley Mill Classic Lager
George Edgar Ale
Golden Grain Lager
Castaway Electric Pilsner

Brewer: Perry Dunn
Two domestic drafts; bottled Corona, Molson, and Labatt.

  They offer a variety of homemade selections including snacks, sandwiches, burgers, soups, salads, ribs and desserts.

The Barley Mill is a replica of an frontier-style bar with 35' stand-up bar, mirrors, stained glass, and stone pillars. Four Victorian mermaid lamps light the seating area and Maltese shields and Byzantine eagles decorate the walls. The ten-hectoliter brewhouse is opposite the bar near the front entrance. They have been winners of the local best bar contest. This is one of four brewpubs owned by the Dunn Group. Clientele is a mix of blue and white collar. Age 19 + required for entry. Opened on June 15, 1989.

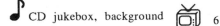 CD jukebox, background   6

  pool, shuffleboard, darts, board games

 $$$ CA, VI

Bonzini's Brew Pub

 (306) 586-3553

4634 Albert Street, South
Regina
S4S 6B4

Located at the corner of Albert Street and Gordon Road in South Regina.

 Mon - Thurs: 11:30 am - 2 am; Fri - Sat.: 11:30 am - 2 am;
Sun: 1 pm - 12:30 am

 Bear Lager
Great Plains Pilsener
Red Tail Ale
Nut Brown Ale
Black & Tan

Brewer: Philip Shaw
Beer is made from malt extract and filtered.
Four guest drafts and 21 bottled beers.

The pub offers pub grub such as toast, fries, meatballs, shrimp, nachos and wings. In addition, there is a large selection of burgers, sandwiches and a variety of pasta dishes. Check out the specials made fresh daily, including the dessert of the day, or their Bonzini's Special Coffee for the designated driver. Wine served; full bar.

This cottage style structure has a large two story turret and stained glass windows, with seating for 150 on a landscaped outdoor patio. The focal point of the interior is a solid oak, U-shaped bar that is 100 feet in length with a nine- foot copper dispenser behind the bar. Exposed beams and neon signs grace the interior with its seating for 200. Opened on June 1991 and owned by NHL vet, Dave Dunn.

♪ live music- special occasions only; background music - juke box (moderate)

EVENTS: Great Caesar Contest (charity event in March)

 5   darts, pool

     free

 CA, VI

Brewsters Brewpub at Cornerstone Inn

 (306) 694-5580

8 Main Street, North
Moose Jaw
S6H 3J6

Located on the corner of Main and Manitoba.

 Mon - Tues: 11 am - 1:30 am, Wed - Sat.: 11 am - 2 am; closed Sunday

Hammerhead Red Ale (1.046)
Palliser Pale Ale (1.046)
Qu'Appelle Valley Brown Ale (1.046)
Big Horn Bitter (1.046)
Shaughnessy Stout (1.058)
Brewsters Barley Wine (1.074)
Seasonal:
  Brewster IPA (1.046)
  Ginger Ale (1.045)
  Original Lager (1.045)

Seasonal (con'td)
  Christmas Ale (1.049,brown ale)
  Flying Frog Lager (1.045)
  Ernest Bay Prem. Pilsner (1.045)
  Wild West Wheat (1.045)
  Rocky Mt. Dark (1.045, lager)
  Continental Light Lager (1.035)
  Cranberry Ale (1.045, pale ale)
  Brewsters Spring Bock (1.055)

Brewer: Stan Gerlach
Beer is all grain, filtered, and served under pressure.
Guest beers include one draft and 15 bottled.

 They offer a limited menu with pub grub and pizzas.

This neighborhood, Canadian brewpub is housed in an 1899 two-storied hotel with refurbished exterior that has been converted to an apartment hotel. The beverage room features ceramic and oak with exterior windows highlighted by stained glass windows. It has a seating capacity of 150. Wine and full bar available. Tours are available and the beverage room offers off-premise sales. They feature a "beer of the week." They began brewing October 1991.

 live music - periodically (blues); background - moderate

 darts, video

 free

 $$$ AE, CA, VI

Brewsters Brew Pub & Brasserie

1832 Victoria Avenue, East
Regina
S4N 7K3

 (306) 761-0784

Located in the east end of Regina, on Victoria Ave. (Transcanada Hwy.).

 Mon - Fri: 11 am - 2 am; Sunday: noon - 8 pm

Hammerhead Red Ale (1.046)
Palliser Pale Ale (1.046)
Qu'Appelle Valley Brown Ale (1.046)
Big Horn Bitter (1.046)
Shaughnessy Stout (1.058)
Brewsters Barley Wine (1.074)
Seasonal:
   Brewster IPA (1.046)
   Ginger Ale (1.045)

Seasonal (cont'd)
   Original Lager (1.045)
   Flying Frog Lager (1.045)
   Ernest Bay Prem. Pilsner (1.045)
   Wild West Wheat (1.045)
   Rocky Mt. Dark (1.045, lager)
   Continental Light Lager (1.035)
   Cranberry Ale (1.045, pale ale)
   Brewsters Spring Bock (1.055)

Beer to go in one-liter bottles and 19-liter kegs.

Choose from wings and ribs, soups and salads, the sandwich and burger bars, and a wide variety of entrees augmented by daily specials. Try the Chicken Kiev, the Halibut 'n Chips or the New York Strip. Desserts include mud pie, New York cheese cake, and their original carrot cake.

Canadian brewpub style in detached building with lots of natural light. It seats 181 inside and 100 on the deck, which also has a loft. Interior decor uses oak and features the brewhouse. They offer a drive through for off-premises sales. Brewery tours offered.

 background - moderate 5

 darts

  free

$$$ AE, CA, VI

Bushwakker Brewing

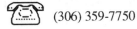 (306) 359-7750

2206 Dewdney Avenue
Regina
S4R 1H3

Located on the corner of Cornwall and Dewdney, in the Strathdee Centre Mall

 Mon - Thurs: 11 am - 1 am; Fri - Sat: 11 am - 2 am; Sun: noon - 9 pm

Granny's Bitter (1.041)
Regina Pale Ale (IPA, 1.041)
Palliser Porter (1.058)
Northern Lights Lager (1.041)
Stubble Jumper Pils (1.048)
Last Mountain Lager (1.047)
Seasonal:
  Pearl Lager (1.034)
  Dark Lager (1.045)

Seasonal (cont'd):
  Harvest Lager (1.053, Maerzen)
  Baron Bock (1.053)
  Summer Wheat (1.041)
  Missiletow Ale (1.076, barley
    wine)
  Cyclone Barley Wine (1.076)
  Wakky Wheat Bock (1.057)
  Chinook ESB (1.057)

Brewer: Scott Robertson
Operates ten hl. brewhouse. Beer to go soon: 22-oz. bottles and 19-liter kegs.

 They have typical pub offering of appetizers, soups, sandwiches, salads, burgers and pasta. Entrees include shepherd's pie, beef pie and bushwakker chili. Entrees are served with homemade beer bread and each entry suggests the house brew to complement the choice. They bill their cuisine as "authentic prairie food" with the Buffalo wings, steamed mussels by the pound, and the Saskatchewan fowl dinner. As if you didn't have enough drinking choices, try a Black & Tan - a blend of the porter & bitter or Sloughshark Lager - a blend of lagers.

The pub is housed in a 75-year-old, restored "catillac" warehouse with post and beam construction with 16" sq. cross sections. The interior decor, described as a converted rustic warehouse, includes an antique, stamped-tin 12' ceiling and old fashioned saloon doors. Lots of natural wood color and shades of green with burnt orange highlights. Clientele varies from professionals, local politicians, labor leaders and civil servants to Bohemians and the Regina police. Seats 150. Happy hour is Monday - Friday from 4 - 7 pm. Homebrewers groups (ALES) meet on 1st Wednesday.

♪ live music occasionally; background music - soft   darts

EVENTS: Medieval Night (near Halloween), Beer Tasting (Sept.), New Years dance.

  free

$$$ AE, CA, DC, VI

**WHERE EVERYONE
FEELS AT HOME.**

Cheers BrewPub & Restaurant
Saskatoon Brewing

2105 8th Street, East #32
Saskatoon
S7H-0T8

 (306) 955-7500

 Brewpub & Off Sales Store: Mon - Sat: 11 am - 2:30 am;
Sunday: 11 am - midnight
Restaurant: Mon - Wed: 11 am - 11 pm; Thurs - Sat: 11 am - midnight;
Sunday: 11 am - 10 pm

 Classic Lager (1.048)
Big Sky Pale Ale (1.044)
Prairie Dark Ale (1.050)
Blackstrap Bock (1.054)

Seasonal:
Pilsner Lite (1.032)
Oktober Fest (1.048)

Brewer: Randy Uytterhagen
Beer is all grain, filtered, and served under pressure.
Two drafts and 24 bottled beers.

 A varied menu offers Cajun, French and Italian. Pub-style foods include Cajun blackened chicken, nachos, quesadillas, and beer battered shrimp. A wide variety of entrees include pasta and filet steak sandwich. The evening specialty is home-smoked salmon. Daily specials include smoked prime rib, chicken en croute, and filet of beef with wild mushroom sauce. Sunday brunch. Wine and full bar available.

This is a European-style, neighborhood English pub located in a strip mall. It features dark stained oak and stained glass windows. Banquet room for 130.

 background (moderate) 4

 darts

 free

 $$$ CA, VI

Clark's Crossing Brewpub

 (306) 384-6633

3030 Diefenbaker
Saskatoon
S7L 7K2

Located in a strip mall on the west side of Saskatoon.

 Mon - Thurs: 11 am - 12:30 am; Fri - Sat: 11 - 2 am; Sun: 2 pm - midnight

 Lager (1.050)
Pilsner (1.050, European amber)
Wheat Ale (1.042)

Brewer: Monty Wood
Beer made from malt extract, filtered, and served under pressure. Three other draft beers and about 20 bottled beers are available.

 They have a pub grub- style menu, with many appetizers, soup, salad, sandwiches, burgers, and pizza. Check for the daily specials. They have a few wines on the menu; full bar.

This is a sports bar which also features many pictures of old Saskatchewan. There are picture windows in the front and the serving tanks are visible in the rear of the pub. The brewhouse is in the basement. Opened October 1990.

 CD jukebox; background music (moderate-loud) 3 and a dish

 pool, pinball, darts

$$$ CA, VI

Fox & Hounds Brewpub

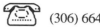 (306) 664-2233

7 Assiniboine Drive
Saskatoon
S7K 4C1

Located in the Canarama Shopping Centre.

 Mon - Wed: 11 am - 12:30 am; Thurs - Sat: 11 - 12:30 am
Sun: noon - midnight

 Dark Ale (1.050, English ale) Seasonal:
Original Lager (1.050) Wheat (1.042)
Light Lager (1.042, American lager) Cranberry Christmas (1.050, dark)
Pilsner (1.050, European amber)

Brewer: Monty Wood
Their beer is made from malt extract, filtered, and served under pressure.
Two other draft beers and about 20 bottled beers are available.

 They have a pub grub- style menu, with many appetizers, soup, salad, sandwiches, burgers, pizza. Check for the daily specials. They have a few wines on the menu; full bar.

The owners have tried to recreate a cozy, old English pub, with dark wood paneling, both carpeted and hardwood floors, stained glass windows, and lots of dark bookcases. The brewhouse is visible in the rear of the pub. Opened in 1989 as Miners Brewpub and reopened later as the Fox & Hounds.

 CD jukebox; background music (moderate)   4 (one is large screen; cable)

 pool, pinball, darts

$$$ CA, VI

Index to Breweries

Brewpubs and Craft Breweries
not Covered in this Guide

Breweries listed below (1) were listed in the first edition or the 1992 supplement, but have closed since then, (2) are still open, but no longer brewing, (3) opened and closed since the first edition, (4) have changed their name, (5) are craft breweries which do not offer tours, (6) were still not brewing at press time, (7) we were unable to obtain information form the brewery, or (8) are private clubs. Entries in italics indicate craft breweries.

United States

Connecticut
Charter Oak   *Bristol*   *closed in 1992*

Florida
Florida	Miami	open, but no longer brewing
Kidders	Ft. Myers	closed in 1993; reopened as The Mill
The Mill	Gainesville	stopped brewing in 1993 (still open)
The Mill	Tallahassee	stopped brewing in 1993 (still open)
Tampa Bay	Tampa	closed in 1992

Hawaii
Honolulu   Honolulu   closed in 1991

Illinois
Berghoff	Chicago	closed in 1993
Chief's	Champaign	closed; reopened as Joe's
Galena Main Street	Galena	opening May 1993?
Tap & Growler	Chicago	closed in 1993

Indiana
Lafayette   Lafayette   opening in July 1993?

Kentucky
Oertels   *Louisville*   *opening in June 1993?*

Louisiana
The Mill   Baton Rouge   closed in 1992

Maine
Lake St. George	*Liberty*	*opening summer 1993?*
Seadog	Camden	opening in summer 1993?

Maryland
British	*Glen Burnie*	*Moved; now called Oxford Brewing*
Frederick	*Frederick*	*opening in May 1993?*

Michigan
Grizzly Peaks   Ann Arbor   opening in June 1993?

New Hampshire
Martha's Exchange   Nashua   opening in June 1993?

SHOCKHOE SLIP 644-3018
1214 E. CARY ST. 11:30 - MIDNIGHT

New Jersey
Clement's　　　　　　　*Vernon*　　　　　　*closed in 1992*

New York
Company B's　　　　　　Orangeburg　　　　never brewed (still open)

North Carolina
Old Heidelberg　　　　　Durham　　　　　　closed; reopened as The French Quarter

Ohio
Gambrinus　　　　　　　Columbus　　　　　opening in May 1993?
Hideaway Hills　　　　　Lancaster　　　　　in a private resort community
Meander　　　　　　　　Youngstown　　　　closed in 1993
New Albany　　　　　　　New Albany　　　　in a private country club
Ronz (Abbie's)　　　　　Dayton　　　　　　closed in 1991

Pennsylvania
Happy Valley　　　　　　State College　　　closed in 1992
Indian Valley　　　　　　Lansdale　　　　　opening September 1993?

Tennessee
Big River　　　　　　　　Chattanooga　　　　opening August 1993?
Smokey Mountain　　　　Knoxville　　　　　opening October 1993?

Vermont
Jasper Murdock　　　　　Norwich　　　　　　opening May 1993?

Virginia
Amdo Rodeo　　　　　　Arlington　　　　　never brewed (still open)
Blue Muse　　　　　　　Roanoke　　　　　opened & closed in 1991; now Lone Star
19th Street　　　　　　　Virginia Beach　　closed in 1991
Potomac River　　　　　*Chantilly*　　　　*opening in May 1993?*
Richbrau　　　　　　　　Richmond　　　　　opening summer 1993?
Virginia　　　　　　　　*Virginia Beach*　*closed in 1993*

Wisconsin
Fox Classic　　　　　　　Appleton　　　　　closed in 1992

Canada

Alberta
Boccalino　　　　　　　　Edmonton　　　　　closed in 1992

Ontario
Elora Mills　　　　　　　*Elora*　　　　　　*opening summer 1993?*
Hometown Breweries　　*London, Ont.*　　*opening August 1993?*
Luxembourg　　　　　　　Oakville　　　　　closed in 1992
Madawaska　　　　　　　Arnprior　　　　　closed in 1992
Queen's Inn　　　　　　　Stratford　　　　　closed in 1992
Snooty Fox　　　　　　　Burlington　　　　closed in 1992
Winchester Arms　　　　　Mississauga　　　closed in 1992

Saskatchewan
Luxembourg　　　　　　　Regina　　　　　　closed in 1992

Further Reading

PERIODICALS

Ale Street News, a bi-monthly tabloid devoted to beer and breweries in New York and surrounding states, available free of charge at most brewpubs and good beer bars in the area, subscriptions available also (Tony Forder, ASN, P.O. Box 5339, Bergenfield, NJ 07621).

Alephenalia, an occaional tabloid devoted to beers distributed by Merchant du Vin (Merchant du Vin, 2505 Third Ave., Suite 324, Seattle, WA 98121).

All About Beer, a bi-monthly magazine for beer lovers (Bosak Publishing, 4764 Galicia Way, Oceanside, CA 92056).

American Brewer Magazine, a quarterly, published by Bill Owens, one of the leaders in the brewpub movement (American Brewer, P.O. Box 510, Hayward, CA 94543).

American Breweriana Journal, a bi-monthly publication of the American Breweriana Association, focuses on breweriana, but contains much up-to-date news on microbreweries and brewpubs as well (American Breweriana Association, P.O. Box 11157, Pueblo, CO 81001).

The BarleyCorn, bi-monthly tabloid devoted to beer and breweries in the Mid-Atlantic states, available free of charge at most brewpubs and good beer bars in the area, subscriptions available also (George Rivers, BarleyCorn, P.O. Box 2328, Falls Church, VA 22042).

Celebrator Beer News, a bi-monthly "brewspaper" covering microbreweries and brewpubs in the western half of the country; published by Tom Dalldorf; available free of charge at most brewpubs and good beer bars in California, subscriptions available also (P.O. Box 375, Hayward, CA 94543).

The Micro Connection, a quarterly newsletter of the Eastern Coast Breweriana Association Micro Chapter, edited by Chris Levesque (ECBA Micro Chapter, P.O. Box 826, South Windsor, CT 06074).

The Moderation Reader, a bi-monthly journal devoted to sensible legislation concerning alcohol consumption, (Gene Ford Publications, 4714 N.E. 50th Street, Seattle, WA 98105-2908)

The New Brewer: the Magazine for Micro and Pub-Brewers, a bi-monthly journal of the Institute for Brewing Studies; for the most part, information is technical or business-oriented (New Brewer, P.O. Box 1679, Boulder, CO 80306-1679).

Northwest Beer Journal, a bi-monthly tabloid devoted to beer breweries in the Northwest, available free of charge at most brewpubs and good beer bars in the Northwest, subscriptions available also (Randy Nilson, Northwest Publishing Co., 2626 Lodgepole Drive SE, Port Orchard, WA 98366).

The Pint Post, a quarterly publication from Larry Baush, who heads the Microbrew Appreciation Society; features Northwest microbreweries and brewpubs (Microbrewer Appreciation Society, 12345 Lake City Way NE, Suite #159, Seattle, WA 98125).

Quick Guide to U.S. Brewpubs and Craft Breweries, bi-annual listing of names, addresses, and phone numbers, $5.00 an issue (WBR Publications, P.O. Box 71, Clemson, SC 29633).

Southwest Brewing News, a bi-monthly tabloid devoted to beer and breweries in the Southwest, available free of charge at most brewpubs and good beer bars in the Southwest, subscriptions available also (Bill Metzger, SBN, 11405 Evening Star Drive, Austin, TX 78739).

What's Brewing, monthly tabloid Newspaper of the Campaign for Real Ale (CAMRA), devoted to the preservation of real ale, real ale breweries, and real ale consumers' rights, (Campaign for Real Ale, 34 Alma Road, St. Albans, Herts., AL1 3BW, United Kingdom).

World Beer Review, a bi-monthly newsletter for beer gourmets, published by Steve Johnson, author of this book; reviews domestic and imported beers, features brewpub & microbrewery openings and closings and covers news of interest to the beer lover; James Robertson's beer review, (WBR Publications, P.O. Box 71, Clemson, SC 29633).

The Yankee Brew News, a quarterly newsletter devoted to beer and breweries in New England, available free at many brewpubs and beer retailers in the region, subscriptions available also (YBN, P.O. Box 8053, J.F.K. Station, Boston, MA 02114).

Zymurgy, the journal of the American Homebrewers Association, published 5 times yearly and frequently has information about brewpubs, Editor-in-Chief: Charlie Papazian (AHA, P.O. Box 1679, Boulder, CO 80306-1679).

BOOKS

All of the books listed below were in print at press time. Titles with an asterisk beside them can be purchased from WBR Publications, P.O. Box 71, Clemson, SC 29633 (please add $3 for postage for first book, $1 for each additional book). Titles generally not carried in bookstores are frequently available from your nearest homebrew supplier (check your Yellow Pages for location).

Beers of North America by Bill Yenne (W.H. Smith Publishers, 1991).

*The Beer Drinkers Guide to Munich by Larry Hawthorne [$8.95] (Honolulu, Freizeit Publishers, 1991).

The Beer Log by James Robertson (Oceanside, Calif., Bosak Publishing, 1992).

Belgian Ale by Pierre Rajotte (Boulder, Colorado, Brewers Publications, 1992).

*Breweries of Wisconsin by Jerry Apps [$19.95] (Madison, University of Wisconsin Press, 1992).

Brewery Adventures in the Wild West by Jack Erickson (Reston, Virginia, RedBrick Press, 1991).

*California Brewin' by Jack Erickson [$11.95] (Reston, Va., RedBrick Press, 1993)

Continental Pilsner by Dave Miller (Boulder, Colorado, Brewers Publications, 1990).

The Essentials of Beer Style: a Catalog of Beer Styles for Brewers and Beer Enthusiasts by Fred Eckhardt (Portland, Oregon, Fred Eckhardt Associates, 1989).

The Gourmet Guide to Beer by Howard Hillman (New York, Facts on File, 1987).

Great Cooking With Beer by Jack Erickson (Reston, Virginia, RedBrick Press, 1989).

*Jay Harlow's Beer Cuisine by Jay Harlow [$16.95] (Emeryville, Calif., Harlow & Ratnor, 1991).

Lambic by Jean-Xavier Guinard (Boulder, Colorado, Brewers Publications, 1990).

The New World Guide to Beer by Michael Jackson (Philadelphia, Pennsylvania, Running Press, 1988).

Pale Ale by Terry Foster (Boulder, Colorado, Brewers Publications, 1990).

Porter by Terry Foster (Boulder, Colorado, Brewers Publications, 1991).

Real Beer and Good Eats: the Rebirth of America's Beer and Food Traditions by Bruce Aidells and Denis Kelly (New York, Knopf, 1992).

Seattle Brews: the Insiders Guide to Neighborhood Alehouses, Brewpubs, and Bars by Bart Becker (Bothell, Wa., Alaska Northwest Books, 1992).

Simon & Schuster Pocket Guide to Beer by Michael Jackson, revised, updated, & enlarged (New York, Simon & Schuster, 1991).

Vienna Märzen by George and Laurie Fix (Boulder, Colorado, Brewers Publications, 1992).

64

5 TA STE EXIT
STRAIGHT
CROSS MAIN
LEFT ON CARY
PAST